PRIMATES

THE BRITANNICA GUIDE TO PREDATORS AND PREY

PRIMATES

EDITED BY JOHN P. RAFFERTY, ASSOCIATE EDITOR, EARTH AND LIFE SCIENCES

Britannica
Educational Publishing

IN ASSOCIATION WITH

ROSEN
EDUCATIONAL SERVICES

Published in 2011 by Britannica Educational Publishing
(a trademark of Encyclopædia Britannica, Inc.)
in association with Rosen Educational Services, LLC
29 East 21st Street, New York, NY 10010.

Distributed exclusively by Rosen Educational Services.
For a listing of additional Britannica Educational Publishing titles, call toll free (800) 237-9932.

First Edition

Britannica Educational Publishing
Michael I. Levy: Executive Editor
J.E. Luebering: Senior Manager
Marilyn L. Barton: Senior Coordinator, Production Control
Steven Bosco: Director, Editorial Technologies
Lisa S. Braucher: Senior Producer and Data Editor
Yvette Charboneau: Senior Copy Editor
Kathy Nakamura: Manager, Media Acquisition
John P. Rafferty: Associate Editor, Earth and Life Sciences

Rosen Educational Services
Alexandra Hanson-Harding: Editor
Nelson Sá: Art Director
Cindy Reiman: Photography Manager
Matthew Cauli: Designer, Cover Design
Introduction by Catherine Vanderhoof

Library of Congress Cataloging-in-Publication Data

Primates / edited by John P. Rafferty.—1st ed.
    p. cm.—(The Britannica guide to predators and prey)
"In association with Britannica Educational Publishing, Rosen Educational Services."
Includes bibliographical references and index.
ISBN 978-1-61530-339-7 (library binding)
1. Primates—Juvenile literature. I. Rafferty, John P.
QL737.P9P6762 2011
599.8—dc22

                                                                2010032414

Manufactured in the United States of America

On the cover: A gorilla named Baghira holds her baby, Kajolu, in their enclosure at Tierpark Hellabrun zoo in Munich, Germany, on January 22, 2010. *Oliver Lang/AFP/Getty Images*

On page x: Coquerel's sifaka (*Propithecus coquereli*). © *Christopher Call Productions*

On pages 1, 28, 46, 74, 92, 145, 174, 194, 228, 262, 264, 272: Gorilla (*Gorillla*). *shutterstock.com*

CONTENTS

107

118

132

power grip

precisio

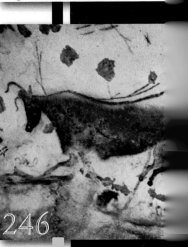

Introduction

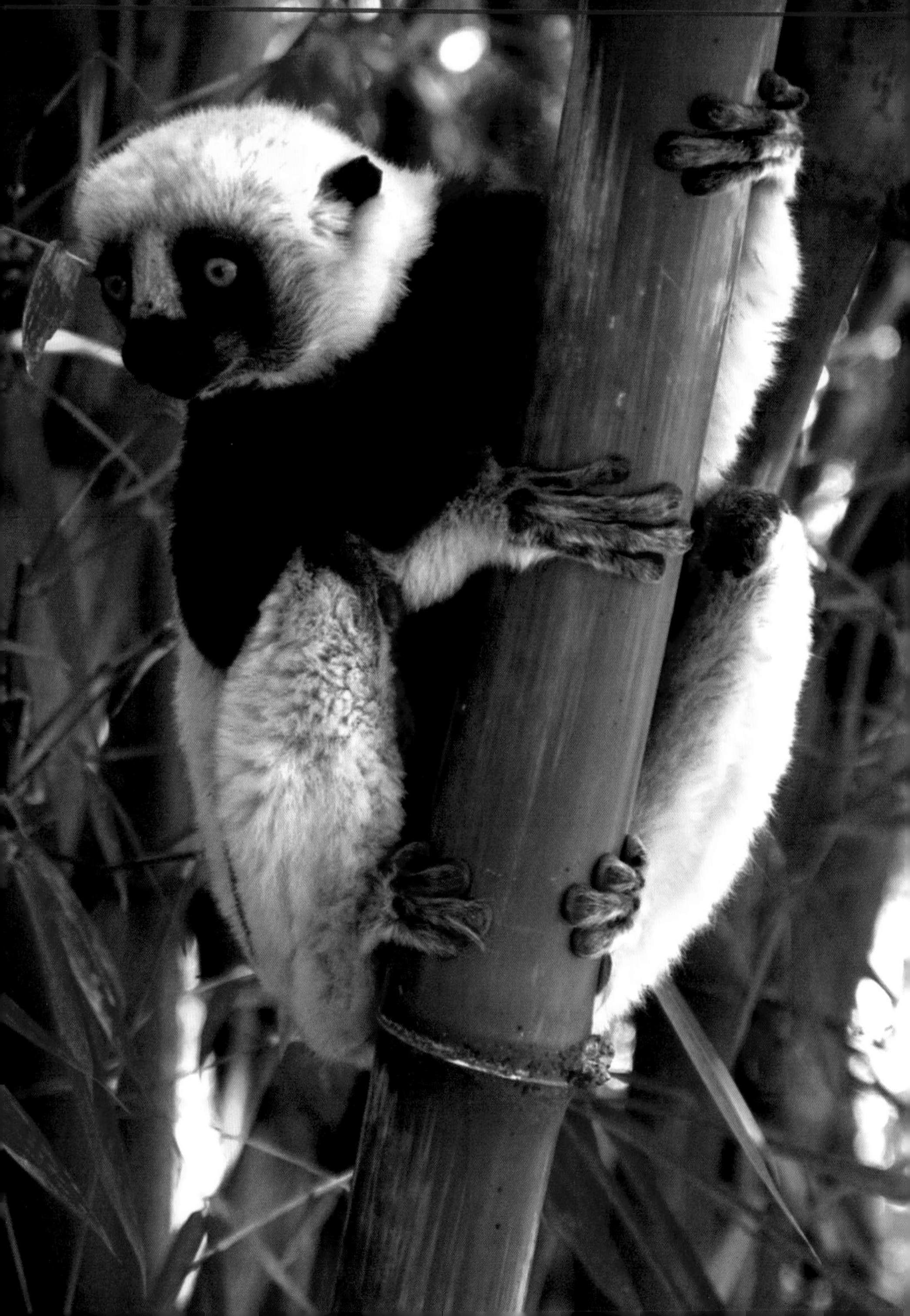

During the Scopes "monkey trial" of 1925, supporting the state of Tennessee's ban on the teaching of evolution, lawyer William Jennings Bryan famously decried evolution's claim that human beings were descended "not even from American monkeys, but from Old World monkeys." Of course, evolutionary theory does not suggest that humans are descended from any living monkey species at all. Over 20 million years ago, however, humans and monkeys did indeed share a common evolutionary ancestor. While political battles over how evolution should be taught still continue, there is no question that humans, apes, monkeys, and a wide variety of other species all fall taxonomically within the order Primates. In this book you will meet all the members of the order, as well as explore the unique development of the human branch of the family tree.

With more than 300 distinct species, primates are in fact the third most diverse order of mammals, encompassing creatures as diverse as lemurs, lorises, and tarsiers, as well as the more familiar monkeys and apes. So what makes all these different animals related? All primates have several traits in common. They are the only mammals that have flat nails on their fingers and toes rather than claws or hooves. They also possess specialized nerve endings in the hands and feet that increase their tactile sensitivity and a big toe separated from the others that is suitable for grasping. However, only a few have an opposable thumb. Compared to other terrestrial mammals, primate brains are larger in proportion to their body weight, with a unique brain structure for visual perception. Primate teeth are also distinct from other mammals, and thus it is relatively easy to recognize fossil remains that belong to this order, the oldest of which date back to the beginning of the Eocene Epoch approximately 56 million years ago.

The evolutionary adaptations common to primates suggest that the first primate species were most likely tree-dwellers and predators, possibly insect eaters. This determination is based on the presence of grasping feet, the tactile sensitivity in the hands and feet, and the forward-facing orientation of their eyes. Modern primate species have evolved to thrive in a variety of environments. The body size of modern primates ranges from the tiny 35-gram (1-ounce) mouse lemur to the large 180-kg (400-pound) gorilla. Primates may travel by leaping or swinging from branch to branch or by walking on either two or four legs. (Humans, however, are the only modern primate species that consistently practice bipedalism.) Non-human primates are widely distributed throughout the tropical regions of Africa, India, Southeast Asia, and South America. A few species are also adapted to life in the more temperate regions of China and Japan. Many primate species are now considered endangered due to loss of habitat, which is particularly acute in Asia and to a lesser extent in Africa and South America.

Primates generally have an extended developmental cycle. Juveniles often remain under the care of adults for a relatively long period to learn the skills necessary to survive and to integrate themselves into the complex social structure of the family or community group. Most primates are omnivorous, eating everything from leaves, stems, and tubers to fruits, vegetables, insects, birds' eggs, crustaceans, snakes, lizards, and small mammals. Such variability in behavior, along with their ability to adapt to a variety of different circumstances, has helped primates survive for tens of millions of years.

Among the more primitive primates, those closest to humanity's evolutionary ancestor are the lemurs. Lemurs are tree-dwellers, and most are nocturnal. They are characterized by large, reflective eyes, monkey-like bodies, and typically long bushy tails. They are generally small. Madame Berthe's mouse lemur is only about 9 cm (3.5 inches) long, whereas the indris grow up to approximately 70 cm (28 inches) long. Lemur-like fossils suggest that these early primates were common in both North America and Europe, but true lemurs survive today only on the island of Madagascar off the African coast. Many lemur species are endangered, and other species, such as the aye-aye, are considered critically endangered.

Primitive primates of Asian forests properly belong to the family Lorisdae, although they are often grouped with lemurs. The habits of lorises are similar to lemurs. They are also nocturnal and arboreal and feed mostly on insects, fruit, and small animals. They are even more closely related to another African primate, the potto. Unlike other primitive primates, lorises, along with pottos and the angwantibos, do not have tails.

Falling somewhere between the primitive lemurs and the higher primate species are the tarsiers, a group found only in the Philippines and other islands of Southeast Asia. Tarsiers are tiny. They measure only about 9–16 cm (3.5–6 inches). This figure excludes their tails, which can be twice as long as their bodies. Tarsiers feed on insects, lizard, and snakes, and they are considered to be the only entirely carnivorous primates. Although they possess nocturnal habits similar to lemurs, the structure of their eyes more closely resembles that of monkeys, apes, and humans. The structure of the placenta and the presence of a dry, hair-covered nose are examples of other anatomical features tarsiers have in common with higher primates.

Nearly 200 species of the order Primates—two-thirds of all primate species—are considered monkeys. All monkeys have tails, even if only a tiny nub. They are distinguished from apes by their slender, narrow-chested bodies. Most live in tropical forests and spend the majority of their time in the treetops. Almost all monkeys are diurnal, that is, they are more active during the day than at night. Monkeys are generally divided, as William Jennings Bryan noted, into Old World and New World species, and Old World monkeys are indeed more closely related to apes than the New World species.

The New World monkeys live primarily in the tropical forests of South America, although some range as far north as southern Mexico. They do not possess the opposable thumb, but some species do have prehensile tails, which are features that do not appear in any Old World species. New World monkeys include the spider monkey, howler monkey, squirrel monkey, capuchin monkey, marmosets, and tamarins. Lesser known New World species include sakis, uakaris, titis, and woolly monkeys. Many of these species are endangered. However, one of the bright spots of monkey conservation involves the recovery of the golden lion tamarin through captive breeding and reintroduction to its native habitat.

Old World monkeys all fall within a single-family classification, but comprise 21 separate genera and more than 100 species. Old World species are known for their wide diversity of habitat, appearance, and habits. They can be found throughout Africa and most of Asia, and one species still occurs on the island of Gibraltar in Europe. Old World monkeys include baboons, langurs, colobus monkeys, macaques, guenons, and mandrills. Not all Old World monkeys, however, are tree-dwellers. Some species are adapted to life on the savannas of Africa, the rocky coastlines of the Red Sea and the Cape of Good Hope, and in the cold mountain regions of China and Japan.

All monkeys are capable of sitting upright, leaving their hands free for a variety of uses. They have large brains and are known for their curiosity and intelligence. Many monkeys use tools to obtain food, and many have been shown to learn from experience and carry those lessons to new tasks. Monkeys are highly social animals, and they living in large troops or extended families of related adult females with one or more unrelated adult males. Juveniles of both sexes remain with the troop until they mature, a period of approximately 6 years for most monkey species. During this period, the young monkey learns how to behave within the complex social structure of the troop.

The apes make up a group of primates that descended from Old World monkeys. Apes are distinguished from monkeys by the complete lack of a tail and by more complex brains. Apes include the families Hylobatidae (gibbons) and Hominidae (chimpanzees, bonobos, orangutans, gorillas, and humans). Gibbons are found in tropical forests of Southeast Asia, while other apes are primarily African, other than orangutans that are found only on the islands of Sumatra and Borneo. The gorilla, chimpanzee, bonobo, and orangutan are called great apes, whereas the gibbons are known as lesser apes. This distinction reflects not only the generally larger size of the hominids, but it also suggests a higher level of intelligence. Great apes have been shown in experiments to recognize themselves in mirrors, learn and communicate in sign language, reason abstractly, and construct simple tools (as opposed to simply using found objects as tools). Apes can stand erect and will occasionally walk upright, although the predominant form of locomotion on the ground in all species except humans remains quadrupedal "knuckle walking." Morphologically, the lower back has only four to six vertebrae. The remainder are fused into the tailbone. In addition, all species possess highly flexible wrists and opposable thumbs.

Against the backdrop of primate evolution, humans and their immediate ancestors are relatively recent developments. The fossil record for hominin species (that is, members of the human lineage) dates back some 6 million years to *Australopithecus*. The most famous specimen in this genus is the fossil skeleton known as "Lucy." The most visible distinguishing characteristics separating hominins from all other primate species are the presence of an erect posture and the ability to walk upright on two feet (bipedal locomotion). Later hominins also possess significantly larger brains than their primate relations, and they demonstrate a number of more sophisticated behavioral characteristics, such as complex tool use and the development of language.

The first appearance of the genus *Homo* dates back approximately 2 million years, with the emergence of *H. erectus*, *H. habilis*, and *H. rudolfensis*, hominin species all estimated to have lived between 2.5 and 1.5 million years ago. *H. erectus* appears to have dispersed quickly through Africa, Europe, and Asia, beginning about 1.7 million years ago, and fossil remains that share common characteristics have been found throughout those regions as recently as 200,000 years ago. Such fossils indicate that *H. erectus* was about the same height and build as modern humans, but it had a smaller brain and flatter face. Other artifacts found with the bones indicate that these early humans used stone tools, cooked food over fires, and had a diet including both meat and vegetable matter. Clearly the mastery of fire was an important development in human evolution, and it appears to have been present as much as 400,000 years ago.

It has not been determined whether *H. erectus* is a direct ancestor of today's humans or whether *H. sapiens* descended from another group. However, it is clear that *H. erectus* was supplanted approximately 200,000 years ago by more modern hominin species, such as *H. neanderthalensis*. The Neanderthals were dominant for only approximately 150,000 years, but they left abundant evidence of their presence in limestone caves from Europe through southwest Asia. The brain size of Neanderthals is similar to that in modern humans, although their faces were larger with a prominent brow ridge and large teeth. The body of the Neanderthal was characterized by a broad chest and shoulders, and it also had muscular upper limbs, and strong, fatigue-resistant legs and feet.

Scientists have in recent years decoded the Neanderthal genome, identifying this species' complete genetic profile. Evidence indicates that Neanderthals were not the direct ancestors of modern humans, but both species certainly overlapped in time and geography. There is some evidence that suggests a level of interbreeding between *H. neanderthalensis* and *H. sapiens* had occurred. A comparison of Neanderthal DNA with that of modern humans indicates a small percentage of the genetic makeup of humans of European and Asian extraction is derived from ancient Neanderthals. Humans from Africa, however, do not appear to share Neanderthal genes. This development appears to support the hypothesis that modern humans, *H. sapiens*, arose in Africa sometime between 150,000 to 100,000 years ago. Populations that spread into areas already populated by *H. neanderthalensis* experienced interbreeding, while the population remaining in Africa did not.

Even as recently as 18,000 years ago, other human species beyond Neanderthals and modern humans may have inhabited the planet. The discovery in 2004 of skeletal remains of a group of diminutive individuals on the Pacific island of Flores, dubbed *H. floresiensis*, is a compelling, but unconfirmed, part of the story of human evolution. Today, however, humanity's closest living genetic relatives are chimpanzees and gorillas, and scientists continue to study primates as a way to understand what it truly means to be human.

CHAPTER 1
THE GENERAL FEATURES OF PRIMATES

I n zoology, a primate is any mammal from the group that includes the lemurs, lorises, tarsiers, monkeys, apes, and humans. The order Primates, with its 300 or more species, is the third most diverse order of mammals, after rodents (Rodentia) and bats (Chiroptera). Although there are some notable variations between some primate groups, they share several anatomic and functional characteristics reflective of their common ancestry. When compared with body weight, the primate brain is larger than that of other terrestrial mammals, and it has a fissure unique to primates called the Calcarine sulcus that separates the first and second visual areas on each side of the brain. Whereas all other mammals have claws or hooves on their digits, only primates have flat nails. Some primates do have claws, but even among these there is a flat nail on the big toe (hallux). In all primates except humans, the hallux diverges from the other toes and together with them forms a pincer capable of grasping objects such as branches. Not all primates have similarly dextrous hands; only the catarrhines (Old World monkeys, apes, and humans) and a few of the lemurs and lorises have an opposable thumb. Primates are not alone in having grasping feet, but as these occur in many other arboreal mammals (e.g., squirrels and opossums), and as most present-day primates are arboreal, this characteristic suggests that they evolved from an ancestor that was arboreal. So too does primates' possession of specialized nerve endings (Meissner's corpuscles) in the hands and feet that increase tactile sensitivity. As far as is known, no other placental mammal has them. Primates possess dermatoglyphics (the skin ridges responsible for fingerprints), but so do many other arboreal mammals. The eyes face forward in all primates so that the eyes' visual fields overlap. Again, this feature is not by any means restricted to primates, but it is a general feature seen among predators. It has been proposed, therefore, that the ancestor of the primates was a predator, perhaps insectivorous. The optic fibres in almost all mammals cross over (decussate) so that signals from one eye are interpreted on the opposite side of the brain, but, in some primate species, up to 40 percent of the nerve fibres do not cross over. Primate teeth are distinguishable from those of other mammals by the low, rounded form of the molar and premolar cusps, which contrast with the high, pointed cusps or elaborate ridges of other placental mammals. This distinction makes fossilized primate teeth easy to recognize. Fossils of the earliest primates date to the Early Eocene Epoch (56 million to 40 million years ago) or perhaps to the Late Paleocene Epoch (59 million to 56 million years ago). Though they began as an arboreal group, and many (especially the platyrrhines, or New World monkeys) have remained thoroughly arboreal, many have become at least partly terrestrial, and many have achieved high levels of intelligence.

SIZE RANGE AND ADAPTIVE DIVERSITY

Members of the order Primates show a remarkable range of size and adaptive diversity. The smallest primate is Madame Berthe's mouse lemur (*Microcebus berthae*) of Madagascar, which weighs some 35 grams (one ounce); the most massive is certainly the gorilla (*Gorilla gorilla*), whose weight may be more than 4,000 times as great, varying from 140 to 180 kg (about 300 to 400 pounds).

Primates occupy two major vegetational zones: tropical forest and woodland-grassland vegetational complexes. Each of these zones has produced in its resident primates the appropriate adaptations, but there is perhaps more diversity of bodily form among forest-living species than among savanna inhabitants. One of the explanations of this difference is that it is the precise pattern of locomotion rather than the simple matter of habitat that governs overt bodily adaptations. Within the forest there are a number of ways of moving about. An animal can live on the forest floor or in the canopy, for instance, and within the canopy it can move in three particular ways: (a) by leaping—a function principally dictated by the hind limbs; (b) by arm swinging (brachiation)—a function particularly of the forelimbs; (c) by a type of movement known as quadrupedalism, in which function is equally divided between the forelimbs and the hind limbs. On the savanna, or in the woodland-savanna biome, which substantially demands adaptations for ground-living locomotion rather than those for tree-living, the possibilities are limited. If bipedal humans are discounted, there is a single pattern of ground-living locomotion, which is called quadrupedalism. Within this category there are at least two variations on the theme: (a) knuckle-walking quadrupedalism, and (b) digitigrade quadrupedalism. The former gait is characteristic of the African apes (chimpanzee and gorilla), and the latter of baboons and macaques, which walk on the flats of their fingers. After human beings, Old World monkeys of the subfamily Cercopithecinae are the most successful colonizers of nonarboreal habitats.

The structural adaptations of primates resulting from locomotor differences are considered in more detail in the section Locomotion, but they do not prove to be very extensive. Primates are a homogeneous group

BRACHIATION

Brachiation is a specialized form of arboreal locomotion in which movement is accomplished by swinging from one hold to another by the arms. The process is highly developed in the gibbon and siamang, which are anatomically adapted for it in the length of their forelimbs, their long hooklike fingers, and the mobility of their shoulder joints. The South American spider monkey, considered a semibrachiator, uses its prehensile tail as a third arm. Spider monkeys both run along branches and swing from them.

Because bipedal locomotion is the terrestrial form of movement in the true brachiators, some researchers believe that the human species may have evolved from a protobrachiator. Other researchers have tried to demonstrate that the so-called knuckle-walking apes (e.g., the gorilla) are descended from brachiating ancestors. They base this theory on the characteristically long arms and curved fingers of knuckle-walkers.

morphologically, and it is only in the realm of behaviour that differences between primate taxa are clearly discriminant. It can be said that the most successful primates (judged in terms of the usual criteria of population numbers and territorial spread) are those that have departed least from the ancestral pattern of structure but farthest from the ancestral pattern of behaviour. "Manners makyth man" is true in the widest sense of the word; in the same sense, manners delineate primate species.

DISTRIBUTION AND ABUNDANCE

The nonhuman primates have a wide distribution throughout the tropical latitudes of Africa, India, Southeast Asia, and South America. Within this tropical belt, which lies between latitudes 25° N and 30° S, they have a considerable vertical range. In Ethiopia the gelada (genus *Theropithecus*) is found living at elevations up to 5,000 metres (16,000 feet). Gorillas of the Virunga Mountains are known to travel across mountain passes at altitudes of more than 4,200 metres (about 13,800 feet) when traveling from one high valley to another. The howler monkeys of Venezuela (*Alouatta seniculus*) live at 2,500 metres (8,200 feet) in the Cordillera de Merida, and in northern Colombia the duru-kuli (genus *Aotus*) is found in the tropical montane forests of the Cordillera Central.

In habitat, primates are predominantly tropical, but few species of nonhuman primates extend their ranges well outside the tropics. The so-called Barbary "ape" (*Macaca sylvanus*)—actually a monkey—lives in the temperate forests of the Atlas and other mountain ranges of Morocco and Algeria. Some populations of rhesus monkey (*M. mulatta*) extended until the middle of the 20th century to the latitude of Beijing in northern China, and the Tibetan macaque (*M. thibetana*) is found from the warm coastal ranges of Fujian (Fukien) province to the cold mountains of Sichuan (Szechwan). One of the most remarkable, however, is the Japanese macaque (*M. fuscata*), which in the north of Honshu lives in mountains that are snow-covered for eight months of the year; some populations have learned to make life more tolerable for themselves by spending most of the day in the hot springs that bubble out and form pools in volcanic areas. Finally, two western Chinese species of snub-nosed monkey, the golden (*Rhinopithecus roxellana*) and black (*R. bieti*), are confined to high altitudes (up to 3,000 metres [about 9,800 feet] in the case of the former and to 4,500 metres [about 14,800 feet] in the latter), where the temperature drops below 0° C (32° F) every night and often barely rises above it by day.

Although many primates are still plentiful in the wild, the numbers of many species are declining steeply. According to the International Union for Conservation of Nature (IUCN), more than 70 percent of primates in Asia and roughly 40 percent of primates in South America,

Red-bellied lemur (Eulemur rubriventer) *in the eastern Madagascar rainforest near Ranomafana.* (Top) © David Curl/Oxford Scientific Films Ltd.

in mainland Africa, and on the island of Madagascar are listed as endangered. A number of species, particularly the orangutan, the gorilla, some of the Madagascan lemurs, and some South American species, are in serious danger of extinction unless their habitats can be preserved in perpetuity and human predation kept under control. The populations of several species number only in the hundreds, and in 2000 a subspecies of African red colobus monkey (*Procolobus badius*) became the first primate since 1800 to be declared extinct.

In the midst of these declines, the populations of some critically endangered primate species have increased. Concerted efforts to breed a type of marmoset, the golden lion tamarin (*Leontopithecus rosalia*), in captivity have been successful; this species's reintroduction to the wild continues in Brazil. The estimated number of western lowland gorillas (*G. gorilla gorilla*), a species thought to be critically endangered, increased when a population of more than 100,000 was discovered in 2008 in the swamps of the Lac Télé Community Reserve in the Republic of the Congo.

NATURAL HISTORY OF PRIMATES

The natural history of primates varies among the different groups. For example, some primates may be restricted to a particular breeding season, whereas others are able to breed throughout the year. Gestational periods range from 54 to 68 days in mouse lemurs to roughly 267 days in humans. Longevity and growth are also type dependent, with apes possessing the longest primate life spans. Such variability also extends to methods of locomotion, diet, and preferred habitat.

REPRODUCTION AND LIFE CYCLE

The stages of the life cycle of primates vary considerably in duration. Among the most primitive members of the group, these stages are broadly comparable to those of other mammals of similar size. Higher in the phylogenetic scale, they are substantially extended. The greatest difference is in the duration of the infant and juvenile stages combined; the least is in the gestation period, which, despite the general belief, cannot be consistently correlated with adult body size. Gibbons, which weigh considerably less than macaques, have a 20 percent longer gestation period.

The clear trend toward prolongation of the period of juvenile and adolescent life is probably to be associated with the corresponding trend toward a progressive elaboration of the brain. The extended period of adolescence means that the young remain under adult (primarily maternal) surveillance for a long period, during which time

Rhesus monkeys (Macaca mulatta). Ylla— Rapho/Photo Researchers

the juvenile acquires, by example from its mother and peers, the knowledge that will allow it to become properly integrated as a fully adult member of a complicated social system. One might therefore expect a close correlation between the period of adolescence, the brain size, and the complexity of the social system; and, insofar as the latter factor can be assessed, this appears to be the case.

BREEDING PERIODS

The reproductive events in the primate calendar are copulation, gestation, birth, and lactation. Owing to the long duration of the gestation period, these phases occupy the female primate (among higher primates anyway) for a full year or more; then the cycle starts again. The female does not usually come into physiological receptivity until the infant of the previous pregnancy has been weaned.

Most lemurs and lorises show one or more discrete breeding seasons during the year, during which time they may undergo more than one reproductive estrous cycle (i.e., period of sexual activity). The breeding seasons are separated by periods of anestrus, which in bush babies and mouse lemurs are accompanied by changes in the skin of the external genitalia (vulva), which closes over, completely sealing the vagina. When living in the wild in the Sudan, the lesser bush baby (*Galago senegalensis*) has an estrus that occurs only twice yearly, during December and August. In captivity, however, breeding seasons may occur at any period in the year. In the wild, birth seasons are closely correlated with the prevailing climate, but in captivity under equable laboratory conditions, this consideration does not apply. For instance, in its native Madagascar, the ring-tailed lemur (*Lemur catta*) has only a single breeding season during the year, conception occurring in autumn (April) and births taking place in late winter (August and September). However, in zoos in the Northern Hemisphere, a seasonal inversion occurs in which the birth period shifts to late spring and early summer. These examples indicate the influence of environmental factors on the timing of the birth seasons.

Reproductive cycles in tarsiers, apes, and many monkeys continue uninterrupted throughout the year, though seasonality in births is characteristic mainly of monkey species living either outside the equatorial belt (5° north and south of the Equator) or at high elevations in equatorial regions, where dry seasons and seasonal food shortages occur. Seasonality of births in macaques (genus *Macaca* species) has been documented in Japan, on Cayo Santiago in the Caribbean (where an introduced population thrives under seminatural conditions), and in India. Observations of langurs in India and Sri Lanka, of geladas in Ethiopia, and of patas monkeys in Uganda have also demonstrated seasonality in areas with well-marked wet and dry seasons. Those within the equatorial belt tend to display birth peaks rather than birth seasons. A birth peak is a period of the year in which a high proportion of births, but not by any means all, are concentrated. Equatorial primates such as guenons, colobus monkeys, howlers, gibbons, chimpanzees, and gorillas might be expected to show a pattern of births uniformly distributed throughout the year, but population samples are as yet too small to make this assumption, and some equatorial monkeys, such as squirrel monkeys (genus *Saimiri*), are strictly seasonal breeders. Even in humans, there is evidence of high birth peaks. In Europe, the highest birth rates are reached in the first half of the year; in the United States, India, and countries in the Southern Hemisphere, in the second half. This may, however, be a cultural rather than an ecological phenomenon, for marriages in certain Western countries reach a peak in the closing weeks of the fiscal year, a fact that undoubtedly has some repercussions on the birth period.

GESTATION PERIOD AND PARTURITION

The period during which the growing fetus is protected in the uterus is characterized by a considerable range of variation among primate species, but it shows a general trend toward prolongation as one ascends the evolutionary scale. Mouse lemurs, for example, have a gestation period of 54–68 days, lemurs 132–134 days, macaques 146–186 days, gibbons 210 days, chimpanzees 230 days, gorillas 255 days, and humans (on the average) 267 days. Even small primates such as bush babies have gestations considerably longer than those of nonprimate mammals of equivalent size, a reflection of the increased complexity and differentiation of primate structure compared with that of nonprimates. Although in primates there is a general trend toward evolutionary increase in body size, there is no absolute correlation between body size and the duration of the gestation period. Marmosets, for example, are considerably smaller than spider monkeys and howler monkeys but have a slightly longer pregnancy (howler monkeys 139 days, "true" marmosets 130–150 days).

An extraordinary and somewhat inexplicable difference exists between the dimensions of the pelvic cavity and the dimensions of the head of the infant at birth in monkeys and humans on the one hand, and apes on the other. The head of the infant ape is considerably smaller than the pelvic cavity, so birth occurs easily and without prolonged labour. When the head of the infant monkey engages in the pelvis, the fit is exact, and labour may be a prolonged and difficult affair, as it is generally with humans. Human parturition, however, is generally a much more extended process than that of monkeys. Like the human infant, the monkey is born head first. Twin births are rare in most monkeys and apes, but marmosets and some lemurs and lorises habitually produce twins.

INFANCY

The degrees of maturation and mother dependency at birth are obviously closely related phenomena. Newborn primate infants are neither as helpless as kittens, puppies, or rats nor as developed as newborn gazelles, horses, and other savanna-living animals. With a few exceptions, primate young are born with their eyes open and are fully furred. Exceptions are mouse lemurs (*Microcebus*), gentle lemurs (*Hapalemur*), and ruffed lemurs (*Varecia*), which bear more helpless (altricial) infants and carry their young in their mouth. Primate life being peripatetic, it is axiomatic that the infants must be able to cling to the mother's fur; just a few species (again, mouse lemurs and ruffed lemurs and a few others) leave their infants in nests while foraging, and lorises "park" their young, leaving them hanging under branches in tangles of vegetation. The young of most higher primates have grasping hands and feet at birth and are able to cling to the maternal fur without assistance; only humans, chimpanzees, and gorillas need to support their newborn infants, and humans do so longest.

It seems likely that the difference between the African apes and humans in respect to postnatal grasping ability is related to the acquisition in man of bipedal walking. One of the anatomic correlates of the human gait is the loss of the grasping function of the big toe, which is aligned in parallel with the remaining digits. Such an arrangement precludes the use of the foot as a grasping extremity. The human infant—and to a lesser degree the gorilla infant—must depend largely on its grasping hands to support itself unaided. The fact that humans are habitually bipedal and that, consequently, the hands are freed from locomotor chores may also be a contributory factor; the human mother can move about and at the same time continue to support her infant. Selection for postnatal grasping, therefore, has not had the high survival value in humans that it has in non-human primates, in which the survival of the infant depends on its ability to hold on tightly. On the other hand, it is well known that newborn human infants can support their own weight, for short periods, by means of their grasping hands. Clearly then, adaptations for survival are not wholly lacking in the human species. Perhaps cultural factors have had the effect of suppressing natural selection for early infant grasping ability. The first factor may be the social evolution of a division of labour between the sexes and a fixed home base, which has allowed the mother to park her infant with other members of the family as babysitters. A second factor may be more peripatetic communities, in which the invention of infant-carrying devices, such as the papoose technique of North American Indians, has made it unnecessary for the infant to support itself. Whatever the biological or cultural reasons, the human infant is more helpless than the young of all other primates.

Once the primate infant has learned to support itself by standing on its own two (or four) feet, the physical phase of dependency is over; the next phase, psychological dependency, lasts much longer. The human child is metaphorically tied to its mother's apron strings for much longer periods than are the nonhuman primates. The reasons for this are discussed below. According to Adolph Schultz, the Swiss anthropologist whose comparative anatomic studies have illuminated knowledge of nonhuman primates since the mid-20th century, the juvenile period of psychological maternal dependency is 2½ years in lemurs, 6 years in monkeys, 7–8 years in most apes (though it now appears to be even longer than this in chimpanzees), and 14 years in humans.

GROWTH AND LONGEVITY

The prolongation of postnatal life among primates affects all life periods, including infantile, juvenile, adult, and senescent. Although humans are the longest-lived members of the order, the potential life span of the chimpanzee has been estimated at 60 years, and orangutans occasionally achieve this in captivity. The life span of a lemur, on the other hand, is about 15 years and a monkey's 25–30 years.

The characteristic growth spurts of human infants in weight and height also occur in nonhuman primates but start earlier in the postnatal period and are of shorter duration. Primates differ from most nonprimate mammals by virtue of a delayed puberty in both sexes until growth is nearly complete; in humans, the peak of the growth spurt in boys comes slightly after the sexual maturity, whereas in girls the growth spurt precedes menarche. There is some controversy over the very existence of an adolescent growth spurt in nonhuman primates. In some species, males are very much larger than females; this extra growth occurs long after sexual maturity and rather rapidly, so it is possibly equivalent to the human growth spurt. The most remarkable case of such postmature growth is seen in orangutans. A male can mature physically in his early teens, or he can spend as much as 20 years as a subadult and then suddenly, within a year, almost double his weight and develop the cheek flanges characteristic of full maturity. It appears that this is related to social conditions; in proximity to a full-grown, dominant male, a subadult male's development will remain suppressed, and when the dominant male moves away (or, in a zoo, is removed from the vicinity), the subadult undergoes a flush of testosterone and matures rapidly.

LOCOMOTION

Primate locomotion, being an aspect of behaviour that arises out of anatomic structure, shows much of the conservativeness and opportunism that generally characterizes the order. Primates with remarkably few changes in their skeletons and musculature have adopted a bewildering variety of locomotor patterns. The "natural" habitat of primates—in the historical sense—is the canopy of the forest. Although many primates have adopted the ground as their principal foraging area during the day, given the opportunity they will return to the trees to sleep at night. Trees provide cover from the climate and protection from predators; they are of course also a source of food. Only the gelada, the hamadryas baboon of the mountainous regions of Ethiopia, and the chacma baboon, which lives on the rocky coast of the Cape of Good Hope, South Africa, are ground sleepers; yet even these animals seek the protection of the cliffs and rocky precipices of their habitats at night. No primate sleeps totally unprotected; as a consequence of their relative immunity from predation, primates are heavy sleepers.

FOUR TYPES OF LOCOMOTION

The essential arboreality of primates has guaranteed the relative uniformity of the locomotor apparatus. Even humans, who have long since abandoned the trees as their principal lodging place, have only partially lost the physical adaptations for tree climbing; their hands, in particular, remain in the arboreal mold. Only the feet have lost their primitive prehensility in adapting to bipedal walking. Primate locomotion can be classified on behavioral grounds into four major types: vertical clinging and leaping, quadrupedalism, brachiation, and bipedalism. Within these major categories, there are a number of subtypes, and within these subtypes, there are an infinite number of variations between species and, by virtue of individual variability, within species. The differences between the four major categories lie principally in the degree to which the forelimbs and hind limbs are used to climb, swing, jump, and run.

Vertical clinging and leaping, for instance, is primarily a function of the hind limbs, as is bipedalism, whereas the arm-swinging motion of brachiation is, of course, performed exclusively with the forelimbs. Quadrupedalism, as its name implies, involves both forelimbs and hind limbs, although not to an equal extent. Some quadrupeds are hind limb-dominated; in others, the forelimb and the hind limb are equally important. The hind limb-dominated

Diademed sifaka (Propithecus diadema). © Christopher Call Productions

primates, such as the langurs and colobus monkeys, employ a large element of leaping in their movements, a less-notable feature of the more generalized quadrupeds such as guenons. The quadrupedal category is inevitably somewhat of a grab bag, and the gaits included in it have not yet been studied critically. One subtype, here designated as slow climbing, differs profoundly from the other subtypes of the category, being somewhat ponderous and devoid of elements of leaping or jumping. The species in this category are lorises and pottos, which are arboreal and nocturnal.

As many authorities who have studied locomotion in free-ranging primate species have pointed out, the classifications of locomotion into categories is a somewhat artificial procedure. A chimpanzee shows a variety of different gaits according to the circumstances of the environment: knuckle walking, climbing, bipedalism, and brachiation. This holds true also for the langurs and colobus monkeys, which are designated semibrachiators, which means that they mainly move quadrupedally (usually with a "galloping gait" rather than walking) but also jump across gaps and occasionally swing by their arms. Although the categories are phrased in behavioral terms, their implications are also anatomic. Brachiation is the mode of locomotion for which the animal is specifically adapted; the anatomic correlates of brachiation are quite unmistakable and can be determined in fossil bones as much as in living animals. In some instances, it may well be that a particular anatomy is misleading. It has been argued that the anatomy of the great apes (including humans), for instance, is that of a brachiator, yet in fact they seldom brachiate (humans rarely and adult gorillas probably never). Watching gorillas, in particular, suggests that what appeared at first to be a locomotor adaptation may actually be a feeding one; the gorilla sits erect amid its food, reaching all around it to pull it in, and thereby saves an enormous amount of energy. The shortened lumbar spine (giving a lowered centre of gravity), broad chest, enhanced mobility of the shoulder joint, and flexible wrist may be related to this feeding style. The gibbons' specializations for brachiation may be derived from these same traits, rather than the other way about.

Changes in climate and geography during the evolutionary history of primates may also have led to structural atavisms in the anatomy of living primates. Many chimpanzees now living in woodland-savanna conditions in Africa, where the trees are widely spaced and generally unsuitable for the classic climbing style of forest-living chimpanzees, have adopted a largely ground-living life. Gorillas and chimpanzees are first and foremost knuckle walkers, but, given an environment like that of a zoo with a cage specially designed with lots of overhead bars and ropes, they will brachiate fairly frequently.

When the subject of primate arboreal locomotion is studied in evolutionary terms by using fossils, it becomes clear that locomotor categories are not discrete but constitute a continuum of change from a forelimb-dominated gait to a hind limb-dominated one. The best single indicator of gait, one that has the added advantage of being strictly quantitative, is the intermembral index. Briefly, the index is a ratio expressed as percentage of arm length to leg length; an index over 100 indicates relatively long arms. This provides a model by means of which the locomotion of an early primate can be inferred by determination of the intermembral index of the fossil skeleton. Animals do not necessarily fall discretely into categories. Species with indexes lying between those of clearly recognizable locomotor types represent transitional types, whose style of locomotion really does manifest features of both of the bracketing categories. Some lemurs have indexes that fall between 65 and 75, and their gait is a combination of vertical clinging and quadrupedalism. The South American spider monkeys (genus *Ateles*), whose index lies between 100 and 108, show a type of locomotion that contains the elements of both quadrupedalism and brachiation.

When the intermembral index is applied to fossil primates, it appears that the earliest primates living in the Eocene Epoch (56 million to 34 million years ago) must have moved about somewhat in the manner of modern vertical clingers and leapers. Quadrupedal gaits were well established during the Miocene Epoch (23 million to 5.3 million years ago) when the two major environmental types of quadrupedal gait— terrestrial and the arboreal—were established, with indexes in the region of 85–100 and 75–85, respectively. Brachiation, associated with a high intermembral index, was established as a way of arboreal life at the end of the Miocene, with the small hominid *Oreopithecus* from Italy. There is direct evidence of bipedalism's extending back four million years, and certain indirect evidence suggests that bipedalism might have evolved in a modified form up to a million years before that.

BIPEDALISM

Some degree of bipedal ability, of course, is a basic possession of the order Primates. All primates sit upright. Many stand upright without supporting their body weight by their arms, and some, especially the apes, actually walk upright for short periods. The view that the possession of uprightness is a solely human attribute is untenable; humans are merely the one species of the order that has exploited the potential of this ancestry to its extreme.

Chimpanzees, gorillas and gibbons, macaques, spider monkeys, capuchins, and others are all frequent bipedal walkers. To define humans categorically as "bipedal" is not enough; to describe them as habitually bipedal is nearer the truth, but habit as such does not leave its mark on fossil bones. Some more precise definition is needed. The human walk has been described as striding, a mode of locomotion defining a special pattern of behaviour and a special morphology. Striding, in a sense, is the quintessence of bipedalism; it is a means of traveling during which the energy output of the body is reduced to a physiological minimum by the smooth, undulating flow of the progression. It is a complex activity involving the joints and muscles of the whole body, and it is likely that the evolution of the human gait took place gradually over a period of 10 million years or so.

The pattern of locomotion of human ancestors immediately preceding the acquisition of bipedalism has long been a matter of controversy, and the question has not yet been resolved. The evidence derived from anatomic, physiological, and biochemical studies for the close affinity of chimpanzees and humans, and the slightly less close affinity of gorillas, would suggest that humans evolved from a knuckle-walking ancestry. There have been claims that the wrist anatomy of australopithecines shows remnant knuckle-walking adaptations. The issue is still hotly debated, and some authorities continue to support a brachiation model for the ancestry of all the apes. Other authorities have proposed other solutions: semibrachiation, for example, and even a form of locomotion similar to that of tarsiers and other clingers and leapers. At the present time, there is insufficient information to elucidate the phylogeny of man's bipedal gait, except that it can be assumed to have involved a large measure of truncal uprightness.

DIET

The diet of primates is a factor of their ecology that, during their evolution, has clearly played an important role in their dispersion and adaptive radiation as well as in the development of the teeth, jaws, and digestive system. Diet is also closely related to locomotor pattern and to body size.

The principal food substances taken by primates may be divided into vegetable (fruits, flowers, leaves, nuts, barks, pith, seeds, grasses, stems, roots, and tubers) and animal (birds, birds' eggs, lizards, small rodents and bats, insects, frogs, and crustacea). The flesh of larger mammals (including primates) is not listed as an important item of nonhuman primate diet, with the sole exception of chimpanzees—it is taken by baboons in special circumstances that are not yet fully understood.

While diet is selective and specific to the order in many mammalian groups, among primates it is difficult to establish any hard and fast rules. Although there are decided preferences for certain food items, catholicity is more characteristic than specificity. Generally speaking, primates are omnivorous, as the physiology of their digestive system attests. Relatively few examples of dietary specialization are to be found. The so-called leaf-eating monkeys, a sobriquet that embraces the whole of the subfamily Colobinae, including colobus monkeys and langurs, are by no means exclusively leaf eaters and according to season include flowers, fruit, and (in some cases) seeds in their diet. The howler monkeys of the New World have a similar dietary preference.

Broadly, however, certain overall dietary preferences are discernible. The leaf-eating langurs have already been mentioned. The apes (other than the mountain gorilla) are substantially fruit eaters. Many of the smaller nocturnal primitive species such as galagos, dwarf lemurs, sportive lemurs, the aye-aye, and the slender loris are substantially insectivorous; the tarsier is probably the only primate that is exclusively carnivorous, feeding on insects, lizards, and snakes. The larger diurnal lemurs (e.g., typical lemurs,

Aye-aye (Daubentonia madagascariensis) *eating a coconut.* Elizabeth Bomford/Ardea London

the sifaka, and the indri) are more vegetarian, including fruit, seeds, and leaves. It seems apparent that size, rather than activity rhythm, governs the nature of the primate diet. The small marmosets of the South American genus *Callithrix* have exclusively diurnal rhythms and are insectivorous and also eat gums, while the slightly larger, but equally diurnal, tamarins (genus *Saguinus*) are more omnivorous. An approximate cutoff point of 500 grams (17.6 oz), known as Kay's threshold, after the primatologist Richard Kay, who first drew attention to it, has been proposed as an upper limit for species subsisting mainly on insects

CIRCADIAN RHYTHM

The circadian rhythm is the cyclical 24-hour period of human biological activity. Within the circadian cycle, a person usually sleeps approximately 8 hours and is awake 16. During the wakeful hours, mental and physical functions are most active and tissue cell growth increases. During sleep, voluntary muscle activities nearly disappear and there is a decrease in metabolic rate, respiration, heart rate, body temperature, and blood pressure. The activity of the digestive system increases during the resting period, but that of the urinary system decreases. Hormones secreted by the body, such as the stimulant epinephrine (adrenaline), are released in maximal amounts about two hours before awakening so that the body is prepared for activity.

The circadian cycle is controlled by a region of the brain known as the hypothalamus, which is the master centre for integrating rhythmic information and establishing sleep patterns. A part of the hypothalamus called the suprachiasmatic nucleus (SCN) receives signals about light and dark from the retina of the eye. Upon activation by light, special photoreceptor cells in the retina transmit signals to the SCN via neurons of the retinohypothalamic tract. The signals are further transmitted to the pineal gland, a small cone-shaped structure that is attached to the posterior end (behind the hypothalamus) of the third cerebral ventricle and that is responsible for the production of a hormone called melatonin. Cyclical fluctuations of melatonin are vital for maintaining a normal circadian rhythm. When the retina detects light, melatonin production is inhibited and wakefulness ensues; light wavelength (colour) and intensity are important factors affecting the extent to which melatonin production is inhibited. In contrast, in response to darkness, melatonin production is increased, and the body begins to prepare for sleep. Sleep-inducing reactions, such as decreases in body temperature and blood pressure, are generated when melatonin binds to receptors in the SCN.

The natural time signal for the circadian pattern is the change from darkness to light. Where daylight patterns are not consistent, as in outer space, regimented cycles are established to simulate the 24-hour day. If one tries to break the circadian rhythm by ignoring sleep for a number of days, psychological disorders begin to arise. The human body can learn to function in cycles ranging between 18 and 28 hours, but any variance greater or less than this usually causes the body to revert to a 24-hour cycle. Even in totally lighted areas such as the subpolar twilight zone, the body has regular cycles of sleep and wakefulness once the initial adjustment has been made.

Any drastic shift in the circadian cycle requires a certain period for readjustment. Each individual reacts to these changes differently. Travel across a number of time zones is commonly accompanied by circadian rhythm stress, sometimes called "jet lag." For example, jet travel between Tokyo and New York City creates a time difference of 10 hours; it usually takes several days for the body to readjust to the new day-night pattern. Too-frequent shifts in circadian patterns, such as several transoceanic flights a month, can lead to mental and physical fatigue. Preflight or postflight adaptation can be achieved by gradually changing one's sleeping patterns to simulate those that will be necessary in the new environment. Space travel is even more extreme. Astronauts first encounter rapid changes in the day-night cycle while in Earth's orbit. Beyond this, the void becomes a constant blackness with no observable distinction between daytime and nighttime.

The circadian cycle can alter the effectiveness of some drugs. For example, the timing of administration of hormonal drugs so as to be in accord with their natural circadian production pattern seems to place less stress on the body and produce more effective medical results.

and a lower limit for those relying on leaves. The reason is that insects are small and hard to catch, and a large animal simply would not be able to catch enough to sustain it during its waking hours. The cellulose and hemicellulose components of leaves, on the other hand, require complex digestive processes, and a small animal would be unable to maintain a constant throughput. Fruit, as a dietary component, suffers from neither of these constraints.

SIZE IN EVOLUTIONARY PERSPECTIVE

In evolutionary terms, increase in size has probably played a large part in determining the direction of primate evolution. Early primates of about 50 million years ago were small forest-living creatures whose molar teeth bore high, pointed cusps but were neither as tall nor as pointed as those of their insectivore-like ancestors, whose molars were ideally adapted for cracking the hard chitinous exoskeletons of insects. This fact suggests that the reduction of the molar cusps was associated with the adoption of a fruit-eating habit. Although this has some validity as a generalization, it should not be taken too literally, as most primates include some insects in their diet and of course there are many almost exclusively insectivorous forms, which have nonetheless reduced the height and acuity of their molar cusps. Increasing body size, a trend that is clearly apparent throughout primate evolution, would have been associated with the adoption of supplementary sources of food. An increase in size and the gradual addition of bulk foods to the diet would in turn have affected the habitat and the pattern of locomotion of primates. Suitable adaptations in this case would have been the facility to climb, leap, and balance in trees.

It is noteworthy that, during evolution, the development of a prehensile foot preceded that of a prehensile hand. Vertical-clinging primates such as the tarsiers or small, squirrel-like quadrupeds such as the marmosets—all of which have prehensile feet but not completely prehensile hands—by remaining or becoming small, have avoided the evolutionary pressures that have impinged on larger primates. A large arboreal primate without entirely prehensile hands is at a considerable disadvantage in moving about in the canopy of trees, but a small one suffers little disadvantage. Amid the large and firm branches, size is no particular hazard, but at the periphery of the crown, where the fruit is most abundant and the branches are slender and flexible, the risk of falling is increased. It is therefore likely that the combination of an increase in body size associated with the inevitable shift toward a bulk diet led first to the evolution of a grasping hand, then to the appearance of a prehensile hand, and finally to an opposable thumb. Four prehensile extremities are obviously more effective than two in defying gravity.

Such adaptations of the forelimbs would have had the effect of equalizing the role of the limbs. The limbs of vertical clingers are functionally disparate, the lower pair being dominantly propulsive and the upper secondary and purely supportive. The limbs of quadrupeds, however, are more homogeneous, both pairs having a propulsive function during running. Thus, it would seem that the transition in locomotor grade between vertical clinging and leaping and quadrupedalism came about as an adaptation to increased body size. Size, diet, ecology, locomotion, and anatomic structure provide a constellation of causes and effects that are critical factors in the evolution of the primates.

FOREST AND SAVANNA

The chief physiognomic features of rainforests, the ancestral home of the order Primates and the principal habitat of nonhuman primates today, are the evergreen broad-leaved trees that collectively form a closed canopy, so opaque to sunlight that the forest floor is in perpetual twilight. Epiphytes (plants that grow on other plants, such as trees) and thick-stemmed lianas (vines that are rooted in soil but which twine around and drape off trees), link one crown to another and provide aerial pathways for monkeys to pass from tree to tree through a continuum of interlacing branches, a three-dimensional maze that provides home, restaurant, shopping districts, and highways for primates. Three strata of rainforests are broadly distinguishable: an understory, a middle story, and an upper story. The understory, consisting

Gibbons (family Hylobatidae*).* Edmund Appel/Photo Researchers, Inc.

of shrubs and saplings, is often "closed," the crowns of the constituent trees overlapping one another to form a dense continuous horizontal layer. The middle story is characterized by trees that are in lateral contact but do not overlap; the highest story, by tall trees, some 50 metres (about 165 feet) or more, that form a discontinuous layer of umbrella-shaped crowns. The occasional "emergent" forest giant may tower above the highest layer of the canopy. There is some evidence, much of it conflicting, that some zonation of forest primates occurs within the forest canopy. The stratification of forest is extremely variable; the number of layers tends to diminish from three to two in secondary forest, dry deciduous forest, and montane forest and from two to one as temperate zone, tropical woodland, or montane woodland supervenes.

Tropical grasslands, or savannas, are also the homes of primates in Africa and Asia; no savanna-living primates exist in South America. Tropical grasslands comprise a mixture of trees and grasses, the proportion of trees to grass varying directly with the rainfall. Areas of high seasonal rainfall support single-story woodlands of tall trees, while lush grasses form the ground vegetation; but, where rainfall is both seasonal and low, the trees consist of stubby xerophilous (dry-loving) shrubs and short, tussocky grasses. The principal primates of the savanna are the ground-living species: in Africa, the vervets, baboons, and patas monkey; and in Asia, the macaques and the Hanumān langur.

Tropical montane forests or tropical rainforests at high altitude also abound in primates in Africa, Asia, and South America. In equatorial Africa, certain primate species have colonized the montane-savanna regions, or moorlands, where the rugged mountainous terrain and seasonal food scarcity support herds of geladas and hamadryas baboons. These high mountaineers of Africa have no ecological counterparts in Asia or South America.

CHAPTER 2
PRIMATE MORPHOLOGY

The basis of the success of the order Primates is the relatively unspecialized nature of their structure and the highly specialized plasticity of their behaviour. This combination has permitted the primates throughout their evolutionary history to exploit the wide variety of novel ecological opportunities that have come their way. Although there are a few highly specialized species among the lower primates (the aye-aye, the tarsier, the potto, and the lorises, for instance), the higher primates, collectively known as the anthropoids, are extremely conservative in their structure; morphologically speaking, they have maintained a position in the evolutionary midstream and have avoided the potential stagnation of specialized life near the banks. Specialization is not always a liability; in times of environmental stability, the specialized animal enjoys many advantages, but, in a rapidly changing world, it is the less-specialized animals that are more likely to survive and flourish. The plasticity of primate behaviour is largely a function of the brain. The primate brain is distinguished by its relatively large size compared with the size of the body as a whole; it is also notable for the complexity and elaboration of the cerebral cortex, the function of which is to receive, analyze, and synthesize the incoming impulses from the sense organs and to convert them into appropriate motor actions, which in turn constitute behaviour.

GENERAL STRUCTURE

Primates are essentially arboreal animals whose limbs are adapted for climbing, leaping, and running in trees. Active arboreal life requires the mechanical assistance of a long tail and sensitive, grasping hands and feet with opposable thumbs and big toes to aid in climbing and to ensure stability on slender branches high above the ground. Active arboreal locomotion also requires a much more accurate judgment of distances than life on the ground; this is facilitated by the development of stereoscopic vision, the anatomic basis of visual judgments in depth. The forward-facing eyes of primates are adaptations for this type of visual precision. A highly developed sense of smell is not nearly as important for animals leading an arboreal life as it is for those on the ground. Many primates thus have a much-reduced olfactory mechanism; noses are shorter, and the nasal conchae (scroll bones) of the nose are reduced in number and complexity compared with most nonprimate mammals—although it should not be overlooked that many lemurs and New World monkeys do enjoy a rich olfactory world, especially in the social sphere.

Above all, the principal evolutionary trend of primates has been the elaboration of the brain, particularly of that portion of the cerebral hemispheres known as the neopallium or neocortex. A neocortex is characteristic of higher vertebrates, such as mammals, which operate under the control of multiple sources of sensory input. In many mammals, the olfactory system dominates the senses, and the cerebral hemispheres consist largely of palaeocortex— the "smell brain"—of lower vertebrates. The arboreal habit of primates has led to a dethronement of the olfactory sense and the accession of a tactile, visually dominant sensory system. This evolutionary trend has resulted in the dramatic expansion and differentiation of the neocortex.

VERTEBRAL COLUMN AND POSTURE

All primates retain collarbones (lost in many mammalian groups), a separate radius and ulna in the forearm, and a separate tibia and fibula in the lower leg. The single exception to this among living primates is the tarsier, in which the fibula becomes fused to the tibia.

The primate vertebral column shows a basic mammalian pattern of components, including an "anticlinal" vertebra situated in the mid-thoracic (upper-back) region of the spinal column and marking the transition between the forelimb and hind limb segments. In a galloping greyhound, the anticlinal vertebra is at the apex of the acute curve of the back. An anticlinal vertebra is characteristic of all quadrupeds and is seen in all primate families except the apes, whose posture is upright or semiupright. The evolutionary trend in the vertebral column is toward shortening the lumbar, sacral, and caudal regions. Extreme shortening in the lumbar region, with complete loss of the caudal (tail) vertebrae, occurs in gibbons, the great apes, and humans. Prehensility of the tail is a specialization of certain New World monkeys, but it appears also for a brief period in the infants of many Old World monkey groups, in which it provides an important mechanical aid to survival.

HANDS AND FEET

With three exceptions, all primates have retained five digits on hand and foot. The exceptions are the spider monkeys and the so-called woolly spider monkey of South America and the colobus monkeys of Africa, which have lost or reduced the thumb. This appears to be an adaptation for locomotion, the rationale for which is not fully understood at present.

All, though to different degrees, possess prehensile (grasping) hands and all (except humans) prehensile feet. The hands of catarrhines show a greater range of precise manipulative activity than those of other primates.

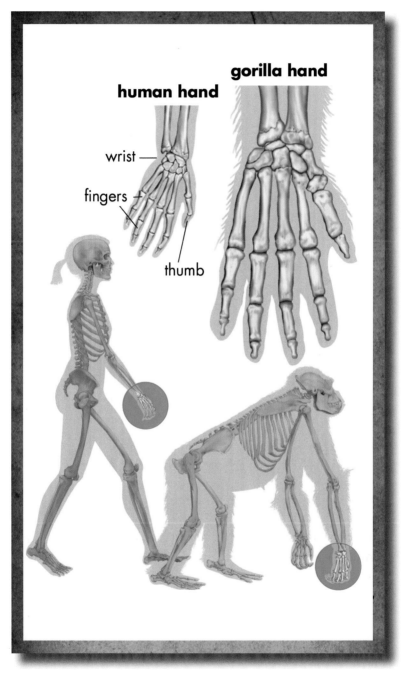

The hand structure of a human being (left) and of a gorilla (right).
Encyclopædia Britannica, Inc.

Lemurs, for example, lack the functional duality of the hands of most apes and Old World monkeys (catarrhines). Duality in hand function has been described in terms of precision and power grips. The power grip of lemurs and lorises is very well developed, but the precision grip is lacking. The New World monkeys show a considerable advance over primitive primates in tactile sensitivity, but they possess less functionally effective hands in prehensile terms than Old World monkeys.

The critical component of the prehensile hand in terms of skilled manipulation is the opposable thumb—a thumb, that is to say, that is capable of being moved freely and independently. The movement of opposition is a rotary movement in which the thumb, swinging about its own axis, comes to face the lower surface of the tips of the fingers. The opposable thumb is the basis of the precision grip that, though present to some extent in all primates, is particularly highly developed in man. Opposability is present to some degree in most primates but varies considerably in its functional effectiveness as an instrument of fine manipulation. Humans and baboons are preeminent in this respect. The apes, having short thumbs and long fingers, are handicapped in relation to delicate manual dexterity but are adept in the coarser elements of hand use, particularly in relation to tree climbing.

TEETH

A dentition with different kinds of teeth (heterodonty)— incisors, canines, and cheek teeth—is characteristic of all primates and indeed of mammals generally. Heterodonty is a primitive characteristic, and primates have evolved less far from the original pattern than most mammals. The principal changes are a reduction in the number of teeth and an elaboration of the cusp pattern of the molars.

Orangutan (Pongo pygmaeus), *female.* Encyclopædia Britannica, Inc.

The dental formula of primitive placental mammals is assumed to have been $5 . 1 . 4 . 3 / 5 . 1 . 4 . 3 = 44$ teeth (the numbers being the numbers respectively of pairs of incisors, canines, premolars, and molars in the upper and lower jaws). No living primate has retained more than two incisors in the upper jaw. The incisors are subject to considerable variation in strepsirrhines. Characteristically, the upper incisors are peglike, one or the other pair often being absent; in the lower jaw, the incisors show a peculiar conformation that has been likened structurally and functionally to a comb. This dental comb is composed of the lower canines and lower incisors compressed from side to side and slanted forward; the most specialized dental combs — seen, for example, in the fork-crowned lemur (genus *Phaner*) and the needle-clawed galago (genus *Euoticus*) — are used for scraping exudates off bark, but other species use the structure for piercing fruit, for nipping off leaves, and for grooming the fur. Canines are present throughout the order but show remarkable variation in size, shape, projection, and function. Characteristically, the teeth of Old World monkeys have a function in the maintenance of social order within the group as well as an overtly offensive role; their function as organs of digestion is relatively unimportant. They are large and subject to sexual dimorphism, being larger in males than females. Great apes have smaller canines than Old World monkeys, though still sexually dimorphic; human canines are smaller still, and there is no size difference between the sexes.

The trend in the evolution of the cheek teeth has been to increase the number of cusps and reduce the number of teeth. Both molars and premolars show this tendency. No living primate has four premolars; primitive primates, tarsiers, and New World monkeys have retained three on each side of each jaw, but in the apes and Old World monkeys, there are only two premolars. The primitive premolars are

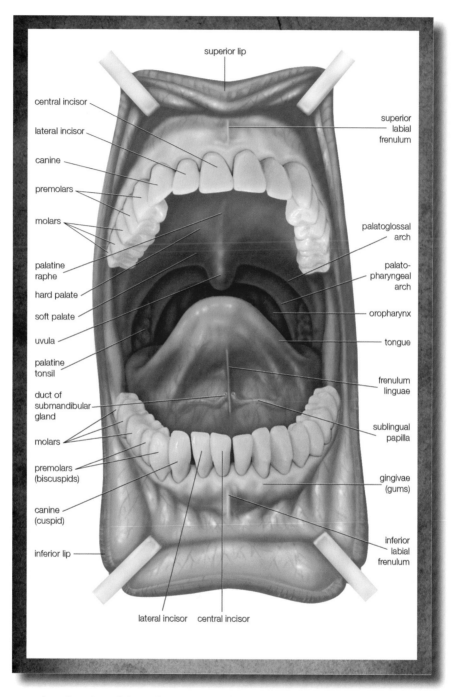

Anterior view of the oral cavity. Encyclopædia Britannica, Inc.

uniform in shape and are unicuspid, but in primates the most posterior premolar tends to evolve either one or two extra cusps (molarization), an adaptation that extends the cheek-tooth row for a herbivorous diet. In species with large upper canines, the most anterior lower premolar assumes a peculiar shape known as sectorial, functioning as a hone for the scythelike canine. In humans, whose canines are small and unremarkable, the first and second premolars are identical in shape and two-cusped.

The trend in the morphology of the molars has been to increase the primitive three cusps to four or five, the less-insectivorous species having four cusps on the molar crown in the upper jaw and five cusps on the lower. A tendency in smaller New World monkeys has been to reduce the molar series from three to two in both jaws.

SNOUTS, MUZZLES, AND NOSES

The reduction of the snout in primates is a correlate of the diminution of the sense of smell, or olfaction. To a great extent, visual acuity and manual dexterity have replaced the sensitive, inquiring nose found in so many nonprimate mammals. A marked reduction in the complexity of the nasal conchae (scroll bones of the nose), the richness of the innervation of the olfactory mucous membrane, and the sensitivity of the moist tip of the nose—the rhinarium—are associated with the reduction in length of the primate snout. Still, although the trend in primate evolution is toward a dethronement of the primacy of the sense of smell, there are still some good snouts to be seen in those lower primates that retain a naked moist rhinarium attached to the upper lip.

Lemurs, lorises, tarsiers, and New World monkeys depend for many aspects of their social and reproductive behaviour on olfactory signals, by means of special scent glands distributed in different regions of the body but congregated principally in the anal and perineal regions (in lemurs and lorises) or in the sternal region (in New World monkeys and tarsiers). Marking behaviour, the placing of scent at various points in the environment, is a prominent feature of the repertoire of communication in these primates. Marking behaviour ceases to be of much importance in the Old World monkeys and apes, with some exceptions such as mandrills, siamangs, concolor gibbons, and even orangutans among the hominoids. All of these primates possess sternal glands, but in all of them the structures by which olfactory signals are given and received are diminished. But all higher primates, including humans, sniff at unfamiliar items of food before placing them in the mouth.

The shape of the nose of higher primates is one of the most reliable means of distinguishing Old World monkeys from New World monkeys at a glance. In New World monkeys (the Platyrrhini, meaning "flat nosed"), the nose is broad, and the nostrils are set wide apart, well separated by a broad septum, and point sideways. In the apes and Old World monkeys (the Catarrhini, meaning "downward nosed"), the nostrils are set close together, point forward or downward, and are separated by a very narrow septum.

Some Old World monkeys—particularly those that have adopted

Male hamadryas (Papio hamadryas). Bruce Coleman/Bruce Coleman Ltd.

NASAL CONCHAE

The nasal conchae, which are also called the turbinates or the turbinals, are thin, scroll-shaped bony elements that form the upper chambers of the nasal cavities. They increase the surface area of these cavities, thus providing for rapid warming and humidification of air as it passes to the lungs. In higher vertebrates the olfactory epithelium is associated with these upper chambers, resulting in keener sense of smell. In humans, who are less dependent on the sense of smell, the nasal conchae are much reduced. The components of the nasal conchae are the inferior, medial, superior, and supreme turbinates.

a ground-living way of life, such as baboons and mandrills, of the subfamily Cercopithecinae—appear to have readopted a long snout during their evolution. This structure, however, is not primarily olfactory in function but seems, rather, to be allometric, more closely related to the large size of the jaws and the prominence of the canine teeth; it should be considered a dental muzzle rather than an olfactory one.

SENSORY RECEPTION AND THE BRAIN

Among mammals in general, the olfactory system is the primary receptor for environmental information; consequently, the brain of most mammals is dominated by the olfactory centres. In primates the sense of smell is considerably less important than the well-developed visual system and highly refined sense of touch. The primate brain is enlarged in the specific areas concerned with vision (occipital lobes) and touch (parietal lobes) and thus takes a characteristic shape throughout the higher primates.

Touch

The skin of the primate hand is well adapted for tactile discrimination. Meissner's corpuscles, the principal receptors

Cotton-top tamarin (Saguinus oedipus) *used in an experiment to determine if music containing calls from others of the same species affected behaviour.* Bryce Richter/University of Wisconsin-Madison

for touch in hairless skin, are best developed in apes and humans, but they can be found in all primates. Structurally correlated with a high level of tactile sensitivity are certain anatomic features of the skin of the hands and feet, such as the absence of pads on the palms and soles and the presence of a finely ridged pattern of skin corrugations known as dermatoglyphics (the basis for fingerprints).

EYES AND VISION

The evolutionary trend toward frontality of the eyes has not proceeded as far in most lemurs as in lorises and more advanced primates. In primitive mammals the central axes of the two bony orbits are 140° apart. In lemurs this angle is considerably less, 60°–70°, and in the apes and monkeys and in the slender loris (genus *Loris*), the divergence has been reduced to 20°. It should be noted that the axes of the eyeballs (as distinct from the bony orbits) in apes and monkeys are, in fact, parallel.

Colour vision is of considerable advantage to arboreal animals living on fruits and insects. Most mammals have both rod and cone receptors in their retinas, and almost all primates have at least two kinds of cones, a short-wavelength (blue) type and a medium–long-wavelength (red-green) type. All, therefore, seem to have well-developed colour vision, the exceptions so far known being some of the nocturnal species: durukulis of South America, the tarsiers, and at least some of the galagos. Catarrhines and howler monkeys have separate red- and green-responding cones, determined by closely linked loci on the X chromosome. In most other investigated platyrrhines (New World monkeys), red and green are determined by alleles at a single locus, again on the X chromosome; thus, males are always dichromatic, whereas females may be either dichromatic (if homozygous) or trichromatic (if heterozygous). It is suggested that, during the evolution of catarrhines, the red-green locus duplicated, one of the daughter loci fixing the red gene and the other the green.

NERVOUS INTEGRATION

The elaboration of touch and vision supplements the senses of smell, hearing, and

Male gorilla (Gorilla gorilla). Kenneth W. Fink/Root Resources

taste, providing the primate with a sensory armament of great range and flexibility. The primate central nervous system is sufficiently refined to deal with the elaborate bombardment of environmental information reaching it. Association areas provide connections between the input and output centres of the brain—the motor and sensory cortex. Association areas are the memory banks where the memory of past experience is encoded in the infinitely complicated plexiform arrangement of the neurons, the brain cells, and their processes. All sensory impulses reaching the cortical centres of the central nervous system are routed through the association areas for conditioning, as it were, before reaching the effector side or output side where the appropriate response is initiated in the cells of the motor cortex. The more highly developed the association areas of the brain are, the more specific and appropriate is the behaviour and the more versatile is the animal in facing environmental demands.

THE BRAIN

The principal evolutionary trend in brain development has been toward elaboration. The neocortex of higher primates possesses highly developed associative functions, an aptitude for receiving, analyzing, and synthesizing the sensory input from visual, olfactory, auditory, gustatory, and tactile receptors and converting them into the appropriate motor responses.

The brain of monkeys and apes is larger, both absolutely and relatively, than that of lemurs, lorises, or tarsiers. For instance, the weight of the simplest anthropoid brain, that of a marmoset, is three times greater than the brain weight of a bush baby of comparative size. This quantitative increase is attributable in part to the elaboration of the regions of the neocortex concerned with tactile and visual sensitivity and in part to the elaboration of the intrinsic pathways connecting one part of the brain with another. The large brain of humans is attributable not so much to an increased nerve cell content as to an increase in the size of the nerve cells and to a greater complexity of the connections linking one cell to another.

The external form of the anthropoid cerebral cortex is characterized by a complicated pattern of folds and fissures (sulci and gyri) in the brain surface. The fissural pattern is seen in its simplest form in the marmosets, but in the larger New World monkeys (capuchins, for instance), the cerebrum is richly convoluted. Gyri and sulci are well marked in Old World monkeys and in the apes, the complexity of the pattern closely approximating the tortuous mazelike pattern seen in humans.

REPRODUCTIVE SYSTEM

The functions of the individual organs of reproductive systems are fairly uniform throughout the primates, but, in spite of this physiological homology, there is a remarkable degree of variation in minor detail of organs between groups—particularly in the external genitalia, which, by their variation, provide a morphological basis for the reproductive isolation of the species. There could be no more effective barrier to mating between different species than incompatibility of the male and female sex organs. In addition, during primate fetal development, the placental connection between fetus and mother can be either of two types. The placentation of lemurs and lorises is epitheliochorial (the bloodstreams of mother and fetus are separated by several layers of cells), whereas the placentation in tarsiers, monkeys, and apes is hemochorial (the maternal bloodstream makes direct contact with the membrane containing the fetus).

Male and Female Genitalia

Among the characteristics of the primate order as listed by the 19th-century zoologist George Mivart, the penis is described as "pendulous" and the testes as "scrotal." In contrast to most other mammals (bats being the principal exception), the primate penis is not attached to the abdominal wall but hangs free. The testes, with a few exceptions among the lemurs, in which they are withdrawn seasonally, lie permanently in the scrotal sac, to which they migrate from their intra-abdominal position some time before birth (in humans) or after birth (in nonhuman primates). In all primates except modern humans, tarsiers, and some South American monkeys, the penis contains a small bone called the baculum, a typically mammalian characteristic. The uterus of female primates shows all grades of transition between the two-horned (bicornuate) uterus, typical of most mammals, to the single-chambered (simplex) uterus of the higher primates and humans.

Variations between primate taxa are demonstrated most strikingly by the glans penis, scrotum, and perineum of the male and by the clitoris and labial folds of the female vulva. In the clitoris, there is in most primates a small bone, the baubellum, homologous with the baculum of the penis. The length and form of the clitoris, which when elongated mimics the penis (as in spider monkeys, for instance), are a potent source of confusion in determining the sex of certain New World primates. The coloration of the male scrotum in forest-living primates, particularly of the guenon (genus *Cercopithecus*) and in drills and mandrills (genus *Mandrillus*), shows an infinite range of variations and provides a species-recognition signal of considerable effectiveness.

The external appearance of the genitalia undergoes seasonal variation in a number of primates. In the male, swellings of the testes and colour changes of the scrotum occur, and, in the female, swelling and coloration of the vulva and perineal region herald ovulation, sometimes most obtrusively. Turgidity and excessive vascularity of the tissues of the perineum are probably characteristic of all mammals, but there are certain primate species in which this engorgement reaches monstrous proportions, notably baboons, mangabeys, some macaques, and chimpanzees. Regions other than the primary sex organs may also be affected by hormones circulating at certain periods of the reproductive cycle. For instance, in the gelada (*Theropithecus*), the skin on the front of the female chest, which normally bears a string of caruncles resembling the beads of a necklace, becomes engorged and brightly coloured. A German zoologist, Wolfgang Wickler, has suggested that this is a form of sexual mimicry, the chest mimicking the perineal region. The observation that geladas spend many hours a day feeding in a sitting posture provides a feasible, Darwinian explanation of this curious physiological adaptation.

PLACENTA

The placenta, the defining characteristic of the eutherian mammals (a class of mammals that includes everything but monotremes, i.e., egg laying mammals such as duck billed platypuses), is a vascular structure that permits physiological interchange of blood and body fluids between the mother and the fetus and the breakdown products of the fetal metabolism; it also provides a two-way barrier preventing the passage of some, but not all, noxious substances and organisms such as bacteria and viruses from one individual to the other and is the source of hormones such as estrogens.

The placenta is a flat, discoid-shaped "cake" in humans, some of the other monkeys and apes, and the tarsiers. In many monkeys, it is bidiscoidal, having two linked portions. The placenta is intimately attached on its outer surface to the endometrium, the lining of the uterus, by fingerlike processes (villi) that embed themselves in the endometrium, where complete vascular connections between the two circulations are achieved. The connection between fetal and maternal circulations appears as two distinct types among primates, a distinction that is believed to have had an important effect on the evolution of the order. In the first type (epitheliochorial), found in the lemurs and lorises, several cellular layers separate the maternal and fetal bloodstreams and thus limit the passage of molecules of serum proteins. In the second type (hemochorial), found in tarsiers, monkeys, and apes, the relationship is much more intimate, there being no cell layers separating the two circulations so that serum proteins can easily pass. In haplorrhines the endometrium becomes highly vascularised about two weeks after ovulation, in preparation for the possible implantation of a zygote; if this does not occur, it is shed via menstruation. The placenta is shed at birth in all primates and, except rarely among humans, is eaten by the mother.

CHAPTER 3
PRIMATE PALEONTOLOGY AND EVOLUTION

The order Primates has been studied with vigour by scientists since the time of Galen of Pergamum. Aristotle and Hippocrates, in the 4th and 3rd centuries BCE, recognized the similarity of man and apes, but it was Galen who demonstrated the kinship by dissection. He wrote, "The ape is likest to man in viscera, muscles, arteries, veins, nerves and in the form of bones." It should be noted that Galen was in fact referring to monkeys, primarily to the Barbary "ape" (a species of macaque, *Macaca sylvanus*), and not to the true apes, which were unknown to Westerners until the 15th century. None of these early scientists saw any evolutionary significance in the similarity of humans and "apes," a correspondence that they regarded as purely coincidental. An inkling of humans' relationship with primates must have penetrated the mind of St. Albertus Magnus, probably the leading naturalist of the Middle Ages, who produced a classification of animal life in his book *De animalibus*. Albertus's classification, which placed man between "apes" (monkeys) on the one hand and "animals" on the other, provides the first whiff of the "missing-link" concept, which later was to befog the issue of humans' place in nature.

The Dark Ages were aptly named as far as knowledge of primates is concerned. The first evidence of a renaissance of interest was in the time of Vesalius, the great Belgian anatomist of the 16th century, who published a comparative anatomy of man and "apes" in order to confound the precepts of Galen. He did not succeed in disproving Galen's assertion that "ape is likest to man," but he unwittingly succeeded in stirring up an interest in the biology of primates that has never flagged since. The first true ape studied as a scientific specimen was a chimpanzee dissected by Edward Tyson, an English anatomist, in 1699. Tyson's specimen, which he called the "Orang-Outang, sive Homo Sylvestris," is housed to this day in the Natural History Museum, London, mounted in a standing position reflecting Tyson's belief that he had discovered the Pygmy, a race of humans known since the time of the ancient Greeks. Tyson wrote of his "pygmie" that it was "no man, nor yet a common ape but a sort of animal between both." It never occurred to Tyson or his contemporaries, who believed that all animals had been created independently in their current image, that humans, apes, and monkeys

BARBARY MACAQUES

Barbary macaque (Macaca sylvana).
Tom McHugh/Photo Researchers

The Barbary macaque (*Macaca sylvanus*), which is also called magot, is a tailless ground-dwelling monkey that lives in groups in the upland forests of Algeria, Tunisia, Morocco, and Gibraltar. It is about 60 cm (24 inches) long and has light yellowish brown fur and a bald pale pink face. Adult males weigh about 16 kg (35 pounds), adult females 11 kg (24 pounds). The species was introduced into Gibraltar, probably by the Romans or the Moors. According to legend, British dominion over the Rock of Gibraltar will end only when this macaque is gone. Because it has no tail, this monkey is sometimes incorrectly called the Barbary ape.

were connected by common evolutionary descent. In 1758 Carolus Linnaeus—the father of animal and plant classification—added the lemurs and bats to the monkeys, apes, and man and called the whole assemblage the Primates. His conclusion was regarded as a grave blow to human dignity, and it was followed by new classifications such as that of Johann Blumenbach in 1776, placing man in a separate order. Man was not again considered part of the primate order until a century later when the English anatomist St. George Mivart, in the climate of post-Darwinian thought, published his classification of primates.

The first evolutionist was a French scholar of the late 18th century, Jean-Baptiste Lamarck, who saw animal life as an uninterrupted continuity in which old species were transformed into new species in a sequence of increasing complexity and perfection. However, it was Georges Cuvier, a rabid antievolutionist, who in 1821 had the historic distinction of describing *Adapis*, the first fossil primate genus ever recognized. Fossils such as *Adapis*, Cuvier believed, were the remains of animals destroyed by past catastrophes such as floods and earthquakes, and living animals were new stocks divinely created to fill the vacuum—a view consistent with the widely held notion that species were immutable. During the early 19th century, a number of geologists and biologists questioned the doctrine of immutability, but it was not until 1859, with the publication of Charles Darwin's *On the Origin of Species by Means of Natural Selection*, that positive evidence was provided, along with a sound alternative theory. The Darwinian contention that humans not only had evolved but had evolved from a simian (apelike) ancestor resulted in acrimonious debate among scientists, theologians, philosophers, and laymen. As influential zoologists and anatomists rose to support Darwin, humanity's primate consanguinity began to be accepted, if not actually relished. Today, few scientists deny that humans and the lower primates belong in the same order; in fact, much current research is directed toward closing the apparent gap between the highest of the nonhuman primates, chimpanzees and gorillas, and humans.

In times past, the public image of primates was largely dictated by prevailing religious beliefs. In Asian countries, where primates abound, monkeys have for a long time been regarded with various degrees of deference that—among Hindus in India, for instance—amounts almost to worship. In Europe and North America, where monkeys and apes are totally absent, no religious sect has attached divine significance to them; in fact, the reverse has been the case, monkeys at various times having been regarded as the personification of evil and depravity, familiars of the devil. This image, however, is fading as a result of instruction in schools and advances in naturalistic presentation of primates in zoos and in the media. The nonhuman primate is generally accepted by Western and other cultures as an animal of peculiar interest to humanity with many amusing and endearing qualities.

The activities of nonhuman primates, however, are less endearing to farmers and agriculturists in certain parts of the world. In South Africa, the chacma baboon (*Papio ursinus*) competes with domestic sheep for grazing lands and is an occasional predator of lambs; in West and Central Africa, native crops are subject to daily assaults by forest-living monkeys; and in India, macaques, which have been accorded a semisacred status, live alongside people in towns and villages and are parasitic upon them for food and shelter.

Scientific interest in nonhuman primates—their structure at all levels and their way of life—is currently in the ascendancy. Their value as research animals has decreased in recent years, as a result of both conservation concerns and ethical qualms, but, at the beginning of the 21st century, 100,000 or more monkeys were still being

Rhesus monkey (Macaca mulatta). © Photos.com/Jupiterimages

consumed annually by laboratories in the study of human diseases, the production of vaccines, experimental organ transplantation, the testing of drugs, and even clinical trials of new cosmetics. Their scientific usefulness has raised important problems of conservation of primate stocks in the wild, and exportation of monkeys is no longer permitted from many countries. Other research fields depending upon observation and experimentation with nonhuman primates include those of endocrinology, neurology, psychology, and sociology. As a result of such studies, much is learned that is of great significance for humans and the betterment of society.

RENEWED INTEREST IN PRIMATE ORIGINS

Beginning in the 1950s, there was a notable expression of interest in primate paleontology. Since then, hardly a year has passed without the announcement of some new major discovery. New sites have been opened up and old discoveries redescribed and reallocated. New techniques in geologic dating, palynology (the study of fossil pollen), paleoclimatology and paleoecology, and taphonomy (the interpretation of fossil sites) have helped to lift primate paleontology into the forefront of the life sciences and have aroused public interest to an unprecedented level. The popularity of all aspects of the evolution of human beings is reflected, for instance, in the spate of books covering this field published during this period.

LOUIS S.B. LEAKEY

(b. Aug. 7, 1903, Kabete, Kenya—d. Oct. 1, 1972, London, Eng.)

Louis Seymour Bazett Leakey was a Kenyan archaeologist and anthropologist whose fossil discoveries in East Africa proved that human beings were far older than had previously been believed. He concluded that human evolution was centred in Africa, rather than in Asia, as earlier discoveries had suggested. Leakey was also noted for his controversial interpretations of these archaeological finds.

Born of British missionary parents, Leakey spent his youth with the Kikuyu people of Kenya, about whom he later wrote. He was educated at the University of Cambridge and began his archaeological research in East Africa in 1924; he was later aided by his second wife, the archaeologist Mary Douglas Leakey (née Nicol), and their sons. He held various appointments at major British and American universities and was curator of the Coryndon Memorial Museum in Nairobi from 1945 to 1961.

In 1931 Leakey began his research at Olduvai Gorge in Tanzania, which became the site of his most famous discoveries. The first finds were animal fossils and crude stone tools, but in 1959 Mary Leakey uncovered a fossil hominin (member of the human lineage) that was given the name *Zinjanthropus* (now generally regarded as a form of *Paranthropus*, similar to *Australopithecus*) and was believed to be about 1.7 million years old. Leakey later theorized that *Zinjanthropus* was not a direct ancestor of modern man; he claimed this distinction for other hominin fossil remains that his team discovered at Olduvai Gorge in 1960–63 and that Leakey named *Homo habilis*. Leakey held that *H. habilis* lived contemporaneously with *Australopithecus* in East Africa and represented a more advanced hominin on the direct evolutionary line to *H. sapiens*. Initially many scientists disputed Leakey's interpretations and classifications of the fossils he had found, although they accepted the significance of the finds themselves. They contended that *H. habilis* was not sufficiently different from *Australopithecus* to justify a separate classification. Subsequent finds by the Leakey family and others, however, established that *H. habilis* does indeed represent an evolutionary step between the australopiths (who eventually became extinct) and *H. erectus*, who may have been a direct ancestor of modern man.

Among the other important finds made by Leakey's team was the discovery in 1948 at Rusinga Island in Lake Victoria, Kenya, of the remains of *Proconsul africanus*, a common ancestor of both humans and apes that lived about 25 million years ago. At Fort Ternan (east of Lake Victoria) in 1962, Leakey's team discovered the remains of *Kenyapithecus*, another link between apes and early man that lived about 14 million years ago.

Leakey's discoveries formed the basis for the most important subsequent research into the earliest origins of human life. He was also instrumental in persuading Jane Goodall, Dian Fossey, and Biruté M.F. Galdikas to undertake their pioneering long-term studies of chimpanzees, gorillas, and orangutans in those animals' natural habitats. The Louis Leakey Memorial Institute for African Prehistory in Nairobi was founded by his son Richard Leakey as a fossil repository and postgraduate study centre and laboratory.

Leakey wrote *Adam's Ancestors* (1934; rev. ed., 1953), *Stone Age Africa* (1936), *White African* (1937), *Olduvai Gorge* (1951), *Mau Mau and the Kikuyu* (1952), *Olduvai Gorge, 1951–61* (1965), *Unveiling Man's Origins* (1969; with Vanne Morris Goodall), and *Animals of East Africa* (1969).

The African continent has contributed the greatest share of significant early finds. Fayum in Egypt; Rusinga, Songhor, Kalodirr, Fort Ternan, Kanapoi, and Koobi Fora in Kenya; Olduvai and Laetolil in Tanzania; Omo and Hadar in Ethiopia; and Sterkfontein, Kromdraai, Swartkrans, and Makapansgat in South Africa are names with which every anthropology student and much of the general public are familiar.

Elsewhere, pieces of this colossal worldwide jigsaw puzzle have been discovered in Europe, notably in Turkey, Greece, Hungary, France, and Italy; in the Siwālik Hills of northwestern India; in China and Burma; in the ever-prolific Middle Eocene Bridger Beds of North America; and in Colombia, Argentina, and Bolivia. The 1990s saw a proliferation of discoveries of the previously impoverished fossil record of New World monkeys.

While new discoveries have clarified the human story, older ones, which had served only to cloud it, have been repudiated. Piltdown man was shown unequivocally to be a fake in 1953; and Galley Hill man in England, the Olmo remains in Italy, and the Calaveras skull in the United States have been shown to be recent intrusions (burials in the case of Galley Hill and Olmo, fraudulent in the case of Calaveras) into Pliocene or Pleistocene levels (5.3 million to 11,700 years ago). Questionable finds from the remoter geologic period of the Eocene and Oligocene epochs (55.8 million to 23 million years ago) have also been reexamined, with the result that a number of confusing fossils have been dismissed.

Progress in constructing the phylogeny of the primates has been bedeviled by a number of controversies concerning taxonomy and nomenclature. New-school and old-school taxonomists have come into conflict. But, with the rapid advances in molecular genetics, in the new concepts of phylogenetic species, and in population anthropology, a fresh equilibrium is slowly being acquired as the pendulum swings between the traditional "splitting," in which every new discovery was provided with a new generic name, and the reactionary "lumping" of such taxa as genera. Finally, cladistic methodology has become virtually universal, and most biologists and palaeontologists today accept the principle that a taxonomic group should be monophyletic (i.e., including only—and all—the descendants of a common ancestor).

RICHARD LEAKEY

(b. Dec. 19, 1944, Nairobi, Kenya)

Richard Erskine Frere Leakey is a Kenyan anthropologist, conservationist, and political figure who was responsible for extensive fossil finds related to human evolution. He also campaigned publicly for responsible management of the environment in East Africa.

The son of noted anthropologists Louis S.B. Leakey and Mary Leakey, Richard was originally reluctant to follow his parents' career and instead became a safari guide. In 1967 he joined an expedition to the Omo River valley in Ethiopia. It was during this trip that he first noticed the site of Koobi Fora, along the shores of Lake Turkana (Lake Rudolf) in Kenya, where he led a preliminary search that uncovered several stone tools. From this site alone in the subsequent decade, Leakey and his fellow workers uncovered some 400 hominin fossils representing perhaps 230 individuals, making Koobi Fora the site of the richest and most varied assemblage of early human remains found to date anywhere in the world.

Leakey proposed controversial interpretations of his fossil finds. In two books written with science writer Roger Lewin, *Origins* (1977) and *People of the Lake* (1978), Leakey presented his view that, some 3 million years ago, three hominin forms coexisted: *Homo habilis*, *Australopithecus africanus*, and *Australopithecus boisei*. He argued that the two australopith forms eventually died out and that *H. habilis* evolved into *Homo erectus*, the direct ancestor of *Homo sapiens*, or modern human beings. He claimed to have found evidence at Koobi Fora to support this theory. Of particular importance is an almost completely reconstructed fossil skull found in more than 300 fragments in 1972 (coded as KNM-ER 1470). Leakey believed that the skull represented *H. habilis* and that this relatively large-brained, upright, bipedal form of *Homo* lived in eastern Africa as early as 2.5 million or even 3.5 million years ago. Further elaboration of Leakey's views was given in his work *The Making of Mankind* (1981).

From 1968 to 1989 Leakey was director of the National Museums of Kenya. In 1989 he was made director of the Wildlife Conservation and Management Department (the precursor to the Kenya Wildlife Service [KWS]). Devoted to the preservation of Kenya's wildlife and sanctuaries, he embarked on a campaign to reduce corruption within the KWS, crack down (often using force) on ivory poachers, and restore the security of Kenya's national parks. In doing so he made numerous enemies. In 1993 he survived a plane crash in which he lost both his legs below the knee. The following year he resigned his post at the KWS, citing interference by Kenyan President Daniel arap Moi's government, and became a founding member of the opposition political party Safina (Swahili for "Noah's ark"). Pressure by foreign donors led to Leakey's brief return to the KWS (1998–99) and to a short stint as secretary to the cabinet (1999–2001). Thereafter he dedicated himself to lecturing and writing on the conservation of wildlife and the environment. Another book with Roger Lewin was *The Sixth Extinction: Patterns of Life and the Future of Humankind* (1995), in which he argued that human beings have been responsible for a catastrophic reduction in the number of plant and animal species living on Earth. Leakey later collaborated with Virginia Morell to write his second memoir, *Wildlife Wars: My Fight to Save Africa's Natural Treasures* (2001; his first memoir, *One Life*, was written in 1983). In 2004 Leakey founded WildlifeDirect, an Internet-based nonprofit conservation organization designed to disseminate information about endangered species and to connect donors to conservation efforts. He also served in 2007 as interim chair of the Kenya branch of Transparency International, a global coalition against corruption.

Leakey's wife, zoologist Meave Leakey (née Epps), conducted numerous paleoanthropological projects in the Turkana region, often in collaboration with their daughter Louise (b. 1972).

THE PRIMATE FOSSIL RECORD

The primate fossil record is thought to have begun as early as the end of the Cretaceous Period, some 65.5 million years ago. Fossil evidence dating to the Paleocene Epoch (65.5 million to 55.8 million years ago) points to the appearance of the first supposed primates, whereas discoveries dating to the Eocene Epoch (55.8 million to 33.9 million years ago) support the idea that the ancestors of lemurs and lorises (Adapidae) and monkeys and apes (Omomyidae) emerged during that time. Evidence uncovered in rocks dating to the Miocene Epoch (23 million to 5.3 million years ago) indicates that some primates adopted a terrestrial existence in response to the conversion of wooded areas to grasslands. The human lineage is thought to have arisen during the Pliocene Epoch (5.3 million to 2.6 million years ago) and diversified during the Pleistocene (2.6 million to 11,700 years ago).

MEAVE G. LEAKEY

(b. July 28, 1942, London, Eng.)

Meave Leakey (née Meave Epps) is a British paleoanthropologist who was part of a family that gained renown for decades of pioneering hominin research in eastern Africa. As a college student, Epps planned to be a marine zoologist, and she earned a B.S. in zoology and marine zoology from the University of North Wales, Bangor. Finding that there was a lack of positions for women on ocean expeditions, she began graduate work in zoology, and from 1965 to 1968 she worked as a zoologist at Tigoni Primate Research Centre outside Nairobi. At the centre, which was administered by Louis Leakey, she conducted doctoral research on the forelimb of modern monkeys, and she obtained a doctorate (1968) in zoology from the University of North Wales. Soon thereafter she joined a team led by Richard Leakey (son of Louis and Mary Douglas Leakey) to explore new fossil sites near Lake Turkana in Kenya. Meave and Richard were married in 1970, and they continued their research in the Lake Turkana area.

In 1989, when Richard shifted his attention to wildlife conservation, Meave became the coordinator of the National Museums of Kenya's paleontological field research in the Turkana basin. She was also the head of the National Museums' Division of Paleontology from

1982 to 2001. In 1994 Leakey led a team that discovered the remains of a previously unknown species—*Australopithecus anamensis*—that was bipedal (walked upright) and, with an age of 4.1 million years, was one of the earliest hominins (modern humans and fossil species more closely related to modern humans than to other living species) then known. One of Leakey's interests was in examining evidence at research sites to determine how the environment might have influenced hominin evolution, such as the development of bipedalism. In 2001 Meave and colleagues reported on the discovery of a 3.5-million-year-old skull that they determined belonged to a previously unknown hominin genus and species—*Kenyanthropus platyops*. The find challenged the conventional view that the specimen's contemporary, *A. afarensis*, was in the direct ancestral lineage of *Homo sapiens*. In 2002 Leakey, along with her daughter Louise, was named an explorer in residence by the National Geographic Society.

In 2007 Leakey was a lead author of a study in *Nature* magazine that went against the prevailing view of the ancestral lineage of *Homo sapiens*, namely, that the species *H. habilis* evolved into *H. erectus* in linear succession. In 2000 the Koobi Fora Research Project, which Leakey and her daughter codirected, had found fossil cranial specimens of *H. habilis* and *H. erectus* that dated from about 1.5 million years ago in an area east of Lake Turkana. The study suggested that the two species coexisted in the area for about 500,000 years. The discovery helped to show that the evolution of hominins was not as simple as a relatively sparse fossil record might have previously suggested. In addition to authoring many published scientific papers, Leakey was coeditor of *The Koobi Fora Research Project, Volume I* (1977) and *Lothagam: The Dawn of Humanity in Eastern Africa* (2003).

CRETACEOUS

The known temporal range of supposed primates was extended to about 65.5 million years ago (Late Cretaceous Epoch) by the discovery in Montana, U.S., of five teeth, representing two species of insectivore-like primates that were assigned in 1965 to a new genus, *Purgatorius*. This diagnosis, based on the characters of one premolar and four molar teeth since augmented by a few complete jaws, is not by any means universally accepted.

Paleocene

The first known supposed primates date to about 60 million years ago, as complete skulls and partial postcranial skeletons are available for the genera *Plesiadapis*, *Ignacius*, and *Palaechthon* from Europe and North America. The skulls show a number of dental specializations, including, in the case of *Plesiadapis*, procumbent rodentlike incisors in the upper and lower jaw and the absence of other antemolar teeth, though the molar teeth show more plausible primate affinities. Recent finds of limb bones, especially finger bones, of *Ignacius* and other genera have suggested that some, perhaps all, of these Paleocene supposed primates may actually belong to the order Dermoptera, whose only living representative is the gliding colugo ("flying lemur") of Southeast Asia. If this is so, then the Paleocene fossil record of primates is reduced to a handful of teeth of dubious status from China and France.

Eocene

The known fossil families of the Eocene Epoch (54.8 million to 33.9 million years ago) include the Tarsiidae (tarsiers), the Adapidae (which include probable ancestors of lemurs and lorises), and the Omomyidae (which include possible ancestors of the monkeys and apes).

The family Adapidae and the related Notharctidae contain two North American genera, *Notharctus* and *Smilodectes*, which are well represented in the

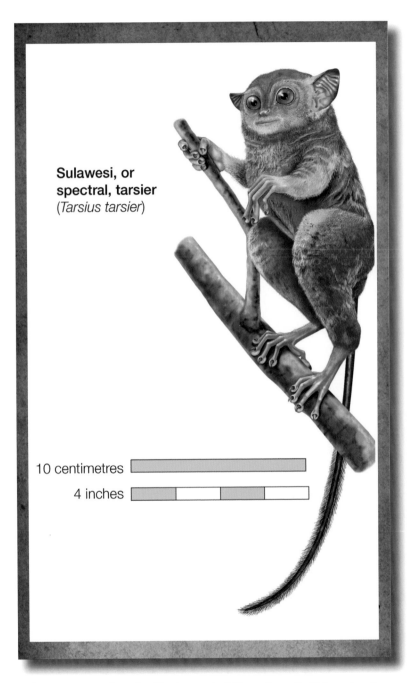

Sulawesi, or spectral, tarsier
(*Tarsius tarsier*)

10 centimetres

4 inches

Sulawesi, or spectral, tarsier (Tarsius tarsier). Encyclopædia Britannica, Inc.

fossil deposits of the Bridger Basin, Wyoming, U.S., and *Adapis, Europolemur, Anchomomys,* and *Pronycticebus* from Europe. *Notharctus* and *Smilodectes* are not thought to be antecedent to living lemurs, though *Notharctus* was not unlike the modern lemurs in size and general appearance. On both morphological and zoogeographical grounds, particularly the structure of the foot bones, the Adapidae may have provided the stem from which the living lemurs and lorises evolved; one genus, *Europolemur,* is even known to have a had a toilet claw, the large claw that in modern species replaces a nail on the second toe of the foot. Representatives of the Omomyidae have been found in North America, Europe, Egypt, and Asia.

The Eocene Tarsiidae, represented by the European species *Necrolemur antiquus,* found in the Quercy deposits of France, and *Afrotarsius chatrathi,* from the Fayum of Egypt, are likely to contain the ancestor of the modern genus *Tarsius.* The tarsier is indeed a "living fossil" (in the best sense of that overworked term), and teeth referred to the modern genus *Tarsius* are known from the Eocene Epoch of China and the Miocene Epoch (23 million to 5.3 million years ago) of Thailand.

Traces of what are probably the earliest monkeylike primates (Simiiformes) come from 45-million-year-old deposits in southern China. *Eosimias,* a tiny fossil known mainly by jaws and a few foot bones, has features that are plausibly argued to be those expected in the earliest ancestors of the Simiiformes. From slightly later, in Burma, come remains of further early simiiforms, *Pondaungia* and *Amphipithecus.* These have been known since the 1920s, but it was only in the 1980s and '90s that further remains were discovered to confirm their simiiform status.

IDA

"Ida" is a nickname for the remarkably complete but nearly two-dimensional skeleton of an adapiform primate dating to the middle Eocene Epoch (approximately 47 million years ago). It is the type specimen and the only known example of *Darwinius masillae*, a species assigned to the adapiform subfamily Cercamoniinae. The specimen, a juvenile female, was named for the daughter of Norwegian paleontologist Jørn Hurum. He was one of the scientists involved in the original description of the specimen. It was so named because his daughter had reached a similar developmental stage during the study.

The specimen was originally hailed by members of the scientific team who described it as a potential "missing link" between primitive primates and anthropoids (that is, the group that includes monkeys, apes and humans). Most scientists, however, regard *Darwinius* as a typical member of the expansive adapiform evolutionary radiation. Adapiforms are one of the earliest and most primitive known groups of fossil primates. Most scientists consider adapiforms as basal members of the suborder that includes lemurs and lorises, which are distantly related to humans and other anthropoids.

The fossilized remains of Ida were unearthed by one or more unknown collectors around 1983 at Grube Messel, a UNESCO World Heritage site near Darmstadt, Ger. The specimen was discovered by splitting the fossiliferous Messel oil shale in which Ida was originally entombed into two pieces, each of which contained part of the nearly complete skeleton. The less complete part was artificially embellished and eventually sold to the Wyoming Dinosaur Center in Thermopolis, Wyo., in 1991. Its more complete counterpart was kept in a private collection for many years before being sold in 2007 to the Natural History Museum of the University of Oslo in Norway.

Because it is based on a single juvenile specimen, the precise affinities of *D. masillae* are problematic. The establishment of lower-level taxonomic relationships among adapiforms heavily relies upon details of adult dental anatomy, but Ida retains most of her deciduous (or milk) teeth in place. What is known of Ida's dentition suggests that *Darwinius* is closely related to contemporaneous adapiforms from Germany and elsewhere in western Europe, such as *Europolemur* and *Godinotia*.

Ida is regarded as a female because a baculum (or os penis) is absent from this virtually complete skeleton. There is ample evidence from Ida's postcranial skeleton to indicate a highly arboreal lifestyle. Functionally important traits include the presence of nails rather than claws on all fingers and toes, an opposable big toe (or hallux) that was well adapted for grasping, and mobile limbs that were capable of wide ranges of motion in three dimensions. As such, *Darwinius* has been interpreted as a generalized arboreal quadruped that was not particularly specialized for leaping. Its relatively large orbits, which delimit the size of the eyeballs, suggest that it may have been nocturnal. Estimates of adult body mass range from 600 to 900 grams (21.1 to 31.7 ounces), similar to that of the extant lesser bamboo lemur (*Hapalemur griseus*).

OLIGOCENE

Information on primate evolution during the Oligocene Epoch (33.9 million to 23 million years ago) rests principally on discoveries in two areas—Texas and Egypt. The earliest platyrrhine fossils were found in South America and are only about 25 million years old, so much remains to be learned about their earliest evolutionary history.

Of unusual interest is the recent discovery of the cranium of a North American omomyid called *Rooneyia*; it is of particular note in view of a belief that primates had disappeared from North America by late Eocene times. *Rooneyia* is also of considerable interest in itself. The skull possesses a mixture of primitive and advanced features, precisely the combination that might be anticipated in a transitional form between lower and higher primates.

But by far the most important Oligocene site is Egypt. From the Fayum (al-Fayyūm) region of the Western Desert, from the Qasr El Sagha and Jebel Qatrani formations, has come the first evidence of the emerging Catarrhini.

A number of different genera have been described from Fayum, including *Catopithecus*, *Proteopithecus*, *Apidium*, *Qatrania*, *Propliopithecus*, *Oligopithecus*, *Parapithecus*, and *Aegyptopithecus*. The first two of these, together with some other primates of uncertain affinities, are from the Sagha Formation, which, technically, is latest Eocene in age, but the deposits are continuous. *Aegyptopithecus* went on to give rise to living catarrhines (Old World monkeys and apes, whose ancestors did not separate until much later, about 25 million years ago). The Fayum seems to depict the cradle of the catarrhines and possibly of the New World monkeys too, since some authors consider the family Parapithecidae (containing *Parapithecus*, *Apidium*, and *Qatrania*) to be closer to the platyrrhines. The other genera represent structural common ancestors of the Catarrhini, which indicates that the catarrhines and platyrrhines had by now become separate, whereas the two modern groups of catarrhines (cercopithecoids and hominoids) had not. From the evidence provided by the Fayum primate fauna, it is evident that quadrupedalism was becoming established as the typical locomotor pattern and that vertical clinging and leaping, the characteristic gait of the Eocene forebears of the fauna, was no longer retained by the genera represented at this site.

MIOCENE

The Miocene Epoch (23 million to 5.3 million years ago) is probably the most fruitful for paleoprimatology. During this time, dramatic changes in geomorphology, climate, and vegetation took place. The Miocene was a period of volcanism and mountain building, during which the topography of the modern world was becoming established. Of particular relevance to the story of primate evolution are the vegetational changes resulting from the formation of mountain ranges. Grasses, known only since the Paleogene Period (65.5 million to 23 million years ago), flourished in the new conditions and in many areas that had previously been forested. Grasslands are known regionally by such names as savanna, Llanos, and prairies. A new type of primate—the ground inhabitant—came into being during this period. The generalized nature of the bodily form of primates, combined with their specialized brain, made this critical step possible.

In the last few decades, considerable additions to the knowledge of ape and human evolution have accrued from Miocene fossil beds in East Africa and Europe. In East Africa, as long ago as the 1930s, the excavations of the inshore islands and Kenyan shores of Lake Victoria by Louis Leakey and a number of colleagues began to illuminate knowledge of human and ape evolution. Renewed excavations at these sites, 17 million to 19 million years old, and exploration of new sites (one of them as much as 24 million years old) in northern Kenya have modified the older conclusions. The genus *Proconsul* is known from a nearly complete skeleton and several other postcranial bones, a large number of jaw and facial fragments, and several partial skulls—only one of them complete, and it had been distorted by pressure of the surrounding rocks during fossilization. Subsequent reconstruction reveals a skull more monkeylike than apelike in its contours; this, along with the forelimb skeleton, which is known in great detail for this species, indicates a body form that most closely resembles that of living monkeys. Leakey concluded that *Proconsul* diverged from the modern ape/human lineage before any of the living members of this group began to diverge from each other, and this led him to classify it in a separate family, Proconsulidae.

Since the 1980s a number of other genera (*Limnopithecus*, *Dendropithecus*, *Afropithecus*, *Kamoypithecus*, and others) have been added to the family. The location of the actual ancestors of living hominoids remained mysterious until previously known specimens from Moroto Island, in Lake Victoria, were reexamined, and fresh material was discovered. In 1997 the description of a new genus and species, *Morotopithecus bishopi*, was announced, and this 20-million-year-old fossil is claimed to show the earliest traces of modern hominoid skeletal features. As, at the same time, traces of the earliest Old World monkeys are known, it appears that, while the Proconsulidae flourished with many genera and species, the hominoids (apes) and cercopithecoids (monkeys) were emerging and beginning to specialize. When, in the Middle Miocene, the proconsulids finally disappeared, it was the Old World monkeys that immediately diversified and took their place; the hominoids, until the rise of the human line, tended to remain mostly an inconspicuous group, remaining rather scarce in the fossil record. The separation of the gibbons (Hylobatidae) from the great ape/human stock (Hominidae) is at present not documented by fossils; indeed, whether there are any fossil gibbons known at all before the Pleistocene is still disputed.

In Europe, an archaic family, Pliopithecidae, was widespread. Remains of the best-known genus, *Pliopithecus*, from the Czech Republic have provided a remarkably complete picture of the habits of this group, which, on this evidence, appears to have possessed bodily forms of a tailed quadruped retaining numerous characteristics of New World monkeys. Long considered to be ancestral gibbons, the pliopithecids are now known to be far removed from gibbons, or indeed any other living primates. Their ancestors diverged from primitive catarrhines before even

Orangutan (Pongo pygmaeus). PRNewsFoto/Smithsonian National Zoo/AP Images

the Proconsulidae became separate. Alongside them in Spain, France, and Hungary occur remains of *Dryopithecus*, which are now classified in the Hominidae; they are close to living human/ape ancestry and show further advances over *Morotopithecus* in the development of the skeletal features characterizing modern hominoids.

In the Siwālik Hills of northern India and Pakistan, remains of several species of the Middle–Late Miocene *Sivapithecus* have been known since the 1870s. It was long suspected that this genus was related to the living orangutan, and this hypothesis was splendidly corroborated in the 1970s with the discovery of the first facial skeleton, which exquisitely combines primitive hominid features with derived orangutan-like states. If the orangutan lineage was now separate, it would be expected that ancestors of the human/gorilla/chimpanzee line would be found at contemporary sites farther west, and this turns out probably to be the case with the discoveries of two additional genera: the poorly known eight-million-year-old *Samburupithecus*, from northern Kenya, and the increasingly complete craniodental discoveries of *Graecopithecus*, from several sites of about the same age in Greece.

One of the most famous of the Late Miocene fossils was the "abominable coalman," so called because the best-preserved remains, a complete skeleton, were found during the 1950s in a lignite mine in northern Italy. *Oreopithecus* possessed a number of dental and bony characters that are typically hominid. The canines were relatively short and stout; the face was abbreviated; and the pelvis was broad and even showed characteristics associated with bipedal walking, as did the vertebral column. The arms were long (the intermembral index being well above 100) and the fingers long and curved. The limb proportions are those of a brachiator. An early argument was that it was a special human ancestor; reanalysis suggested that it might be an Old World monkey that had developed brachiating features convergently with gibbons; new studies have placed *Oreopithecus* firmly in the Hominidae, but, within this family, its exact position is still unclear. The human line is not thought to have separated from that of the chimpanzee by this period, yet the *Oreopithecus* pelvis undeniably shows biomechanical stress patterns expected of a partial biped. That the end of the *Oreopithecus* story has not yet been heard is certain. A final twist is that the sites at which it is found seem to have formed an isolated swampy region, probably an island, on which the (somewhat impoverished) fauna had been evolving in isolation for some considerable time, perhaps even a million years or more.

LLUC

"Lluc" is the nickname for the nearly complete upper and lower jaws and much of the associated facial region of an adult male hominid found in 2004 at the Abocador de Can Mata site in Catalonia, Spain. Lluc is the only known specimen of *Anoiapithecus brevirostris*, a species that dates to the middle of the Miocene Epoch (roughly 11.9 million years ago). It was recovered during a salvage operation designed to rescue fossil specimens and associated data threatened by impending construction activities.

Lluc differs from other Miocene forms of the superfamily Hominoidea in having a nearly flat and relatively orthognathic (vertically oriented) face that contrasts markedly with the more prognathic (forward-projecting) face of most other living and fossil apes. The specimen resembles living and fossil members of the genus *Homo* (humans) in this regard, but this similarity is thought to be the result of convergent evolution, because fossil members of the human lineage (such as *Australopithecus*) lack a similarly vertical face.

Anoiapithecus, so far characterized by a single species, displays a unique combination of anatomical features that are considered to be both primitive and derived with respect to earlier hominoid primates. Its primitive characteristics primarily relate to detailed aspects of dental morphology, including its relatively low-crowned teeth. Those features resemble conditions that are found in much older African hominoids, such as *Proconsul*, a genus from the early Miocene. Other traits found in *Anoiapithecus* ally it with younger and more-advanced hominoids, including the group containing living great apes and humans (classified as the family Hominidae). For example, the molars of *Anoiapithecus* are covered by a thick layer of enamel, and its lower jaw is robust. The deep, short face of *Anoiapithecus* frames a pear-shaped opening for the nasal aperture, which is characteristic of modern great apes and humans. The maxillary sinus of *Anoiapithecus* appears to be reduced, probably as a result of its relatively deep facial proportions.

Reconstructing the evolutionary relationships of Miocene apes has proven to be difficult for at least two reasons. First, the diversity of Miocene apes was much greater than that which characterizes the group today. Second, these Miocene apes show a baffling pattern of characters, indicating that parallel and convergent evolution occurred commonly within the group. *Anoiapithecus* has been interpreted as being a basal member of the Hominidae. According to this view, *Anoiapithecus* occupies a branch of the evolutionary tree intermediate between modern great apes and humans on the one hand and a diverse group of (mainly African) fossil apes on the other.

Some scientists have argued that the discovery of *Anoiapithecus* and related fossil apes in Eurasia indicates that the common ancestor of living great apes and humans evolved somewhere on that landmass, rather than in Africa as others have suggested. According to this hypothesis, the common ancestor of living African apes and humans would have returned to Africa sometime later in the Miocene, while the ancestor of living orangutans remained in Eurasia. Other scientists dispute this hypothesis, pointing to the relatively poor quality of the African fossil record during the middle and late Miocene.

PLIOCENE

The Pliocene Epoch (5.3 million to 2.6 million years ago) was very similar to the present in terms of its geomorphology and climate. Discounting the effects of recent human influence on the distribution of forest and savanna in the tropics, the face of the land cannot have differed much from today. Thus, one would expect that, during the Pliocene (given the effectiveness of environmental selection), essentially modern forms of primates would have made their appearance. Yet no fossils referable to modern ape lineages are known during the Pliocene, and monkey families are scarcely better known. *Libypithecus* and *Dolichopithecus*, both monkeys, were probably ancestral colobines, but neither genus can be placed in a precise ancestral relationship with modern members of this subfamily. What did characterize the Pliocene was the rise in Africa of the human line, with *Ardipithecus ramidus* at 4.4 million years ago in Ethiopia.

PLEISTOCENE

The Pleistocene Epoch (2.6 million to 11,700 years ago) is the epoch of hominin (protohuman) expansion. Knowledge of nonhuman primates, except for some selected Old World monkeys, is surprisingly sketchy. No ape fossils are known until relatively recent times, and monkeys have been identified in only a few regions in Africa and even fewer in Asia—e.g., *Cercopithecoides*, *Paracolobus*, and *Rhinocolobus* (members of the subfamily Colobinae) and *Gorgopithecus* and *Dinopithecus* (related to the living genus *Papio*), from South African deposits. *Simopithecus*, a giant ancestral forerunner, according to most authorities, of the present-day genus, *Theropithecus* (gelada), was unearthed from Olduvai Gorge and South Africa and was recently discovered also in India. It is possible that the *Papio-Theropithecus* divergence can be pushed well back into the Pliocene.

One genus of the Pleistocene that is neither ape nor monkey in the sense that these taxa are interpreted today is *Gigantopithecus*. The romantic story of the discovery of the gargantuan molar teeth of *Gigantopithecus blacki* by the German-Dutch paleontologist G.H.R. von Koenigswald in a Chinese pharmacy has often been told. His boldness in erecting a new genus on such apparently slender grounds has been amply justified by the subsequent discovery of several massive jaws from Kwangsi in South China, which are apparently about a million years old, and by numerous teeth from caves in China and Vietnam. In one such cave (Tham Khuyen), *Gigantopithecus* and *Homo* teeth occur in the same deposits, dated as recently as 475,000 years ago. Furthermore, the discovery of an enormous jaw in the Dhok Pathan deposits of the Siwālik Hills of India, from the earliest Pliocene, has provided a respectably long period of existence for this aberrant giant-toothed hominoid genus. Clearly, *Gigantopithecus* was a member of the

Hominidae related to the orangutan, with divergent dental specializations that were possibly adaptive for foraging in grassland where tree products were unavailable and ground products available but hard to get, which makes it an orangutan lineage that ran for a while in parallel with that of humans.

CLASSIFICATION

Traditionally, the order Primates was divided into Prosimii (the primitive primates: lemurs, lorises, and tarsiers) and Anthropoidea (the bigger-brained monkeys and apes, including humans). It is now known that one of the "prosimians," the tarsier, is actually more closely related to the "anthropoids," so the classification of the primates has had to be revised. The two suborders recognized today are Strepsirrhini (lemurs and lorises) and Haplorrhini (tarsiers, monkeys, and apes, including humans). The present classification was adopted in the early 1970s, when the logic of phylogenetic systematics was beginning to be appreciated, and the taxonomy of the order Primates was reorganized so as to make taxa equivalent, as far as possible, to clades. In this classification, the order is divided into the suborders Strepsirrhini and Haplorrhini, and these in turn are divided into infraorders.

The two suborders differ in such features as the nose, eyes, and placenta. The muzzle of strepsirrhines is moist and bare, like a dog's; haplorrhines have a nose covered with downy hair. Strepsirrhines have a reflective layer, the *tapetum lucidum*, behind the retina, which increases the amount of light for night vision, while haplorrhines have no tapetum but, instead, an area of enhanced vision, the *fovea*. This difference is consistent, even though not all strepsirrhines are nocturnal or all haplorrhines diurnal. Finally, the uterine wall of haplorrhines is elaborated and vascularised

Male red colobus monkey (Piliocolobus badius temminckii). © Starin

each month for possible pregnancy, forming a *hemochorial* placenta (with intimate contact between maternal and fetal bloodstreams) if pregnancy occurs and requiring it to be shed, in menstruation, if there is no fertilization. Strepsirrhines have no uterine preparation, no menstruation, and a much-less-intimate *epitheliochorial* placenta. All indications are that these two suborders separated very early, perhaps 60 million years ago. The Strepsirrhini divide further into Lemuriformes (lemurlike) and Lorisiformes (lorislike) infraorders, while the Haplorrhini divide into Tarsiiformes (tarsiers) and Simiiformes ("anthropoids"—i.e., monkeys, apes, and humans). The Simiiformes divide in turn into Platyrrhini (New World monkeys) and Catarrhini (Old World monkeys and hominoids). A group of fossil mammals called the Paromomyiformes, known mainly from the Paleocene, have usually been classified as primates, but the eminent primate specialist Robert D. Martin has long argued that their connection with authenticated primates is tenuous, to say the least, and, in the 1990s, the paleontologist K.C. Beard discovered hand bones and other material that suggest strongly that some of these fossils may actually belong not to Primates but to the order Dermoptera.

There has been a good deal of discussion about the relationships of primates to other mammals. In the 1930s it was proposed that the tree shrews (small Southeast Asian mammals, family Tupaiidae), hitherto classed in the order Insectivora, belong to the order Primates—or at least that they are closely related. This has turned out to be wrong; Martin has shown in detail how they differ from Primates and how the error arose. Tree shrews are nowadays placed in their own order, Scandentia. In the 1980s the mammalogist Jack Pettigrew discovered that the Megachiroptera, the suborder of bats (order Chiroptera) that contains the fruit bats or "flying foxes" (family Pteropodidae), share aspects of the visual system with primates, and he proposed that they are in effect flying primates, having evolved wings independently from other bats (suborder Microchiroptera, the echolocating, mostly insectivorous smaller bats). Later he found that the colugos, so-called "flying lemurs" (sole living representatives of the order Dermoptera) of the Southeast Asian rainforests, share the same features. Molecular data, however, confirm that, whereas primates and colugos really are closely related, the bats form a monophyletic group. Therefore, either the primates, colugos, and all bats shared a common ancestor with those specializations of the visual system, which the Microchiroptera then lost, or these features were developed independently by (1) primates and colugos and (2) Megachiroptera. Molecular data are equivocal as to whether bats are the sister group to primates and colugos, so these two competing hypotheses cannot yet be tested.

CHAPTER 4
LEMURS

The lemurs (suborder Strepsirrhini) constitute a group that generally includes all primitive primates except the tarsiers. More specifically, lemurs are any of the indigenous primates of Madagascar. However, in the broad sense, the term *lemur* applies not only to the typical lemurs (family Lemuridae) but also to the avahis, sifakas, indris, and aye-ayes of Madagascar, in addition to the lorises, pottos, and bush babies of Southeast Asia and Africa. Defined more narrowly, the designation excludes the last three (the Lorisiformes).

GENERAL FEATURES

Most lemurs of Madagascar and the nearby Comoros Islands have large eyes, foxlike faces, monkeylike bodies, and long hind limbs. Lemurs range in length (excluding the tail) from about 9 cm (3.5 inches) in Madame Berthe's mouse lemur (*Microcebus berthae*) to nearly 70 cm (about 28 inches) for the indri (*Indri indri*). The bushy tails of lemurs can be longer than their bodies; the indri, however, has only a stub of a tail. Except for the aye-aye, lemurs have woolly fur that is reddish, gray, brown, or black; some species are variously patterned with white. Among other markings, they may also have eye-rings or crown patches.

Lemurs are less intelligent than monkeys. Their sense of smell is more acute but their vision less so. Although some species are at times active during the day, their eyes seem to be adapted for nocturnal life, trading acuity for increased sensitivity in low light conditions. All lemurs are characterized by a reflective layer (tapetum) behind the retina in the eye, but no fovea or macula lutea; a hairless, moist tip to the muzzle; a noninvasive (epitheliochorial) placenta; comblike forward-directed lower front teeth (with the exception of the aye-aye); and a claw ("toilet claw") on the second toe of the foot.

Lemurs are docile, gregarious animals; some species live in groups of 10 or more. Most of their time is spent in the trees eating fruit, leaves, buds, insects, and small birds and birds' eggs, but diet varies among different species. Some, for example, are mainly insectivorous, whereas others feed almost exclusively on foliage. All breed seasonally, and females may have only one fertile day during the entire year. Single offspring are usually born after two to five months' gestation. The newborn lemur then clings to its mother's underside until it is old enough to ride on her back.

A number of lemurs are rare or endangered. Several either were not discovered until the late 20th century or were rediscovered after having been thought extinct. Remains exist of species larger than any of today's lemurs. Some of these may have survived until only 500 years ago. They were probably exterminated by overhunting or habitat modification by the Malagasy people, who arrived on the island less than 2,000 years ago.

LEMUR DIVERSITY

The "true lemurs" (family Lemuridae) include five genera and about 18 species. The best known of these is the ring-tailed lemur (*Lemur catta*), commonly seen in zoos. It is unique both in its habitat (some dry and rocky areas of Madagascar) and for its striped tail (all other lemurs have solid-coloured tails). Troops are made up of several males and females, and the females are the dominant sex. A male marks the troop's territory by slashing the trunk of a small tree with a horny spur on his wrist, making an audible click,

30 centimetres

12 inches

ring-tailed lemur
(*Lemur catta*)

Ring-tailed lemur (Lemur catta). Encyclopædia Britannica, Inc.

and leaving a scented scar on the tree. Members of the related genus *Eulemur* include the black lemur (*E. macaco*), in which the male is black and the female is reddish brown. The rare black-and-white or black-and-red ruffed lemurs (genus *Varecia*) live in rainforests on the eastern side of Madagascar. The gentle lemurs, or lesser bamboo lemurs (genus *Hapalemur*), and the highly endangered greater bamboo lemurs (*Prolemur simus*) feed on bamboo stems in the eastern and northwestern rainforests of the island.

Gray mouse lemur (Microcebus murinus). Encyclopædia Britannica, Inc.

There are at least 10 species of sportive lemurs (family Megaladapidae) that live throughout Madagascar in both rainforests and dry forests. They are solitary and nocturnal, feeding on leaves and flowers, which are digested in their enormous cecum with the aid of bacteria. Bacterial fermentation enables energy to be extracted from the large quantity of otherwise indigestible cellulose in the lemur's diet.

The dwarf lemurs (*Cheirogaleus*), along with the mouse (*Microcebus*), Coquerel's (*Mirza*), hairy-eared (*Allocebus*), and fork-crowned (*Phaner*) lemurs, make up the family Cheirogaleidae, which in many respects are the most primitive living lemurs. Dwarf lemurs store fat in their tails and are dormant (estivate) during dry periods; they live in monogamous pairs. Mouse lemurs, which eat insects and fruit, are the smallest living primates.

Strepsirrhine primates first emerged in the Early Eocene Epoch (some 50 million years ago), though their origins may be traced to the preceding Paleocene Epoch. These Eocene lemuroids were abundant in North America and Europe, and some are known from complete skeletons. By the close of the Eocene (approximately 34 million years ago), strepsirrhines had practically disappeared from the Northern Hemisphere. The lemur lineage continued in tropical forests, however, and they were particularly successful in Madagascar, where they were relatively free from competition with more-advanced primates. No fossil deposits are known in Madagascar between the Mesozoic Era (251 million to 65.5 million years ago) and recent times, so the fossil history of the island's lemurs is unknown.

TYPES OF LEMURS

Any study of Earth's primitive primates typically emphasizes the examination of suborder Strepsirrhini, a group that encompasses the typical lemurs (lemurs, avahis, and other members of family Lemuridae), as well as the lorises, indris, aye-ayes, sifakas, and other forms. In addition, tarsiers are typically grouped with other primitive primates, but they are not classified in suborder Strepsirrhini. Tarsiers are described below for convenience.

AVAHIS

The avahis (*Avahi*), which are also called woolly lemurs, are long-legged arboreal lemurs of Madagascar. Avahis have short arms, a short muzzle, and a round head with small ears hidden in woolly fur. Nocturnal and vegetarian, they live in small groups in both rainforests and patches of dry forests, typically clinging vertically to the trees. Groups consist of a male, a female, and their young. Single young are born after about five months' gestation.

The eastern avahi (*Avahi laniger*), which lives in rainforests, is grayish brown to reddish, is about 28 cm (11 inches) long and 1.2 kg (2.6 pounds) in weight, and has a furry reddish tail of about body length or longer. The three species that live in western Madagascar's dry forests are smaller, weighing only 800 grams (28 ounces). They are lighter gray with a cream-coloured underside. The Betsiboka avahi (*A. occidentalis*) has a light facial mask and broad dark rings around the eyes, whereas the recently described Sambirano avahi (*A. unicolor*) lacks these facial markings. An additional species from the Bemaraha district was described scientifically only in 2005 and was named *A. cleesei* after the British comedian and conservation supporter John Cleese. These three western species all have very small distributions and are in danger of extinction. Avahis are related to sifakas and the indri; all are primates of the leaping lemur family, Indridae.

AYE-AYES

The aye-aye (*Daubentonia madagascariensis*) is a rare squirrel-like primate of Madagascar. It is the sole living representative of the family Daubentoniidae. Nocturnal, solitary, and arboreal, most aye-ayes live in rainforests, but some have been discovered more recently in the dry forests of western Madagascar.

The aye-aye is about 40 cm (16 inches) long, excluding the bushy 55- to 60-cm (22- to 24-inch) tail. Covered with long, coarse, dark brown or black fur, it has a short face, large eyes, and ever-growing incisors like those of

aye-aye
(*Daubentonia madagascariensis*)

30 centimetres

12 inches

Aye-aye (Daubentonia madagascariensis). Encyclopædia Britannica, Inc.

rodents. Its hands are large, and its fingers, especially the third, are long and slender. All the fingers have pointed claws, as do the toes except for the large opposable flat-nailed great toes. The aye-aye constructs a large ball-like nest of leaves in forked tree branches and feeds mainly on insects and fruit. It locates wood-boring insect larvae by tapping the tree with the long third finger, apparently listening for the hollow sound of the channels the grubs make through the wood, and then uses this finger to extract the insects. It also uses the third finger to dig the pulp out of fruit. The female bears a single young. The aye-aye is critically endangered and protected by law. Successful breeding colonies have been established in a few zoos outside Madagascar.

BUSH BABIES

The bush babies (family Galagidae), or galagos, are a group of several species of small, attractive arboreal primates native to sub-Saharan Africa. They are gray, brown, or reddish to yellowish brown, with large eyes and ears, long hind legs, soft, woolly fur, and long tails. Bush babies are also characterized by the long upper portion of the feet (tarsus) and by the ability to fold their ears. They are nocturnal, and they feed on fruits, insects, and even small birds, but a major component of the diet of most species is gum (tree exudate). This they extract by gouging holes in trees and scraping the bark, using their toothcombs (forward-tilted lower incisor and canine teeth). Galagos cling to and leap among the trees; the smaller forms, such as the lesser bush baby (*Galago senegalensis*), are extremely active and agile. When they descend to the ground, they sit upright, and they move around by jumping with their hind legs like jerboas. Gestation is about three to four months; young usually number one or two.

Bush babies, or galagos (Galago senegalensis). George Holton/Photo Researchers

Before 1980 only six species were recognized, but studies since then, especially of their vocalizations, have resulted in the identification of perhaps as many as 20 species. The lesser bush baby and its relatives, which weigh 150–200 grams (5–7 ounces), live in the thornbushes and tree savannahs from Senegal in the west to Somalia in the east and southward to Kwazulu-Natal, South Africa, although one species, the dusky bush baby (*G. matschiei*), is restricted to the rainforests of eastern Congo (Kinshasa). They feed on gum, insects, pods, flowers, and leaves. The larger Allen's bush baby (*G. alleni*) and its relatives live in the rainforests of west-central Africa, where they feed on fallen fruits and the insects that they find in them; they may be generically distinct.

The dwarf bush babies, with their long, slender snouts, are now placed in a separate genus, *Galagoides*. The

Zanzibar bush baby (*Galagoides zanzibaricus*) and Grant's bush baby (*G. granti*) and their relatives live in East African coastal forests from Kenya to Mozambique and Malawi and on the islands of Zanzibar and Pemba. The tiny Prince Demidoff's bush baby (*G. demidoff*), which weighs only 70 grams (2.5 ounces), is widespread and common in African rainforests from Sierra Leone to Uganda. Even smaller is the Rondo bush baby (*G. rondoensis*), first described in 1997, which weighs just 60 grams and is restricted to a few coastal forests in southeastern Tanzania.

The needle-clawed bush babies are classified in another genus, *Euoticus*. The two species live in the rainforests of west-central Africa. They feed on tree exudate, clinging upside-down to the bark of a tree by digging in their sharp-pointed clawlike nails, stabbing the bark with specialized canine and premolar teeth, and then scraping up the gum that flows out. The final genus, *Otolemur*, contains the largest species, the brown greater galago (*O. crassicaudatus*), with an average weight of 1.2 kg (2.6 pounds), though some weigh up to 1.8 kg (4 pounds). It lives in coastal forests and woodlands in southeastern Africa. One or two slightly smaller closely related species live in Angola and East Africa.

INDRIS

Indris (*Indri indri*) are slender, long-limbed primates found in the forests of Madagascar. The largest of the lemurs, it is 60–70 cm (24–28 inches) long, with a rudimentary tail and large hands and feet. The round head has a pointed face and round, furry ears. Its fur is black, with white on the head, throat, forearms, and buttocks; the relative proportions of white and black vary geographically. Active during the day and thoroughly arboreal, the indri clings to trees and climbs in an upright position as it feeds on leaves, fruit, flowers, and other vegetation.

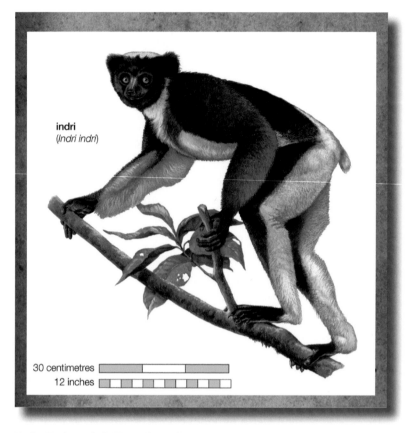

indri
(*Indri indri*)

30 centimetres
12 inches

*Indri (*Indri indri*)*. Encyclopædia Britannica, Inc.

The indri is an endangered species found only in remote parts of northeastern Madagascar, where it is protected by law. It is related to sifakas and avahis; together they constitute the leaping lemurs, family Indridae.

LORISES

Lorises make up any of about eight species of tailless or short-tailed South and Southeast Asian forest primates. Lorises are arboreal and nocturnal, curling up to sleep by day. They have soft gray or brown fur and can be recognized by their huge eyes encircled by dark patches and by

their short index fingers. They move with great delibera-
tion through the trees and often hang by their feet, with
their hands free to grasp food or branches.

The slender loris (*Loris tardigradus,* now generally classified as two or more species) of India and Sri Lanka is
about 20–25 cm (8–10 inches) long and has long, slender
limbs, small hands, a rounded head, and a pointed muzzle.
It feeds mostly on insects (predominantly ants) and is solitary. The female usually bears a single young after five or
six months' gestation.

The five slow lorises (genus *Nycticebus*) are more robust
and have shorter, stouter limbs, more-rounded snouts, and

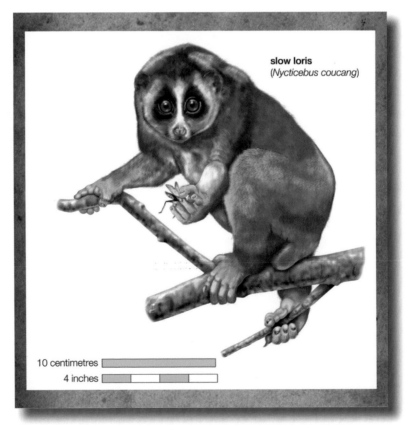

Slow loris (Nycticebus coucang). Encyclopædia Britannica, Inc.

smaller eyes and ears. They are found in Indonesia and on the Malay Peninsula. The smallest species (*N. pygmaeus*), restricted to forests east of the Mekong River, is about 25 cm (about 10 inches) long; the larger *N. coucang* and its relatives, widespread in Southeast Asia, are about 27–37 cm (about 11–15 inches) long. Slow lorises move more slowly than slender lorises; they feed on insects, small animals, fruit, and vegetation. The females bear one (sometimes two) young after about six months' gestation. Lorises are related to the pottos and angwantibos of Africa; together they constitute the family Lorisidae.

POTTOS

The potto (*Perodicticus potto*), which is also called bush bear, tree bear, or softly-softly, is a slow-moving tropical African primate. It is a nocturnal tree dweller found in rainforests from Sierra Leone eastward to Uganda. It has a strong grip and clings tightly to branches, but when necessary it can also move quickly through the branches with a smooth gliding gait that makes it quite inconspicuous. It feeds on fruit, small animals, and insects (especially larvae) and curls up to sleep by day in tree hollows. Its length is about 35 cm (14 inches), excluding its furry 5–10-cm (2–4-inch) tail. It has large eyes, sturdy limbs, stublike second fingers and toes, and dense woolly fur, which is grizzled reddish in colour. A ridge of short, blunt spines formed by the neck vertebrae runs down the nape. The spines are covered by thin, highly innervated skin and are thought to be sensitive to the movements of potential predators when the potto tucks its head between its arms in a defensive posture. Gestation is six months; single young are typical.

It is now thought likely that pottos constitute several species, but in 1996 primatologists were stunned when a new genus and species, the false potto (*Pseudopotto martini*), was announced. It was said to be slightly smaller than a potto, longer-tailed, and without the neck spines. The animal was described on the basis of a single skeleton, the remains of an animal that had been imported from Cameroon and lived several years in the Zürich Zoo, where it had been identified as a potto. There is controversy over whether it might have been an abnormal potto. Despite the controversy, many specialists would agree that, unlikely as it might seem that such a distinctive animal could have remained unknown for so long a time, live false pottos may really exist, waiting to be discovered.

Two related but much smaller primates called angwantibos (*Arctocebus calabarensis* and *A. aureus*) live only in the rainforests of west-central Africa. They measure 24 cm (9.5 inches) long and are yellowish in colour, with a long, thin snout. Like the potto, they are tailless, but the third finger as well as the second is reduced to a tiny stub. They too feed on small insects and other slow-moving invertebrates. Pottos and angwantibos are related to the lorises of Southeast Asia; together they constitute the family Lorisidae.

SIFAKAS

Sifakas (*Propithecus*) are leaping arboreal lemurs found in coastal forests of Madagascar. There are nine species. Sifakas are about 1 metre (3.3 feet) long, roughly half the length being tail. They have a small head, large eyes, and large ears that in most species are partially hidden in their long silky fur. Colour varies both within and between species but is usually white with darker markings. Vegetarian and active during the day, sifakas live in small family groups; females are dominant to males. Sifakas cling vertically to upright stems and tree trunks and sit in forked tree branches; they move by springing as far as 9–10 m

Crowned sifaka (Propithecus coronatus). © Christopher Call Productions

(30–33 feet) from tree to tree. One young, usually, is born after about five months' gestation.

Verreaux's sifaka (*P. verreauxi*) is white with dark shoulders and sides, sometimes with a dark crown cap. Coquerel's sifaka (*P. coquereli*) is somewhat similar; it lives in the thorny forests of Madagascar's southern desert. Two other species live in the dry forests of western Madagascar. The larger diademed sifaka (*P. diadema*), silky sifaka (*P. candidus*), and Milne-Edwards's sifaka (*P. edwardsi*) live in the rainforests of eastern Madagascar. Milne-Edwards's sifaka is black or brown, generally with a white patch on the back and flanks, whereas the diademed sifaka, or simpoon, has a beautiful coat of white, which becomes silvery on the back, light gold on the hindquarters, and black on the crown and nape. The black, or Perrier's, sifaka (*P. perrieri*) lives in the dry northwestern highlands of Ankarana, and the golden-crowned, or Tattersall's, sifaka (*P. tattersalli*), first described scientifically in 1988, lives only in the Daraina region of the northeast. Both species are critically endangered. Sifakas are related to avahis and the indri; all are primates of the leaping lemur family, Indridae.

TARSIERS

Tarsiers are small leaping primates found only on various islands of Southeast Asia, including the Philippines. There are roughly six living species, and all belong to the genus *Tarsius* in family Tarsiidae. Tarsiers are intermediate in form between lemurs and monkeys, measuring only about 9–16 cm (3.5–6 inches) long, excluding a tail of about twice that length. Tarsiers are lemurlike in being nocturnal and having a well-developed sense of smell. However, like monkeys, apes, and humans, the nose is dry and hair-covered, not moist and bald as is that of lemurs. The eyes and placenta are also simiiform in structure.

The tarsier's small brain has an enormous visual cortex to process information from the large goggling eyes, the animal's most striking feature. The size of the eyes and visual cortex is probably made necessary by the absence of a reflective layer (tapetum) that the eyes of most other nocturnal mammals possess. The tarsier is also unusual in having especially long ankle bones (tarsals, hence the name tarsier), a short body, and a round head that can be rotated 180°. The face is short, with large, membranous ears that are almost constantly in motion. The fur is thick, silky, and coloured gray to dark brown. The tail is scaly on the underside like a rat's; in most species it has an edging or terminal brush of hair.

Tarsiers are the only entirely carnivorous primates, preying on insects, lizards, and snakes. Clinging upright to trees, they press the tail against the trunk for support. Their grip is also aided by the tips of their digits, which are expanded into disklike adhesive pads. Tarsiers move through the forest by launching themselves from trunk to trunk propelled by their greatly elongated hind limbs.

Adults live in monogamous pairs and keep in contact vocally during the night, defending territory against other pairs using extremely high-pitched calls. On the island of Celebes (Sulawesi) these calls are duets—different but complementary calls made by the male and female. Single young are born in a fairly well-developed state, furred and with eyes open, after a gestation of perhaps six months.

Tarsiers live on the islands of the southern Philippines, Celebes (Sulawesi), Borneo, Bangka, Belitung, the Natuna Islands, and Sumatra. Species differ so much across this range that some authorities are inclined to classify them in different genera. In Indonesia and Malaysia the Western tarsier (*Tarsius bancanus*) has huge bulging eyes, making the head broader than it is long; it also has the longest feet, and its tail is tufted at the tip. It thrives in both old-growth and secondary forests but can also be found in low scrubby vegetation, even around villages. The South Sulawesi, or spectral, tarsier (*T. tarsier*, formerly called *T. spectrum*) is primitive, with smaller eyes, shorter feet, and a hairier tail. There are several species on Celebes (Sulawesi) and on its offshore islands, but most have not yet been described scientifically. The most distinctive is the high-mountain pygmy tarsier (*T. pumilus*). Until it was rediscovered in 2008, the last living pygmy tarsier specimen was seen in 1921. The Philippine tarsier (*T. syrichta*) has a totally bald tail, and the feet are also nearly hairless. Human settlement in its habitat threatens its continued existence.

Family Tarsiidae is classified with monkeys, apes, and humans (infraorder Simiiformes) in the suborder Haplorrhini, but it constitutes a separate infraorder, Tarsiiformes.

CHAPTER 5

MONKEYS

M onkeys make up nearly 200 species of tailed primate, with the exception of lemurs, tarsiers, and lorises. The presence of a tail (even if only a tiny nub), along with their narrow-chested bodies and other features of the skeleton, distinguishes monkeys from apes. Most monkeys have a short, relatively flat face without great prominence of the muzzle, although baboons and mandrills are notable exceptions. The vast majority of species live in tropical forests, where they move on all four limbs. All but the durukuli of tropical Central and South America are active during the day, moving frequently in bands as they search for vegetation, birds' eggs, smaller animals, and insects to eat. Monkeys are capable of sitting upright, and, consequently, their hands are freed for many manipulative tasks. Except for a few Old World forms, monkeys are predominantly arboreal, leaping from limb to limb in their travels among the trees. Their hands and feet are both used for grasping and typically have five digits, the thumb and big toe being divergent from the others. Commonly, the digits have flattened nails, but the marmosets have claws on all digits except the big toe, which bears a nail. On the ground, monkeys walk with the entire sole of the foot touching the ground but with the palm of the hand raised. They almost never walk on two legs (bipedally) and can stand erect for only short periods, if at all.

GENERAL FEATURES

Monkeys have large brains and are known for their inquisitiveness and intelligence. Brain development, combined with the freeing of the hands and well-developed vision, allows them a great latitude of activity. Most are good at solving complex problems and learning from experience, but they do not quite reach the cognitive levels of great apes. Some, especially the capuchins (genus *Cebus*), spontaneously use objects as tools (e.g., stones to crack nuts). Others, such as baboons, readily learn to use sticks to obtain food. However, in strong contrast to the great apes (gorillas, chimpanzees, and orangutans), most monkeys do not appear to be very good at learning from each others' experience—individuals more or less have to learn new behaviours for themselves. A significant exception is the Japanese macaque (*Macaca fuscata*). In field experiments, these monkeys were introduced to new foods such as sweet potatoes and candies wrapped in paper. Once a few individuals had solved the problems of getting at the new foods, their innovations gradually spread throughout entire troops. These experiments have had implications in redefining cultural behaviour.

Monkeys are highly social animals, and almost all live in troops consisting of several females with young and either a single male (as in hamadryas baboons, mandrills, most guenons, and most langurs) or several males (as in savannah baboons and macaques). Usually, but not universally, the females stay in the troop in which they were born and are thus closely related to each other. Males join new troops on maturity, and so they are unrelated to each other and somewhat antagonistic. Like humans and apes, female monkeys nurse their young and have a menstrual cycle, albeit less copious. In some species, sexual activity is strictly confined to the period around ovulation (estrus); in others, there appears to be little or no restriction. Some species breed all year round; others have a period several months long during which they experience no sexual cycles (anestrus).

OLD WORLD MONKEYS VERSUS NEW WORLD MONKEYS

Monkeys are arranged into two main groups: Old World and New World. Old World monkeys all belong to one family, Cercopithecidae, which is related to apes and humans, and together they are classified as catarrhines (meaning "downward-nosed" in Latin). The New World monkeys are the platyrrhines ("flat-nosed"), a group comprising five families. As their taxonomic names suggest, New World (platyrrhine) and Old World (catarrhine) monkeys are distinguished by the form of the nose. New World monkeys have broad noses with a wide septum separating outwardly directed nostrils, whereas Old World monkeys have narrow noses with a thin septum and downward-facing nostrils, as do apes and humans. Old World monkeys have hard, bare "sitting pads" (ischial callosities) on the buttocks; New World monkeys lack these. Many Old World monkeys have thumbs that can be opposed to the other fingers and so can handle small objects precisely. None

From left, head of a saki (Pithecia) *and a macaque* (Macaca). Drawing by R. Keane

of the New World monkeys has such manual dexterity. Indeed, in the hands of many species, the main divergence is between the index and middle fingers; in a few species, the thumb is reduced or even absent. Some New World monkey species have prehensile tails capable of supporting the entire body weight or of grasping, for example, a proffered peanut. No Old World monkeys have this ability, and macaques are nearly tailless.

New World monkeys live primarily in tropical South America, especially the Amazon rainforests; the range of a few species extends northward as far as southern Mexico or southward into northern Argentina. Among the smaller New World forms that have endeared themselves to humans with their antics and their tamability are the alert marmosets, often tufted and colourfully arrayed, and the inquisitive squirrel, woolly, and capuchin monkeys— all of which exhibit in marked degree the curiosity and cleverness ascribed to monkeys generally. Larger New World species include the acrobatic spider monkeys and the noisy howlers. Other New World monkeys include uakaris, sakis, and titis.

Old World monkeys live throughout Africa, on the Red Sea coast of Arabia, and in Asia from Afghanistan to Japan and southeast to the islands of the Philippines, Celebes, Bacan, and Timor. Some Old World monkeys have been successfully naturalized in Gibraltar, France, Mauritius, Belau, and a few islands of the West Indies. Old World monkeys include many that are often seen in zoos, especially the beautifully coloured African guenons (e.g., mona, diana, white-nosed, green, vervet, and grivet monkeys), colobus, mangabeys, and the chiefly Asiatic macaques. The macaques include the Barbary "ape" of North Africa and the Rock of Gibraltar—the only macaque outside Asia and the only wild monkey inhabiting any part of Europe today—and the rhesus monkey of the Indian subcontinent, which has been used considerably in medical research. The graceful langurs include the hanuman, or sacred monkey, also of southern Asia. Among the more unusual monkeys are the large and strikingly coloured African drills and mandrills, the proboscis monkey of Borneo, and the rare and bizarre snub-nosed monkeys of China and Vietnam. The Old World monkeys are divided into two subfamilies: Cercopithecinae and Colobinae. The cercopithecines have cheek pouches, in which they store food; these include baboons, macaques, guenons, and their relatives. The colobines lack cheek pouches but have complicated three- or four-chambered stomachs, where bacterial fermentation of cellulose and hemicellulose occurs and thereby enriches the nutrient content of their diet, which consists partially of leaves and seeds. Colobines include colobus monkeys, langurs, and their relatives.

Because the ecological niches that they occupy are similar, there are many parallels between Old and New World monkeys. In particular, the squirrel monkeys (genus *Saimiri*) of the New World and the talapoin (genus *Miopithecus*) of West-Central Africa are remarkably convergent; both are small (about 1 kg [2.2 pounds]) and greenish, live in large troops along rivers, and breed seasonally. Other aspects of each group's evolution, however, are unique. No New World monkey lives on the savanna or has a multichambered cellulose-fermenting stomach, and no Old World monkey is nocturnal like the durukuli. The closest analogue to the complex society of the spider monkey is found not in an Old World monkey but in the chimpanzee.

AFRICAN MONKEYS

Africa is home to several species of catarrhines. Some of these forms, such as the baboons, are familiar sights in zoos worldwide. Catarrhine monkeys include the mangabeys, drills, and guenons, as well as the mandrill, a species recognizable by its coloured patches of bare skin.

BABOONS

There are five living species of baboons (*Papio*). These large, robust, and primarily terrestrial monkeys are found in dry regions of Africa and Arabia. Males of the largest species, the chacma baboon (*Papio ursinus*), average 30 kg (66 pounds) or so, but females are only half this size. The smallest is the hamadryas, or sacred baboon (*P. hamadryas*), with males weighing about 17 kg (about 38 pounds) and females only 10 kg (22 pounds), but this still places them among the largest monkeys. Baboons range from 50 to 115 cm (20–45 inches) long, not including the 45–70-cm (18–28-inch) tail, which is carried in a characteristic arch. All species have long snouts with the nostrils located at the end; male baboons have long daggerlike canine teeth.

Unlike most monkeys, few baboons live in tropical forests; most are found in savanna and semiarid regions, where they rove on the ground. They regularly climb trees, however, and here they sleep, keep watch, and sometimes feed. Baboons eat a variety of plants and animals, including grass and grass seeds, fruit, pods, roots, and tubers that they dig out of the ground. They also eat rodents, birds, and even gazelle fawns that they find hiding in long grass. In South Africa they are said to kill lambs, and everywhere they are known as crop raiders.

The five species of baboon replace each other geographically across the open country of Africa from parts of the Sahara southward. The chacma, which lives in southern Africa south of the Zambezi River, is brown or blackish in colour. The much smaller yellow baboon (*P. cynocephalus*) is found from the Zambezi northward to the Kenya coast

Anubis, or olive, baboon (Papio anubis). Norman Myers/Photo Researchers

and Somalia. The anubis, or olive baboon (*P. anubis*), is only slightly smaller than the chacma and olive in colour; the male has a large mane of hair over the head and shoulders. The anubis baboon has a wide range, from the hinterland of Kenya and Ethiopia through the grasslands and Sahel westward to Mali. It is also found in the less-arid highlands of the Sahara, such as Tibesti and Aïr. The small red Guinea baboon (*P. papio*) is restricted to far western Africa, and males have a cape of hair. These four species are often referred to collectively as savannah baboons, and they have much in common. All live in large cohesive troops numbering from 10 to several hundred. In most cases, females will remain with the troop in which they are born, but males nearing maturity will leave and try to join a different troop. Within each troop there is a dominance hierarchy among adult males. They threaten each other and often fight, and the dominance ranking is constantly changing. The dominance hierarchy of females is much more stable; females are genetically related to each other and rarely fight. Dominant members of each sex have the first choice of favoured foods and mating partners; they also keep order within the troop, chasing and threatening subordinates that are fighting or otherwise causing a disturbance.

The female baboon has a menstrual cycle lasting about 35 days. As estrus approaches, she develops large cushionlike swellings incorporating the vulva, perineum, and anus; these make her attractive to the males, which then compete to consort with her. The most dominant male will mate with more estrous females than will any other males and thus will father a high proportion of the next generation. After ovulation, the female's swellings rapidly subside, and she is no longer attractive to the adult males. A single infant is born after a gestation of five to six months. The young are conspicuously black in colour and are permitted a great deal of freedom in their behaviour.

The fifth species, the hamadryas baboon (*P. hamadryas*), differs in appearance from the savannah baboons in that females are brown, but males are silvery gray with an enormous cape of hair on the neck and shoulders. Hamadryas baboons live in the semidesert hills along the African and Arabian coasts of the Red Sea. The small groups of hamadryas rove on their own during the day, then come back together in the evening and sleep on cliffs (not in trees, like most savannah baboons).

The ranges of hamadryas and anubis baboons meet in Africa, and here the two species hybridize. Observations of these hybrids have shown that much of the difference in behaviour between the two species is genetic. For example, the ability of hybrid males to herd females seems to be greater the more they physically resemble hamadryas. Along the Awash River of Ethiopia, the hamadryas/anubis border and its hybrid zone moves back and forth according to climate; after a run of dry years, the hamadryas area moves upriver, whereas a run of wetter years results in the anubis's expanding downstream. This study (begun in the mid-1960s) and others like it have provided significant information on various evolutionary processes, including adaptation, genetics, and gene flow between different but related species.

Baboons belong to a large family of Old World monkeys (Cercopithecidae). Other long-faced monkeys, especially the mandrill and drill, the gelada, and the Celebes macaque, are sometimes referred to as baboons, but among these only the gelada is closely related. In the Guyanas and Belize, the term *baboon* is colloquially applied to the howler monkey.

COLOBUS MONKEYS

The dozen or so species of colobus monkeys are native to eastern, central, and western Africa. These long-tailed tree-dwellers are generally gregarious. They are active during the day and strong enough to make long leaps between trees. The three genera of colobus are all more or less thumbless and can be distinguished by colour: black-and-white colobus (genus *Colobus*), red colobus (genus *Piliocolobus*), and olive colobus (genus *Procolobus*).

The five species of black-and-white colobus are slender, with long silky fur. Although the black colobus (*C. satanas*) is completely black, the other four species are partially white. The young are white at birth. The best-known species is the Abyssinian colobus, or mantled guereza (*C. guereza*), of the East African mountains, including Mount Kenya and Kilimanjaro. This colobus has a long beautiful veil of white hair along each flank and a long white brush on the tail. The pelts are valued by native populations as ornaments, and at one time European demand for the fur was so great that large numbers of these monkeys were

guereza, or Abyssinian, black-and-white colobus
(*Colobus guereza*)

30 centimetres

12 inches

Guereza, or Abyssinian, black-and-white colobus (Colobus guereza). Encyclopædia Britannica, Inc.

slaughtered annually. Black-and-white colobus are about 55–60 cm (22–24 inches) long, with a tail that is significantly longer than the body. Adult females weigh about 8 kg (18 pounds), adult males 9.5 to 10 kg (21 to 22 pounds). They live in small groups of 1 or 2 males and 3 to 10 females. Each group lives in a territory in the trees, which the males mark by a "jumping-roaring display" consisting of a loud rattling call accompanied by a vigorous display of leaping about and dropping from tree crown to lower branches.

The five or more species of red colobus are brown or black with red markings and are about half a metre (1.6 feet) long, excluding the 40–80-cm (16–32-inch) tail. In large species, such as the bay colobus (*Piliocolobus badius*) of West Africa, both sexes average 8 to 8.5 kg (18 to 19 pounds), though the Zanzibar red colobus (*P. kirkii*) weighs only 5.5 kg (12 pounds). Unlike black-and-white colobus, red colobus tend to live in large troops sometimes numbering 60 or more, with each troop including several adult males. Red colobus are not territorial, and they do not have such loud calls or dramatic displays. In many regions they are extremely abundant, but, where their forest habitat has been altered by logging or fire, they are much less resilient than black-and-white colobus. Several races of the red colobus are endangered, and some subspecies of red colobus have apparently become extinct since the middle of the 20th century. The other colobus species are declining in population and are variously listed as vulnerable or rare. The olive colobus (*Procolobus verus*) is a small monkey, weighing only 4.5 kg (10 pounds), with short olive-coloured fur. It lives in West Africa, where it is not especially rare but is very quiet and secretive and therefore seldom seen. Neither red nor olive colobus survive very long in captivity.

Red and olive colobus share an unusual feature not seen among black-and-white colobus. Like some other Old World monkeys, the females have very large periodic swellings around the sex organs, but, uniquely, the subadult males also develop swellings, and these exactly mimic those of the female. It is thought that the swellings allow young males to remain in the troop without being evicted by adult males, as their so-called perineal organ is lost with maturity.

The three genera of colobus monkeys are classified in the subfamily Colobinae, which also includes leaf monkeys such as langurs. All Colobinae have complex stomachs adapted to fermenting a vegetarian diet. Colobinae is a subfamily of Old World monkeys (family Cercopithecidae).

DeBrazza's Monkey

DeBrazza's monkey (*Cercopithecus neglectus*) is a large, brightly coloured guenon. The species is widely distributed through central Africa and into Ethiopia and

DeBrazza's monkey (Cercopithecus neglectus). Robert C. Hermes— The National Audubon Society Collection/Photo Researchers

western Kenya, particularly in forests near rivers and swamps. DeBrazza's monkey is a white-bearded primate with speckled yellow-gray fur and a white stripe along each thigh. Hands, feet, and tail are black. On the forehead is a browband of white-tipped red hairs surmounted by a black band; the cheek fur is grizzled black and yellow. DeBrazza's monkey is rather heavy-set, with females weighing 4 kg (9 pounds) and males 7.5 kg (about 17 pounds). It has a less lively nature than some of the other guenons and is less arboreal, living more on the forest floor.

DIANA MONKEYS

The diana monkey (*Cercopithecus diana*) is an arboreal species of guenon named for its crescent-shaped white browband that resembles the bow of the goddess Diana. It is generally found well above the ground in West African rainforests. Its face and much of its fur are black. It has a white beard, chest, and throat; there are a white stripe along each thigh and a deep reddish patch on the back. On the inside of the thighs, the fur is whitish, yellowish, or reddish. The roloway monkey (*C. d. roloway*) is a subspecies or closely related species with a longer beard and broader diadem (browband). The diana monkey is active, hardy, and readily tamed. Although engaging when young, it is less friendly as an adult.

DRILLS

The drill (*Mandrillus leucophaeus*) is a large short-tailed monkey found from southeastern Nigeria to western Cameroon and on Bioko Island. As a result of hunting and deforestation, the drill is now highly endangered. The drill, like the related mandrill, was formerly thought to be a forest-dwelling baboon, but it is now known to be related to some of the mangabeys; all of these primates belong to the Old World monkey family, Cercopithecidae.

Like the mandrill, the drill is a stout-bodied quadrupedal monkey with vividly coloured buttocks. The drill is slightly smaller, the male being about 82 cm (32 inches) long. Males are larger than females. Drills have a black face with a crimson lower lip. The hairs around the face

drill
(*Mandrillus leucophaeus*)
male

30 centimetres
12 inches

Male drill (Mandrillus leucophaeus). Encyclopædia Britannica, Inc.

and the tuft behind each ear are yellowish white. The rest of the fur is olive-brown. The drill is also like the mandrill in being active during the day, omnivorous, mainly terrestrial, and gregarious. Small groups consisting of one male and up to 20 females may come together to form troops of over 100. A powerful animal, the drill can fight ferociously if molested.

GELADAS

The gelada (*Theropithecus gelada*) is a large baboonlike monkey that differs from true baboons in having the nostrils some distance from the tip of the muzzle. The gelada inhabits the mountains of Ethiopia and lives in groups among steep cliffs and high plateaus. Terrestrial and active during the day, it feeds on leaves, grasses, roots, and tubers.

The gelada is a stocky primate with white eyelids, brown fur, a tufted tail, and a bald pink chest. The male bears a long, heavy mane and may be more than 70 cm (28 inches) long, excluding the somewhat shorter tail. Weight is about 19 kg (42 pounds), but the female is markedly smaller, only 12 kg (26 pounds). The female has a necklacelike row of bead-shaped fleshy growths along the edges of the bare chest patch. The social group consists of a male and several females. However, groups often combine with each other and with bachelor groups of males to form a large foraging herd several hundred strong. The gelada belongs to the Old World monkey family, Cercopithecidae.

GUENONS

There are more than 20 species of guenons, a widely distributed group of African monkeys characterized by bold markings of white or bright colours. Guenons are slim, graceful quadrupedal monkeys with long arms and legs, short faces, and nonprehensile tails that are longer than the combined head and body length of about 30–65 cm (12–26 inches). Males of the large species weigh over 9 kg (20 pounds) and females as much as 5 kg (11 pounds); males of the smaller species are only 4 kg (9 pounds), females 2.5 kg (about 6 pounds). Guenons are known for the beauty of their soft, dense fur, which in many species has a speckled appearance produced by the alternation of two colours along each hair shaft. The bodies of guenons are commonly grayish, reddish, brown, green, or yellow.

In general, these monkeys are arboreal forest dwellers. The basic social unit is the family, consisting of one male and two or three females and young. The families are territorial, and the males utter loud barks or chirps as spacing calls, but families of different species will often combine for foraging, at times associating for long periods. Guenons forage for leaves, fruit, and other vegetation and possibly for insects and other small animals; several species raid crops. Breeding seems to occur at any time of year; single young are born after a gestation period of approximately five to seven months, depending on the species. Numerous species can be tamed, and they are

The moustached monkey (Cercopithecus cephus) is a species of guenon. Toni Angermayer/Photo Researchers

commonly seen in zoos owing to their hardiness, activity, good nature, and habit of grimacing at observers. With good care, their life span may exceed 20–30 years.

Guenons are primates of the family Cercopithecidae (Old World monkeys). *Chlorocebus* species include the grivet (*C. aethiops*) of northeastern Africa, the vervet (*C. pygerythrus*) of eastern and southern Africa, and the green monkey (*C. sabaeus*) of West Africa. These largely ground-dwelling guenons are sometimes known collectively as savanna monkeys because they are found in open country or in woodland, as opposed to rainforest. They are greenish with pale yellow or white underparts and black faces. The grivet has a white tuft on the tip of the tail and a thin white browband that continues into back-swept white whiskers. The vervet has shorter whiskers and black hands, feet, and tail tip. The green monkey has yellow whiskers, grayish hands and feet, and a yellow and black tail. Savanna monkeys live in larger social groups than other guenons, consisting of several males and 10 or more females and their young.

Species of the genus *Cercopithecus* have patches of short contrasting fur on the nose. The large spot-nosed guenon, or putty-nosed monkey (*C. nictitans*), is a common West African form with gray-flecked black fur and an oval yellowish or white nose spot. Among other species with nose patches are the lesser spot-nosed guenon (*C. petaurista*) and the redtail (*C. ascanius*), both with heart-shaped white nose spots.

Some guenons are generally known by other names, among them the diana monkey (including the roloway), the owl-faced monkey (also called Hamlyn's monkey), the mona monkey, and DeBrazza's monkey. Other guenons include the patas monkey (genus *Erythrocebus*), the talapoin, or mangrove monkey (genus *Miopithecus*), and the robust Allen's swamp monkey (genus *Allenopithecus*).

HAMADRYAS

The hamadryas (*Papio hamadryas*), which is also called sacred baboon or Arabian baboon, is a large, powerful monkey that inhabits the plains and open-rock areas of the Red Sea coast, both in Africa (Eritrea, the Sudan) and on the opposite coast in Yemen and Saudi Arabia. The hamadryas is the smallest baboon species, with a body length of about 60–70 cm (24–28 inches) and weight of up to 18 kg (40 pounds). Females are brown, but males are silvery gray with an enormous cape of hair on the neck and shoulders.

The hamadryas also differs from other baboons in its social behaviour. Instead of maintaining a large cohesive troop, hamadryas split during the day into groups consisting of a single male and his "harem" of up to six (or more) females. Each male herds his females strictly—chasing them, rounding them up, and, if necessary, biting them on the nape of the neck; he supposedly mates only with the females of his own group. The remaining males form bachelor bands. Sometimes a male will join another male's group and act as follower or apprentice, eventually taking over from the lead male. Other males will attempt to kidnap juvenile females and thus start their own new group. The male-led groups and bachelor bands come back together in the evening on cliffs, where they join together to sleep in herds numbering up to several hundred.

The hamadryas was sacred to Thoth, the ancient Egyptian god of learning. Many mummified bodies of these baboons have been unearthed, and the hamadryas is said to have been trained by the Egyptians to perform many tasks.

MANDRILLS

The mandrill (*Mandrillus sphinx*) is a colourful and primarily ground-dwelling monkey that inhabits the rainforests of equatorial Africa from the Sanaga River (Cameroon) southward to the Congo River. It is stout-bodied and has a short tail, prominent brow ridges, and small, close-set, sunken eyes. The adult male has bare coloured patches of skin on both the face and the buttocks. On the face, the cheeks are ribbed and range in colour from bright blue to violet, with scarlet along the bridge and end of the nose. The buttock pads are pink to crimson, shading to bluish at the sides. The long body fur is olive to brown, and the small beard and the neck fur are yellow; the eyes are framed in black. The adult male is about 90 cm (3 feet) long, including the tail stub, and weighs up to 35 kg (77 pounds), which makes it the largest of all Old World monkeys. The female, also with bare face and buttocks, is duller in colour and considerably smaller, only about 13 kg (29 pounds) on average.

Mandrill (Mandrillus sphinx). Russ Kinne/Photo Researchers

Like baboons, females develop swellings on their hindquarters when they are in estrus.

Mandrills feed on fruit, roots, insects, and small reptiles and amphibians. They live in troops consisting of a male and several (occasionally up to 20) females along with their young. At times several troops come together and travel in enormous aggregations of 100 or more. They are threatened by deforestation of their habitat for agriculture and lumbering as well as by hunting; their flesh is considered to be delicious and fetches high prices in local markets.

The mandrill, along with the related drill, were formerly grouped as baboons in the genus *Papio*. Both are now classified as genus *Mandrillus*, but all belong to the Old World monkey family, Cercopithecidae.

MANGABEYS

Mangabeys make up a group of 11 species of slender, rather long-limbed monkeys found in African tropical forests. They are fairly large quadrupedal monkeys with cheek pouches and deep depressions under the cheekbones. Species range in head and body length from about 40 to almost 90 cm (16–35 inches) and weigh up to about 11 kg (24 pounds) in males and 6 kg (13 pounds) in females; the tail is about as long as the head and body. Mangabeys are highly social and generally quiet, and they feed on seeds, fruit, and leaves. Their large front teeth enable them to bite into fruit that is too tough-coated for other monkeys.

Mangabeys of the genus *Cercocebus* are short-haired with speckled pale grayish brown to dark gray fur; they have light-coloured eyelids, often bright white. They spend much of their time on the ground and usually carry their long, tapering tails forward over their backs. The white-collared or red-capped mangabey (*C. torquatus*), the largest species, lives in west-central Africa and is gray with a white "collar" around the neck and a red crown. The white-naped mangabey (*C. lunulatus*) is restricted to a small region between the Nzo-Sassandra river system in Côte d'Ivoire and the Volta River in Ghana. The sooty mangabey (*C. atys*), a dark, uniformly gray species with a pale face, is found from the Nzo-Sassandra system westward to Senegal. Four paler, browner species live in

sooty mangabey
(*Cercocebus atys*)

30 centimetres

12 inches

Sooty mangabey (Cercocebus atys). Encyclopædia Britannica, Inc.

Central and East Africa: the agile mangabey (*C. agilis*), a slender monkey that has a small whorl of hair on the front of the crown and lives in Congo (Kinshasa) north of the Congo River westward into Gabon; the golden-bellied mangabey (*C. chrysogaster*), which lacks a whorl and has a bright golden orange underside and is restricted to the region south of the Congo River; the Sanje mangabey (*C. sanjei*), discovered quite unexpectedly in 1980 living in the Udzungwa Mountains and Mwanihana forest of Tanzania; and the Tana River mangabey (*C. galeritus*), a small species that has long crown hair diverging from a part and is found only in forests along the lower Tana River in Kenya. The Tana River mangabey, which numbers only 1,000–2,000 and is in danger of extinction, lives alongside rivers, where it benefits from periodic flooding to feed on fungi, insects, and seedlings. It lives in small troops with one or two males as well as several females and young. The troops move across open grassland between small patches of gallery forest—an unusual practice for mangabeys. In the morning and the evening, the males produce loud spacing calls consisting of a series of deep whoops that rise into screeches.

Mangabeys of the genus *Lophocebus* spend more time in the trees than *Cercocebus* and are long-haired with unspeckled black fur. They do not have white eyelids, and they carry their tails more upright, usually in a curve or question-mark shape. The gray-cheeked mangabey (*L. albigena*) is found from eastern Nigeria eastward into Uganda; it has a gargoylelike face with thinly haired gray or white cheeks and scruffy hair on the crown. Living in dispersed troops of several males and females, they rest between feeding bouts characteristically sprawled along branches or in tree forks. The black mangabey (*L. aterrimus*) has long curved gray whiskers on the cheeks and a coconut-like crest on the crown; it replaces the gray-cheeked species south of the Congo River. The little-known Opdenbosch's mangabey (*L. opdenboschi*) has a shorter crest, and the thick straight cheek whiskers are black like the body; it is confined to a few gallery forests on the rivers south of the Congo.

A fourth species of *Lophocebus*, *L. kipunji*, recognized by some scientists exists in two populations in the Eastern Arc forests of Tanzania: one in the Ndundulu forest in the Udzungwa Mountains, the other in the Southern Highlands. These animals are often classified as a separate genus, *Rungwecebus*, due to genetic and morphological characteristics that separate it from other mangabeys, and it is commonly known as the kipunji. It is light brown in colour with white on the midline of the underside and white toward the end of the tail. There is a long, broad crest of hair on the crown. Vocalizations of the species, which have been heard only in the Southern Highlands population, seem rather different from those of other species of *Lophocebus*. The total number of kipunji appears to amount to fewer than 500 in each population.

Much remains to be learned about these unusual monkeys, so classification at the species level is unclear. Mangabeys are placed in different genera because it is realized that they are not closely related to each other, but each has its nearest affinities with other groups of the family Cercopithecidae (Old World monkeys): genus *Cercocebus* is closely related to mandrills and drills, whereas *Lophocebus* and *Rungwecebus* are closely related to baboons and geladas.

MONA MONKEYS

The mona monkey (*Cercopithecus mona*) is a primate commonly found in West African tropical rainforests. It was introduced to the island of Grenada during the 18th century via the slave trade, and a wild population has established itself there. The mona monkey is a speckled reddish brown in colour, with white underparts and an oval patch of white on each side of the tail. Its face is marked by a pale band across the forehead and a thin black stripe between each eye and ear. The mona monkey is lively and is one of the most widely exhibited members of the guenon group of African monkeys. Related species such as Campbell's monkey (*C. campbelli*) and the crested guenon (*C. pogonias*) are sometimes loosely referred to as monas. All belong to the Old World monkey family, Cercopithecidae.

OWL-FACED MONKEYS

The owl-faced monkey (*Cercopithecus hamlyni*), which is also called Hamlyn's monkey, is an arboreal guenon found in tropical forests east of the Congo basin. The owl-faced monkey is greenish gray with black underparts and forelimbs; the lower back and base of the tail are silver-gray. It is named for the white streak running down the length of the nose, which gives it an owl-like appearance, but some individuals living at high altitudes, especially in the bamboo forest of Mt. Kahuzi, Democratic Republic of the Congo (Kinshasa), lack this streak. Owl monkeys eat fruit and other vegetation and live in groups consisting of a male and several breeding females.

PATAS MONKEYS

The patas monkey (*Erythrocebus patas*) is a long-limbed and predominantly ground-dwelling primate found in the grass and scrub regions of West and Central Africa and southeast to the Serengeti plains.

The adult male patas monkey has shaggy fur set off by a white mustache and white underparts, and its build is like that of a greyhound; the female has a similar but less-striking pattern and build. It is about 50–70 cm (20–28 inches) long, excluding the tail of about the same length. Males average 12.5 kg (27.5 pounds), the female only 6.5 kg (14 pounds). Omnivorous and quadrupedal, it generally lives in troops consisting of a single male with up to half a dozen females and their young; the dominant female leads the troop, the male being peripheral. Upon sighting a predator such as a cheetah, the male makes himself conspicuous, finally running off at high speed and drawing the predator away from the females and young hiding in nearby long grass. Small bachelor male troops constantly try to invade breeding troops and mate with the females or oust the troop male. Single births occur during the wet season after a gestation period estimated at five to six months. The young develop quickly, with females maturing at three years and males at four— a shorter period of immaturity than observed in many smaller monkeys.

The patas monkey is an Old World monkey (family Cercopithecidae) related to guenons. Because of its colour, white facial marking, and habits, it has also been called the hussar, military, or dancing red monkey, as well as the red guenon.

SWAMP MONKEYS

Swamp monkeys (*Allenopithecus nigroviridis*) are small heavily built primates of the Congo River basin. They are dark olive in colour, with orange or whitish undersides. The head and body length is about 450 mm (18 inches), and there is a somewhat longer tail; females weigh 3.7 kg (8 pounds) on average, males 6 kg (13 pounds). They live in groups of about 40, mainly in swamp forest, where they spend as much time on the ground as they do in the trees foraging for fruit and invertebrates. Swamp monkeys can swim and will jump into the water to escape predators.

The swamp monkey is in many respects intermediate between the guenons and the group consisting of baboons, mangabeys, and macaques. The swamp monkey's skull resembles that of guenons, but, as with baboons and mangabeys, the female develops sexual swellings during estrus. The teeth possess characteristics of both groups. All of these primates belong to the Old World monkey family, Cercopithecidae.

TALAPOINS

Talapoins (*Miopithecus*) make up either of two small species of monkeys found in swamp forests on each side of the lower Congo River and neighbouring river systems. They are the smallest of the Old World monkeys, weighing less than 2 kg (4.4 pounds). *M. talapoin*, which lives south and east of the river in Angola and the Democratic Republic of the Congo (Kinshasa), has been known to science since the 18th century, whereas *M. ogouensis*, living north and west of the river in the Republic of the Congo (Brazzaville) and Gabon, was recognized as a distinct species in the 1990s. Both species have long tails and greenish upperparts, but the colour of their fur and several other parts of the body is different and varies among individuals.

Talapoins live in huge troops, usually of 50 to 100, but, in the vicinity of villages, they often number well over 100 and raid root crops, especially manioc. Manioc contains high concentrations of poisonous hydrogen cyanide (HCN) and is left by farmers to leach in running water for days before it can be prepared. During this time, talapoins test the leaching roots and eat those that they consider to be safe. Troops of talapoins sleep in trees along watercourses, and when disturbed they drop into the water and swim away. Within the troop, various social behaviours such as aggression, play, and grooming are observed among small groups and individuals.

Talapoins belong to the Old World monkey family, Cercopithecidae. They have sometimes been included with the guenons in the genus *Cercopithecus*, but talapoins' smaller size and the development of sexual swellings in females during estrus warrant their classification as a separate genus.

ASIAN MONKEYS

The most diverse groups of Asian catarrhine monkeys include the langurs, macaques, the snub-nosed monkeys, and the doucs. Earth's largest continent is also home to the bonnet monkey, the simakobu, the proboscis monkey, and others.

Bonnet monkey (Macaca radiata). Warren Garst/Tom Stack & Associates

BONNET MONKEYS

The bonnet monkey (*Macaca radiata*) is a macaque of southern India named for the thatch of long hair forming a cap, or "bonnet," on the head. It is grayish brown with a hairless pink face. It is about 35–60 cm (14–24 inches) long, excluding its long tail. Average adult females weigh about 4 kg (9 pounds), adult males 6.7 kg (15 pounds). This agile monkey sometimes raids gardens or stores of food.

CELEBES CRESTED MACAQUES

The Celebes crested macaque (*Macaca nigra*), which is also called black macaque, is a mainly arboreal Indonesian monkey named for the narrow crest of hair that runs along the top of the head from behind the overhanging brow. The Celebes crested macaque is found only in the Minahasa region on the island of Sulawesi (Celebes) and on nearby Bacan Island, where it was probably introduced by humans.

Stump-tailed and covered with dark brown or black fur, its body is 55–65 cm (22–26 inches) long. Adult females weigh about 5.5 kg (12 pounds) and adult males nearly 10 kg (22 pounds). The long, flat muzzle is black and nearly hairless. Active during the day and primarily arboreal, this monkey feeds on fruit in its tropical forest habitat. Troops are large, usually numbering 20 or more, and each troop includes several adult males. A closely related species, the Gorontalo macaque (*M. nigrescens*), lives just southwest of Minahasa, and at least five other species of macaques live in other parts of Sulawesi. Although sometimes incorrectly called apes, Celebes macaques are monkeys belonging to the family Cercopithecidae.

DOUCS

Doucs (*Pygathrix*) make up a group of three colourful species of langur monkeys found in the tropical forests of central and southern Vietnam, southern Laos, and northeastern Cambodia. Doucs are among the most strikingly coloured primates. The head is brownish, but the body appears blue-gray owing to black-and-white bands on each hair. The tail and long cheek whiskers are white, as are the rump patch and the throat, which is bordered by a necklacelike red line. The vivid orange-yellow face has slanting, almond-shaped eyes. Doucs grow to more than a half metre (20 inches) long, not including the tail, which is slightly longer than the body. Males weigh 11 kg (24 pounds), females about 8.5 kg (19 pounds).

The red-legged douc (*P. nemaeus*) lives from 14° to 20° N latitude. The legs are maroon below the knees, and the forearms are white. The black-shanked douc (*P. nigripes*) is found south of 14° N and has black legs, gray arms, and a darker face. The ranges of the two species overlap, apparently with very little interbreeding, in the Southern Highlands of Vietnam. In the 1990s a third species, the gray-legged douc (*P. cinerea*), was discovered in Vietnam in a few isolated forests around 14° N.

Doucs have been only briefly studied in the wild. Their troops vary in size from 4 to 50 or more, with up to a dozen males and twice as many females. They eat mostly young leaves but also consume fruit, flowers, and seeds. Because of extensive deforestation in Vietnam and Laos, all species, especially the gray-legged, are in danger of extinction. Doucs and other langurs are primates classified in the family Cercopithecidae (Old World monkeys).

LANGURS

Langur is a general name given to numerous species of Asian monkeys belonging to the subfamily Colobinae. The term is often restricted to nearly two dozen species of leaf monkeys but is also applied to various other members of the subfamily.

Leaf monkeys and other langurs are gregarious, diurnal, and basically arboreal monkeys with long tails and slender bodies. The limbs, hands, and feet are also long and slender. Depending on species, the head and body are about 40 to 80 cm (16 to 31 inches) long and the tail about 50 to 110 cm (20 to 43 inches); weight varies from 5.5 kg (12 pounds) in the smallest species, the white-fronted langur (*Presbytis frontata*) of Borneo, up to 15 kg (33 pounds) in the female and 19 kg (42 pounds) in the male of the Himalayan langur (*Semnopithecus schistaceus*). Leaf monkeys have long fur, and many species have characteristic caps or crests of long hair. Colour varies among species but is commonly gray, red, brown, or black, and adults usually have black faces. The colour of the young, born singly after five to six months' gestation, differs from that of adults and possibly serves to arouse the protective instincts of the adults. Mothers are protective but allow other females to help care for the young. Like the related colobus monkeys of Africa, langurs have large, complex stomachs adapted to a diet of leaves, fruit, and other vegetation.

The gray, or Hanuman, langur (*S. entellus*) of the Indian subcontinent is almost black when newborn and gray, tan, or brown as an adult. Regarded as sacred in Hinduism, it spends a good deal of time on the ground and roams at will in villages and temples of India and Nepal, raiding crops and the stores of merchants. The Hanuman langur usually lives in bands of about 20 to 30, though some troops number over 100. In some regions troops include several dominance-ranked adult males, though elsewhere there is only a single adult male per troop. In single-male troops, surplus males live in small bachelor bands that occasionally attempt to oust a troop leader. If successful, one of the bachelors takes over the troop and attempts to kill the unweaned infants in order to bring the females quickly back into estrus (mating condition).

Leaf monkeys of genus *Trachypithecus* are also called brow-ridged langurs. They live in Southeast Asia from Bhutan and southern China to Java and are smaller and more arboreal than Hanuman langurs. The newborn are a bright golden colour. There are 10 to 15 species, including the beautiful golden langur (*T. geei*) from Bhutan, the spectacled langur (*T. obscurus*) from the Malay Peninsula, with white eye rings and pink muzzle, and a group of black langurs with white markings on the head and body, including François' langur (*T. francoisi*) and its relatives, which live in the limestone country of northern Vietnam, Laos, and parts of southeastern China (Kwangsi). The purple-faced langur (*T. vetulus*) of Sri Lanka and the rare Nilgiri langur (*T. johnii*) of southern India may be more closely related to the Hanuman.

Leaf monkeys of the genus *Presbytis* are confined to Malaysia and western Indonesia, where they are mostly known by the local name *surili*; brow-ridged langurs of this region are generally called *lutung*. Most of the 10 or so *Presbytis* species are white on the underside and on the inner aspect of the thigh, contrasting sharply with the dark upper side. The newborn are white with a thick dark line from crown to rump and another at right angles across the shoulders ("cruciger" pattern). Most species live in small territorial groups of one male and two to four females with their young, but one, the joja (*P. potenziani*) of the Mentawai Islands of Indonesia, is unique among Old World monkeys in that it always lives in monogamous pairs.

The three genera of langurs commonly called leaf monkeys are *Presbytis*, *Trachypithecus*, and *Semnopithecus*; other langurs belong to the genera *Pygathrix*, *Rhinopithecus*, *Nasalis*, and *Simias* and include the proboscis monkey and simakobu. Several species are endangered. Langurs and colobus monkeys make up the subfamily Colobinae of the Old World monkey family, Cercopithecidae.

PROBOSCIS MONKEYS

The proboscis monkey (*Nasalis larvatus*) is a long-tailed arboreal primate found along rivers and in swampy mangrove forests of Borneo. Named for the male's long and pendulous nose, the proboscis monkey is red-brown with pale underparts. The nose is smaller in the female and is upturned in the young. Males are 56–72 cm (22–28 inches) long and average 20 kg (44 pounds), but females weigh only about 10 kg (22 pounds). The tail is about the same length as the body. Proboscis monkeys live in groups of about 20 consisting of a single male and up to a dozen females; males live in bachelor groups. The young have blue faces and are born singly, apparently at any time of year; gestation is estimated at five to six months. Proboscis monkeys wade upright through water, which makes them exceptional among monkeys in being habitually bipedal.

Despite government protection, habitat destruction has caused a decline in the population of this species. Proboscis monkeys belong to the same subfamily as langurs and colobus monkeys of the family Cercopithecidae.

MACAQUES

The macaques (*Macaca*) comprise any of about 20 species of gregarious Old World monkeys, all of which are Asian except for the Barbary macaque of North Africa. Macaques are robust primates whose arms and legs are of about the same length. Their fur is generally a shade of brown or black, and their muzzles, like those of baboons, are doglike but rounded in profile, with nostrils on the upper surface. The tail varies between species and may be long, of moderate length, short, or absent. Size differs between the sexes and between the species; males range in head and body length from about 41 to 70 cm (16 to 28 inches) and in weight from about 2.4 kg (5.3 pounds) in females and 5.5 kg (12 pounds) in males of the smallest species, the crab-eating macaque (*M. fascicularis*), to a maximum of about 13 kg (29 pounds) in females and 18 kg (about 40 pounds) in males of the largest species, the Tibetan macaque (*M. thibetana*).

Macaques live in troops of varying size. The males dominate the troop and live within a clear but shifting dominance rank order. The ranking of females is longer-lasting and depends on their genealogical position. Macaques are somewhat more arboreal than baboons but are equally at home on the ground; they are also able to swim. Depending on the species, they live in forests, on plains, or among cliffs and rocky terrain. Macaques are omnivorous, and they possess large cheek pouches in which they carry extra food. Breeding occurs year-round in some (mostly tropical) species, but, among those living outside the tropics, it is seasonal. Single young are born after about six months' gestation and become adult at four years. Macaques are considered highly intelligent but may be bad-tempered as adults.

The seven species of short-tailed macaques on the Indonesian island of Sulawesi (Celebes) vary in appearance from the distinctive Celebes black "ape" (*M. nigra*) at the northern end of the island to the less-specialized Moor macaque (*M. maura*) in the south. Most of the Sulawesi species are in danger of extinction. Crab-eating, or long-tailed, macaques (*M. fascicularis*) of Southeast Asia have whiskered brown faces; they live in forests along rivers, where they eat fruit and fish for crabs and other crustaceans. In the 1950s they were used extensively in studies that led to the development of the polio vaccine. Macaques in general, including the rhesus monkey (*M. mulatta*), are the monkeys most widely used in biomedical research. Rhesus monkeys are native to northern India, Myanmar (Burma), Southeast Asia, and eastern China, formerly as far north as Beijing.

The Formosan, or rock macaque (*M. cyclopis*), is closely related to the rhesus monkey and lives only in Taiwan. Japanese macaques (*M. fuscata*) are larger, more muscular, and shaggy-haired, with pink faces and very short furry tails. These monkeys are important figures in myths and folktales and are seen in representations of the Buddhist adage "See no evil, hear no evil, speak no evil."

Liontail macaques, or wanderoos (*M. silenus*), are black with gray ruffs and tufted tails; an endangered species, they are found only in a small area of southern India. Closely related to liontails are the pigtail macaques (*M. nemestrina*), which carry their short tails curved over their backs. Inhabiting rainforests of Southeast Asia, they are sometimes trained to pick ripe coconuts. Another close relative is the bokkoi (*M. pagensis*), found only on the Mentawai Islands of Indonesia.

Stump-tailed macaques (*M. arctoides*) are strong, shaggy-haired forest dwellers with pink or red faces and very short tails. Another short-tailed species is the Père David's macaque (*M. thibetana*), which lives in mountain forests of southern China; it is sometimes called the Tibetan macaque but is not in fact found there. Often confused with the stump-tail, Père David's macaque is in fact more closely related to the longer-tailed Assam macaque (*M. assamensis*) from the eastern Himalayan foothills and northern Myanmar. The bonnet monkey (*M. radiata*) and the toque macaque (*M. sinica*), from southern India and Sri Lanka, respectively, have hair on the top of the head that grows from a central whorl, in contrast to the short hair of the forehead and temples.

The genus *Macaca* is a primate classified in the family Cercopithecidae (Old World monkeys), along with baboons, mangabeys, guenons, langurs, and colobus monkeys.

RHESUS MONKEYS

The rhesus monkey (*Macaca mulatta*) is a sand-coloured primate native to forests but also found coexisting with humans in northern India, Nepal, eastern and southern China, and northern Southeast Asia. The rhesus monkey is the best-known species of macaque and measures about 47–64 cm (19–25 inches) long, excluding the furry 20–30-cm (8–12-inch) tail. Females average about 8.5 kg (19 pounds) and males 11 kg (24 pounds). In both sexes the rump and legs are orange.

Rhesus monkeys can thrive in a variety of climates and habitats. Their natural diet consists of fruits, seeds, roots, herbs, and insects, but, in areas of human habitation, they also eat crops and search through garbage for food. Rhesus monkeys live in groups consisting of several adults of both sexes and their young; males leave the troop at maturity, whereas females tend to stay in the troops in which they were born. Because the rhesus monkey is held sacred in some parts of India and is the object of tolerant affection on the part of many Brahmans, it is especially common around temples. Here groups may number 50 to 200 or more, whereas in forests 12 to 20 is usual.

Hardy in captivity, the rhesus monkey is a highly intelligent, lively animal that is docile when young but may become bad-tempered as an adult. It has also been an important experimental animal for medical and psychological research. The determination of the Rh (from rhesus) factor in human blood involves reaction with the blood of this monkey, and a rhesus was the first monkey to be rocketed into the stratosphere. The rhesus monkey and other macaques are classified in the family Cercopithecidae (the Old World monkeys).

SNUB-NOSED MONKEYS

Snub-nosed monkeys (*Rhinopithecus*), which are also called snub-nosed langurs, make up a group of four species of large and unusual leaf monkeys found in highland forests of central China and northern Vietnam. They have a broad, short face with wide-set slanting eyes and a short, flat nose with forward-facing nostrils.

The golden snub-nosed monkey (*R. roxellana*) lives in the coniferous montane forests of central China at elevations of 1,800–2,700 metres (6,000–9,000 feet), where the temperature drops below freezing in winter and rises only to about 25° C (77° F) in summer. They have rich golden-brown to golden-red fur, and the tail is about the same length as the body. Males have a long mantle of black and golden hairs on the back; their bodies measure about 62 cm (24 inches) long, and they weigh 16–17 kg (35–37 pounds). Females are slightly smaller, weighing only about 9–10 kg (20–22 pounds). The trefoil-shaped face of the golden snub-nosed monkey is pale blue, and adult males develop strange red swellings at the corners of the mouth. The scientific name refers to Roxellana, consort of the Ottoman sultan Süleyman the Magnificent, who had reddish gold hair and, by some accounts, a snub nose.

The black snub-nosed monkey (*R. bieti*) is black above and white below, with a greenish face and a forward-curling tuft of hair on the crown of the head. It is longer-bodied and shorter-tailed than the golden species but weighs about the same. Found only along the divide between the Yangtze and Mekong rivers in the southern Chinese province of Yunnan, it lives at elevations up to 4,000 metres (about 13,100 feet) in mainly coniferous forests, which are snow-covered for much of the year. The gray snub-nosed monkey (*R. brelichi*) is somewhat smaller, long-tailed, and dark gray with a red patch on the crown and a white patch between the shoulders. It lives only on Mt. Fanjing in southern China (Kweichow province) at about 1,500 metres (about 4,900 feet).

The Tonkin snub-nosed monkey (*R. avunculus*) is the smallest and has a long tail and long, slender fingers and toes. It is black above and strikingly white below and around the face, with the face itself being dark greenish with prominent brick-red lips. This species is confined to the tropical forests of the Na Hang district of northern Vietnam.

The Tonkin species has been recorded only in small groups of up to 30, but this may be because it is so rare that its population is scattered and fragmented. The three Chinese species, however, live in troops up to 500 strong and thus form the largest social groups of any nonhuman primate. These troops divide at times into small groups consisting of one adult male and three to five adult females and their young. This may improve foraging success in their highly seasonal montane environments. All snub-nosed monkeys are leaf eaters, but their diet also includes flowers, fruits, and seeds. The two large high-mountain species (the golden and the black) also eat lichens and often travel or forage on the ground.

There are some 8,000 to 10,000 golden snub-nosed monkeys in the wild, and they are not in immediate danger of extinction. The black and gray species, however, number fewer than 1,500 each; the gray is protected, but the black is hunted, and its habitat is being deforested to provide cattle pasture. The Tonkin is one of the most endangered primates in the world, having little effective protection and a total population below 250. Snub-nosed monkeys are closely related to the douc and were formerly classified in the same genus. Langurs and other leaf monkeys are primates belonging to the Old World monkey family, Cercopithecidae.

NEW WORLD MONKEYS

The New World is the home to the platyrrhine monkeys. There are several interesting forms, found from southern Mexico to northern Argentina. Some of the best known include the howler monkeys, spider monkeys, and marmosets.

DURUKULIS

The durukulis (*Aotus*), which are also called owl monkeys or night monkeys, are a group of several species of closely related nocturnal monkeys. Durukulis live in Central and South America and are distinguished by their large yellow-brown eyes. The durukuli is round-headed, with small ears and dense, soft, grizzled gray or brown fur. Weight ranges from 780 to 1,250 grams (1.7 to 2.7 pounds), and length is 25 to 50 cm (10 to 20 inches), not including the bushy tail, which is about the same length and hangs straight down, incapable of coiling or grasping.

Durukulis live in dry and wet tropical forests from Panama to Argentina. These monogamous monkeys, often in family groups of two to five individuals, can be seen with the fathers carrying the young. They sleep together in tree hollows during the day and emerge at night to feed on fruit, nectar, insects, and other small animals. Durukulis are fairly sedentary, and on moonlit nights they can be observed making soft clicks or chirrs, melodius whoops, and low hoots.

These primates belong to the family Cebidae, but species-level taxonomy is unclear in this genus, with as many as nine distinct and geographically disparate species recognized by some authorities. Taxonomy is further complicated by the fact that different populations have from 46 to 56 chromosomes. The monkeys, while fairly common, have not been heavily hunted, although they are in some demand as laboratory animals.

Howler Monkeys

Howler monkeys (*Alouatta*) make up a group of tropical American monkeys noted for their roaring cries. Several species of howlers are widely distributed through Central and South America. These are the largest New World monkeys and generally attain lengths of about 40–70 cm (16–28 inches), excluding the 50–75-cm (20–30-inch) tail. Howlers are stoutly built bearded monkeys with a hunched

black-and-gold howler
(*Alouatta caraya*)
female

30 centimetres

12 inches

Female black-and-gold howler monkey (Alouatta caraya). Encyclopædia Britannica, Inc.

appearance and thickly furred prehensile tails that are naked on the underside of the tip to afford a better grip. The hair is long and thick and, depending on species, is typically black, brown, or red. Howlers are characterized by expansion of the hyoid bone into a large shell-like organ in the throat that gives resonance to the voice. In connection with the enlarged hyoid, howlers have a large throat, protruding jaws, and high sloping faces.

Howlers live in groups within territories whose boundaries are mapped out by howling matches with neighbouring clans. Their voices carry for 3 to 5 km (2 to 3 miles) and can be heard at dusk, at dawn, and during rainstorms. Howlers are slow-moving monkeys that commonly sit on the topmost branches, rarely descending to the ground. They feed primarily on leaves. When on the move, howlers progress in orderly groups usually led by an old male. Births are usually single and occur at any time of year.

Because of their diet, temperament, and other factors, howlers are difficult to maintain in captivity. The red howler (*A. seniculus*) has the largest distribution, but it is heavily hunted in some areas for its meat. Other howler species are critically endangered within parts of their ranges. The *Alouatta* genus is one of several within the family Atelidae, which also includes woolly monkeys, spider monkeys, and woolly spider monkeys. All are found only in the Western Hemisphere.

MARMOSETS

Marmosets (family Callitrichidae) are small long-tailed South American monkeys. Similar in appearance to squirrels, marmosets are tree-dwelling primates that move in a quick, jerky manner. Claws on all the digits except the big toe aid them in scampering along branches, where they primarily eat insects in addition to fruit, tree sap, and other

Common marmoset (Callithrix jacchus). Art Wolfe/Tony Stone Images

small animals. Marmosets are active during the day and live in small groups. The gestation period is four to six months, depending on species; twins are the norm, with single births being about as common as triplets. Marmosets have been kept as pets since the early 17th century, but they require knowledgeable care to remain healthy.

There are three groups of marmosets: the "true" marmosets, the tamarins, and Goeldi's monkey (*Callimico goeldi*). Also called Goeldi's marmoset, this species is found only in the western Amazon River basin. Black in colour and maned, it differs from other marmosets in that it possesses a third set of molars and does not bear twins. Though Goeldi's monkey was formerly thought to be an evolutionary intermediate between marmosets and the other New World monkeys, molecular genetics now indicate that it is a member of the marmoset family.

The "true" marmosets (genus *Callithrix*) have short lower canine teeth (short-tusked), whereas marmosets with relatively long lower canines (long-tusked) are known as tamarins (genera *Saguinus* and *Leontopithecus*). The pygmy marmoset (*C. pygmaea*) is the smallest "true" marmoset and lives in the rainforests of the Amazon River's upper tributaries. The length of the head and body of the pygmy marmoset is about 14 cm (6 inches), and the tail is somewhat longer. Adults weigh only about 90 grams (3 ounces), whereas other species of the family attain 600 grams (1.3 pounds) or more. The common marmoset (*C. jacchus*) lives in the scrub forest (*caatinga*) of northeastern Brazil. Weighing 400 grams, it is about 15–25 cm (6–10 inches) long, excluding the 25–40-cm (10–16-inch) tail. The marbled brown-and-white fur is dense and silky, and there are white tufts on the ears and black-and-white rings on the tail. Five *Callithrix* species live in different tropical forests along Brazil's Atlantic coast. In the rainforests south of the Amazon River, there may be a dozen or more additional species—three were discovered

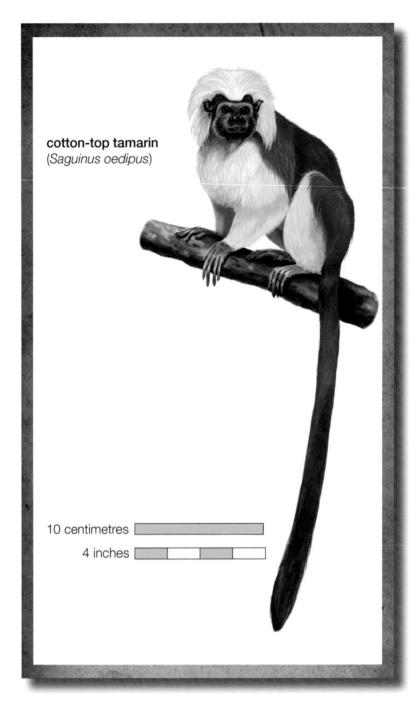

cotton-top tamarin
(*Saguinus oedipus*)

10 centimetres

4 inches

*Cotton-top tamarin (*Saguinus oedipus*). Encyclopædia Britannica, Inc.

in the 1990s, and several others were awaiting description; these vary widely in colour and in the amount of fur on the ears. The short canine teeth and long lower incisors of these marmosets are used to gnaw at tree bark and leave characteristic notches from which sap flows. "True" marmosets breed in monogamous pairs and live in a social organization in which the older young assist in feeding, carrying, and educating the infants. The presence of a breeding pair suppresses the sexual development of the young of both sexes until they leave the group.

Lion tamarins (genus *Leontopithecus*) are named for their thick manes, and all four species are endangered, three of them critically; one (*L. caissara*) was first discovered in 1990. Lion tamarins are larger than "true" marmosets and have long, slender hands and fingers, which they use to hook insects from crevices. The golden lion tamarin (*L. rosalia*), found only in fragmented forest habitats in the Brazilian state of Rio de Janeiro, is particularly striking, with a thick mane, black face, and long silky, golden fur. The fur of the other three species is partly black. Lion tamarins appear to have a social organization similar to that of "true" marmosets, but reproductive suppression appears to be behavioral rather than physiological, and some tamarins appear to tolerate a polyandrous system in which two males share in the rearing of infants of a single female.

There are at least 12 species in the tamarin genus *Saguinus*. Although they lack the manes of lion tamarins, some have notable features. The emperor tamarin (*S. imperator*) of the southwestern Amazon basin, for example, has a long white mustache complementing its long grizzled fur and reddish tail, whereas the mustached tamarin (*S. mystax*) has a small white upswept mustache. The cotton-top tamarin (*S. oedipus*), found in Colombia and Panama, has a scruffy white crest of hair on the top of its head. The golden-handed tamarin, *S. midas*, is named for the mythological Greek king.

GOLDEN LION TAMARINS

The golden lion tamarin (*Leontideus rosalia*), which is also called the golden lion marmoset, is a species of tamarin that possesses a thick, lionlike mane, black face, and long, silky, golden fur. A striking-looking animal, it is found only in fragmented forest habitats in the Brazilian state of Rio de Janeiro, where it is listed as endangered.

SAKIS

There are seven species of sakis, a group of arboreal South American monkeys that have long nonprehensile furred tails. The "true" sakis of the genus *Pithecia* are approximately 30–50 cm (12–20 inches) long, not including the bushy, tapering tail of 25–55 cm (10–22 inches). Females generally weigh less than 2 kg (4.4 pounds) and males more than 2 kg. These sakis are covered with long, coarse hair that falls like a hood on the head and a cape over the shoulders.

The male pale-headed saki (*P. pithecia*) is black with a whitish face surrounding the dark muzzle, but the female is grizzled gray with a gray face and a white line on either side of the muzzle. The other four species, including the monk saki (*P. monachus*), are grizzled gray with less difference between the sexes. Sakis are active by day (diurnal) and live in monogamous pairs. They feed on fruit, leaves, and especially seeds, which they grind in their powerful jaws. Births are single; the young at first cling to the female's belly and later are carried on her back until they are able to travel independently. They are gentle in captivity but nervous and difficult to keep.

Bearded sakis (*Chiropotes*) are not as well known as true sakis. Each of the two species is about 40–45 cm (16–18 inches) long, excluding the heavily furred tail, which ranges in length from slightly shorter to slightly longer than the body. Females weigh 2.5 kg (6 pounds) on average,

pale-headed saki
(*Pithecia pithecia*)
male

10 centimetres

4 inches

Pale-headed saki (Pithecia pithecia). Encyclopædia Britannica, Inc.

males about 3 kg (7 pounds). They have dense coats of long, primarily black hair, and the tails are rounded. On the head, their bouffant hair parts in the centre, grows thickly along the sides of the face, and extends into a full, heavy beard. Bearded sakis are diurnal and live in small groups with several individuals of both sexes, and their diet is similar to that of true sakis.

Related to uakaris, sakis belong to the family Pitheciidae of the order Primates.

SPIDER MONKEYS

Spider monkeys (*Ateles*) are large, extremely agile monkeys that live in forests from southern Mexico to Brazil. In spite of its thumbless hands, this lanky potbellied primate can move swiftly through trees, using its long tail as a fifth limb.

Spider monkeys weigh about 6 kg (13.2 pounds) and are 35–66 cm (14–26 inches) long, excluding the heavily furred tail, which is longer than the body. The coat, of variable length and fineness, ranges among the several species from gray to reddish, dark brown, or black. Most have a black face with white eye rings, but some have a flesh-coloured face.

The monkeys live in bands numbering up to 35 animals but forage in smaller groups, roaming the highest branches during the day. They feed most intensively early in the day, relishing fruit supplemented by nuts, seeds, buds, flowers, and leaves as well as spiders and bird eggs. They do not normally descend from the trees and will leap or drop spread-eagled from one tree to another. Spider monkeys are dextrous with their tails as well as their hands. They pick up objects with the tail as well as hang from branches by using the tail alone.

Spider monkeys that are hunted for food sometimes remove the arrows with their hands and attempt to stem the bleeding. Wary of humans, they will break off tree branches and try to drop them on intruders and bark like terriers when approached. Spider monkeys also produce a variety of other sounds. When separated from their fellows, they call to one another in a whinnying voice like a horse. They are also capable of prolonged screams.

Single young are born in seclusion after a gestation period of about 139 days and are dependent on the mother for a year. Time between births ranges from two to five years.

Widely hunted for food by local people, spider monkey populations are decreasing owing to logging and land clearing. Spider monkeys are susceptible to malaria and are used in laboratory studies of the disease.

Four to eight species of spider monkeys are recognized, depending on the taxonomic criteria used. The woolly spider monkey is of a different genus, but all are primates of the family Cebidae.

Squirrel Monkeys

The squirrel monkey (*Saimiri*) is the most abundant primate of riverside forests in the Guianas and the Amazon River basin. Each of the five species possesses a circle of black hairless skin around the nose and mouth set against an expressive white face. Their short, soft fur is gray to olive green, with whitish underparts. Squirrel monkeys are 25–40 cm (10–16 inches) long, not including the heavy nonprehensile tail, which is at least as long as the body. Hands, arms, and feet are yellow to orange. Common squirrel monkeys (*Saimiri sciureus*) have olive or grayish crowns and are found only in South America, whereas the endangered Central American squirrel monkeys (*S. oerstedii*) have black crowns and reddish backs. The common and Central American species both have hair on the ears, unlike the bare-eared squirrel monkey (*S. ustus*) of central Brazil.

Squirrel monkeys form larger groups than any other New World monkey—one group of 300 was counted in a pristine Amazonian rainforest. They are also among the most vocal of primates, communicating with at least 26 different calls, including barks, purrs, screams, peeps, and squawks. Exceptionally agile jumpers and runners, these monkeys prefer life in the trees, though they will occasionally descend to the ground. They are active

Common squirrel monkey (Saimiri sciureus). © Gerry Ellis Nature Photography

during the day and move single file after a leader along frequently used pathways in the treetops. At night, they sleep huddled together on branches, tails wrapped around their bodies. Squirrel monkeys and capuchin monkeys sometimes forage together, eating fruit, leaves, buds, tree gum, insects, spiders, and small vertebrates. Females give birth to a single baby after a gestation of about six months. The baby rides the mother's back jockey-style for the first few weeks of life and remains dependent on the mother for a year.

Attractive, gentle, affectionate, and clean, squirrel monkeys were popular pets in the United States until the capture and importation of wild primates as pets was outlawed in 1975. They seem to fare best when kept with others of their kind and may live up to 20 years under favourable conditions. Squirrel monkeys are primates of the family Cebidae.

TITIS

Titis (*Callicebus*) are a group of about 20 species of small arboreal monkeys that have long furred tails and are found in South American rainforests, especially along the Amazon and other rivers. Titis have long, soft, glossy fur and rather flat, high faces set in small, round heads. Even the largest species weighs less than 2 kg (4.4 pounds), and they measure about 25–60 cm (10–24 inches) long, with a tail of about the same length. Titis may be dark brown, gray, reddish, or blackish, depending on the species, with lighter or differently coloured underparts, face, limbs, and tail. They live in monogamous, territorial groups and are active during the day. When resting together in trees, titis intertwine their tails, but the tail is used for balance while foraging for fruit, bird eggs, insects, and small vertebrates. Breeding is not seasonal. The single offspring clings to the male except when being fed. Titis are New World monkeys belonging to the family Pitheciidae, order Primates.

UAKARIS

Uakaris (*Cacajao*) make up a group of several types of short-tailed South American monkeys with shaggy fur, humanlike ears, and distinctive bald faces that become flushed when the animal is excited. In two of the three colour forms, the face is bright red. Uakaris are about 35–50 cm (14–20 inches) long, excluding their strangely short 15–20-cm (6–8-inch) nonprehensile, or nongrasping, tails.

The monkeys live in troops of about 15 individuals and are diurnal (active during the day), feeding mainly on fruit. Acrobatic and athletic, they launch themselves from high branches, bouncing on small tree limbs to leap from one tree to another with arms outstretched.

There are two species and three main colour forms of this primate, and all are either endangered or vulnerable. The faces of red uakaris (subspecies *C. calvus rubicundus, C. calvus novaesi*, and *C. calvus ucayalii*) are bright red, and the coats range from reddish brown to red-orange. They live in flooded forests along the upper Amazon River and its tributaries in eastern Peru and western Brazil. The white, or bald, uakari (*C. calvus calvus*) is a different colour form of the same species. It has whitish fur and lives only in the Mamiraua Reserve along the upper Amazon in Brazil. Because of its vermilion face, local people call it the "English monkey." The face, shoulders, arms, hands, and feet of the black-headed uakari (*C. melanocephalus*) are black, and the coat is chestnut-coloured with a saddle of reddish or yellowish hair. It lives in southern Venezuela, southeastern Colombia, and northwestern Brazil. Males are particularly red, which leads some scientists to speculate that the colour attracts females; in fact, since male uakaris pale with malaria, the bright colour may help females to select healthy mates.

Uakaris are captured by Amazonian Indians; the young are kept as pets, the adults eaten. In general, uakaris do not do well in captivity. They belong to the family Cebidae and are one of the few New World monkeys without a prehensile tail.

WOOLLY MONKEYS

Woolly monkeys are densely furred South American primates found in rainforests of the western Amazon River basin. Each of the five species averages 40–60 cm (16–24 inches) in length, excluding the thick and somewhat longer prehensile tail. Females weigh 7 kg (15.5 pounds) on average, males a little more. The common, or Humboldt's, woolly monkeys (*Lagothrix lagotricha* and related species) have short fur that, depending on the species, is tan, gray, reddish, or black; some have darker heads. The head itself is large and round, with a bare black or brown face. Their bodies are thick with sturdy limbs, and their protruding bellies have given them the Portuguese name *barrigudo*, or "big belly."

Woolly monkeys are active during the day. Gregarious, they live in small groups and are often found in the company of capuchins, howlers, and other monkeys. They are rather slow-moving and generally travel on all fours, although they often swing by their hands, feet, and tail or by their tail alone. On the ground they are able to stand erect, using the tail for support.

Woolly monkeys mature at about four years and bear single young after seven to eight months' gestation. Diet in the wild consists primarily of fruit and leaves, but in captivity they accept almost any food, which can result in nutritional problems. Although placid and gentle, they need attention and must be coddled to some extent. They appear to weep when upset, and those kept as pets enjoy playing hide-and-seek.

The yellow-tailed, or Hendee's, woolly monkey (*Oreonax flavicauda*) is very different from *Lagothrix* and is not closely related, hence its classification as a separate genus. This species has silky mahogany-coloured fur, a whitish nose, and a yellow stripe on the underside of the tail. It is restricted to the cloud forests of northern Peru and is critically endangered; little is known of its behaviour, its ecology, or even its range. The other woolly monkeys are becoming rarer as their habitat is destroyed. Both genera belong to the family Atelidae of the New World monkeys.

WOOLLY SPIDER MONKEYS

Woolly spider monkeys (*Brachyteles*), which are also called muriquis, are extremely rare. These primates live only in the remaining Atlantic forests of southeastern Brazil. The woolly spider monkey is the largest monkey in South America and is intermediate in structure and appearance between the woolly monkeys (genus *Lagothrix*) and the spider monkeys (genus *Ateles*). Its thick fur, heavy body, and protruding abdomen are similar to those of woolly monkeys, while its reduced thumbs and long limbs resemble those of spider monkeys.

The woolly spider monkey is 45–63 cm (17–25 inches) long, excluding the 65–80-cm (26–32-inch) prehensile tail; females average 8 kg (17.6 pounds), males 9.6 kg (21.2 pounds). Its body is yellowish or brown, and the face is hairless. Recent study has shown that there are two species. The southern muriqui (*B. arachnoides*), from the states of Rio de Janeiro and São Paulo, has a black face and no thumb at all, and the male's canines are much longer than the female's. In the northern muriqui (*B. hypoxanthus*), from Bahia, Minas Gerais, and Espiritu Santo, the face is mottled pink and black, there is a rudimentary thumb, and the two sexes have canines of the same size.

Both species are active by day and move among the treetops, gathering their food of leaves, seeds, and fruit and frequently hanging by their tails. Field studies report small, flexible social groups. Some behavioral variations observed between species, such as the degree of competition between the males, may be correlated with the difference in canine teeth.

Woolly spider monkeys are more closely related to woolly monkeys than to spider monkeys, but all belong to the family Atelidae of New World monkeys. They are considered critically endangered, as their forest habitats are extremely fragmented.

CHAPTER 6
APES

Apes (superfamily Hominoidea) are tailless primates that belong to the families Hylobatidae (gibbons) and Hominidae (chimpanzees, bonobos, orangutans, gorillas, and human beings). Apes are found in the tropical forests of western and central Africa and Southeast Asia. Apes are distinguished from monkeys by the complete absence of a tail and the presence of an appendix and by their more complex brains. Although human beings are categorized zoologically as members of the broader ape superfamily, they are usually placed within their own subcategories on account of their larger brain size, more advanced cognitive abilities (particularly the ability to speak), and striding two-legged gait.

The gorilla, chimpanzee, bonobo, and orangutan are called great apes in recognition of their comparatively large size and humanlike features; the gibbons are called lesser apes. The great apes are much more intelligent than monkeys and gibbons. Great apes, for example, are able to recognize themselves in mirrors (monkeys and other nonhumans cannot, with the exception of bottlenose dolphins). They can also reason abstractly, learn quasi-linguistic communication, at least when taught by humans, and learn in captivity to make simple tools (though some populations of orangutans and chimpanzees make tools in the wild). The great apes were formerly classified in their own family, Pongidae, but, because of their extremely close relation to humans and the fact that orangutans, gorillas, and chimpanzees are not as closely related to each other as chimpanzees are to humans, all are now grouped with humans in the family Hominidae. Within this family gorillas, chimpanzees, and humans make up the subfamily Homininae, while orangutans are placed in their own subfamily, Ponginae. Within Homininae, humans are often placed in their own "tribe," Hominini, while gorillas and chimpanzees are grouped in the tribe Gorillini. All nonhuman apes have been classified as endangered species.

Gibbons (family Hylobatidae) typically move about by swinging (brachiation), and it has been theorized that the ancestors of all apes may once have moved in this way. Nonhuman apes can stand or sit erect with great facility, and occasionally they walk upright, especially when carrying an object. Apes have broad chests, scapulae on the back, and full rotation at the shoulder. There is a pad of cartilage (meniscus) between the ulna and the carpal bones in the wrist that gives the wrist great flexibility. The lumbar section of the spine (lower back) has only four to six vertebrae instead of the seven or more of Old World monkeys. There is no external tail; instead, the remnant three to six vertebrae are fused into the tailbone, or coccyx.

The gibbons and the orangutan are arboreal, while the gorilla, chimpanzee, and bonobo spend some or much of their time on the ground. African apes (gorilla, chimpanzee, and bonobo) travel on the ground by quadrupedal knuckle walking, in which the long fingers of the forelimbs are folded under to provide support for the body. Fruits and other plant material are the chief foods, though small invertebrates are eaten occasionally by all apes, and chimpanzees hunt large vertebrates, especially monkeys. Most apes lodge at night in trees, and all except gibbons build nests for sleeping. Group size ranges from the virtually solitary orangutan to the sociable chimpanzees and bonobos, which may live in bands of 100 or more.

Hominidae and Hylobatidae diverged about 18 million years ago, but the evolutionary history of the apes includes numerous extinct forms, many of which are known only from fragmentary remains. The earliest-known hominoids are from Egypt and date from about 36.6 million years ago. Fossil genera include *Catopithecus* and *Aegyptopithecus*, possible successive ancestors of both the Old World monkeys and the apes. Later deposits have yielded such fossils as *Pliopithecus*, once thought to be related to gibbons but now known to be primitive and long separated from them. Closer to the modern apes are *Proconsul*, *Afropithecus*, *Dryopithecus*, and *Sivapithecus*, the latter being a possible ancestor of the orangutan.

HOMINIDAE

Family Hominidae is one of the two living families of the ape superfamily Hominoidea, the other being the Hylobatidae (gibbons). Hominidae includes the great apes—that is, the orangutans (genus *Pongo*), gorillas (*Gorilla*), and chimpanzees and bonobos (*Pan*)—as well as human beings (*Homo*). Formerly, humans alone (with their extinct forebears) were placed in Hominidae, and the great apes were placed in a different family, Pongidae. However, morphological and molecular studies now indicate that humans are closely related to chimpanzees, while gorillas are more distant and orangutans more distant still. Since classification schemes aim to depict relationships, it is logical to consider humans and great apes as hominids, that is, members of the same zoological family, Hominidae. Within this family there are considered to be two subfamilies. One (called Ponginae) contains only the orangutans, and the other (Homininae) contains humans and the African great apes. Subfamily Homininae in turn is divided into two "tribes": Gorillini, for the African great apes and their evolutionary ancestors, and Hominini, for human beings and their ancestors. Following this classification, members of the human tribe, that is, modern human beings and their extinct forebears (e.g., the Neanderthals, *Homo erectus*, various species of *Australopithecus*), are frequently referred to as hominins.

It has been proposed (though not generally accepted) that chimpanzees and bonobos be placed in their own tribe, called Panini, since they are relatively distant genetically from Gorillini, or even that they should be placed within the same tribe (Hominini) and genus (*Homo*) as humans, since their ancestors separated relatively recently (about 5 million years ago).

BONOBOS

The bonobo (*Pan paniscus*), which is also called pygmy chimpanzee, is a species of ape that was regarded as a subspecies of the chimpanzee (*Pan troglodytes*) until 1933, when it was first classified separately. The bonobo is found only in lowland rainforests along the south bank of the Congo River in the Democratic Republic of the Congo. Closely resembling the chimpanzee in both physical appearance and mode of life, the bonobo is more slender, with longer limbs, a narrower chest, and a rounder head with a less-protruding face. Bonobos are not much smaller than chimpanzees—males weigh around 39 kg (86 pounds) and females about 31 kg (68 pounds), but both are the same height, standing 115 cm (3.8 feet) tall when erect.

Bonobos feed mainly in trees and descend to the ground to move to other trees. They eat mostly fruits (which they often share with one another) and other vegetation, such as herbs and roots. In some places, food is washed in streams. The diet is supplemented by invertebrates such as caterpillars and earthworms. In rare instances, they have been observed eating bats, flying squirrels, and even young duikers (small antelopes). Unlike chimpanzees, bonobos do not hunt monkeys but instead play with and groom them.

bonobo or pygmy chimpanzee
(*Pan paniscus*)
male

30 centimetres

12 inches

Bonobo, or pygmy chimpanzee (Pan paniscus), *male*. Encyclopædia Britannica, Inc.

Furthermore, the phenomena of infanticide, cannibalism, and lethal invasion seen among chimps have never been observed among the bonobo. Relationships between separate communities also differ—individuals often intermingle. Adult males do not intermingle but, unlike chimpanzees, are not hostile. The egalitarian and peaceful bonobo society might have evolved as a result of reduced competition due to the abundance of food in their habitats.

Bonobos are active during the day and move on all fours by knuckle walking. They make beds from leafy branches, but, in the wild, tool use is mostly limited to leaf umbrellas and branch dragging during intimidation displays. They form communities usually numbering from 30 to more than 100 individuals occupying a home range area of 22–60 square km (8.5–23 square miles). Each community is in turn composed of "parties," groups of 6–15 individuals that forage together but whose membership is continually changing. Bonobo females and their young form the core of most groups, and males tend to follow the lead of mature females. Females unite against adult males, and mothers help their adult sons to promote their dominance rank. Thus, although adult males are larger in size than adult females, the former cannot be said to dominate the latter. Males groom and share food least frequently with other males, whereas females groom and share food mostly with other females. Males and females, old and young, mate and use a variety of sexual behaviours to promote social bonding. Female bonobos are sexually active for more of the time than their chimpanzee counterparts; they bear offspring at roughly five-year intervals and resume copulating with males within a year of giving birth. Bonobos sometimes mate in a face-to-face position, which is rarely seen among chimpanzees.

The number of bonobos in the wild is shrinking because of human destruction of forests and illegal hunting of bonobos for meat. The bonobo is an endangered species; at the end of the 20th century, the estimated population was fewer than 40,000. Bonobos are not often kept in captivity.

CHIMPANZEES

The chimpanzee (*Pan troglodytes*) is a species of ape that, along with the bonobo, is most closely related to humans. Chimpanzees inhabit tropical forests and savannas of equatorial Africa from the Gambia in the west to Lake Albert, Lake Victoria, and northwestern Tanzania in the east. Individuals vary considerably in size and appearance, but chimpanzees stand approximately 1–1.7 metres (3–5.5 feet) tall when erect and weigh about 32–60 kg (70–130 pounds). Males tend to be larger and more robust than females. Chimpanzees are covered by a coat of brown or black hair, but their faces are bare except for a short white beard. Skin colour is generally white except for the face, hands, and feet, which are black. The faces of younger animals may be pinkish or whitish. Among older males and females, the forehead often becomes bald and the back becomes gray.

NATURAL HISTORY

Chimpanzees awaken at dawn, and their day is spent both in the trees and on the ground. After a lengthy midday rest, late afternoon is usually the most intensive

West African, or masked, chimpanzee (Pan troglodytes verus). Helmut Albrecht/ Bruce Coleman Ltd.

feeding period. In the trees, where most feeding takes place, chimps use their hands and feet to move about. They also leap and swing by their arms (brachiate) skillfully from branch to branch. Movement over any significant distance usually takes place on the ground. Though able to walk upright, chimpanzees more often move about on all fours, leaning forward on the knuckles of their hands (knuckle walking). At night they usually sleep in the trees in nests they build of branches and leaves. Chimpanzees are unable to swim, but they will wade in water. The chimpanzee diet is primarily vegetarian and consists of more than 300 different items, mostly fruits, berries, leaves, blossoms, and seeds but also bird eggs and chicks, many insects, and occasionally carrion. Chimpanzees also hunt, both alone and in groups, stalking and killing various mammals such as monkeys, duikers, bushbucks, and wild pigs. They also appear to use certain plants medicinally to cure diseases and expel intestinal parasites.

The female chimpanzee bears a single young at any time of year after a gestation period of about eight months. The newborn weighs about 1.8 kg (4 pounds), is almost helpless, and clings to the fur of the mother's belly as she moves. From about 6 months to 2 years, the youngster rides on the mother's back. Weaning takes place at about 5 years. Males are considered adults at 16 years of age, and females usually begin to reproduce at about 13 years, but often only two offspring survive during her lifetime. The longevity of chimps is about 45 years in the wild, 58 in captivity.

Chimpanzees are an endangered species; their population in the wild has been reduced by hunting (primarily for meat), destruction of habitat from logging or farming, and commercial exportation for use in zoos and research laboratories. Lions and leopards also prey upon chimpanzees.

SOCIAL BEHAVIOUR

Chimpanzees are lively animals with more extraverted dispositions than either gorillas or orangutans. They are highly social and live in loose and flexible groups known as communities, or unit groups, that are based on associations between adult males within a home range, or territory. Home ranges of forest-dwelling communities can be as small as a few square kilometres, but home ranges covering hundreds of square kilometres are known among savanna communities. A community can number from 20 or fewer to well over 100 members. Each consists of several subgroups of varying size and unstable composition. Social dominance exists, with adult males being dominant over adult females and adolescent males. Within a community, there are twice or three times as many adult females as adult males; the number of adults is about equal to the number of immature individuals. Communities usually divide into subgroups called parties, which vary widely in size. The dominance hierarchy among male chimpanzees is very fluid; individuals associate with each other and join and leave different subgroups with complete freedom. The dominant (alpha) male of a group can monopolize ovulating females through possessive behaviour. On the other hand, gang attack by subordinate males can expel an alpha male. Males spend all of their lives in the community they are born in, but occasionally a juvenile male may transfer to another community with his mother. In contrast to males, most females leave their group of birth to join a neighbouring group when they mature at around age 11. Female chimpanzees spend most of their time with their young or with other females. Those with dependent offspring are more likely to range alone or in small parties within narrow "core areas." Females have been known to form coalitions against a bullying adult male or newly immigrated female.

Relations between different chimp communities tend to be hostile. Intruders on a group's home range may be attacked, and adult males engage in boundary patrol. On rare occasions, a group may invade a neighbouring territory that is much smaller in size, and fatalities among the smaller group result. Infanticide and cannibalism by adult males, and to a lesser extent by adult females, have been observed. Victimized infants are not only those of neighbouring groups but also those born to newly immigrated females. Between- and within-group competition among individuals of the same sex is the likely cause of such violence. Sometimes a male and female will form a consortship, engaging in exclusive mating relationships by leaving other members of the group and staying in the periphery of the group range. This strategy, however, brings increased risk of attack by neighbouring groups.

Chimpanzees exhibit complex social strategies such as cooperation in combat and the cultivation of coalitions and alliances via ranging together, reciprocal grooming, and the sharing of meat (sometimes in exchange for mating opportunities). An alpha male, for instance, may interfere with his rival in grooming with a third party because such a coalition might jeopardize the alpha's status. On the other hand, the third party might show strategic opportunism in such a situation, since his assistance to either side could determine which of his superiors prevails. Chimpanzees, therefore, appear to have some concept of "trade." They console, reconcile, and retaliate during fighting and so share emotions and aspects of psychology similar to those found in humans: self-recognition, curiosity, sympathy, grief, and attribution. Although chimps take care of orphaned infants, they also tease handicapped individuals, conceal information that would bring disadvantage to themselves, and manipulate others for their own advantage by expressing deceptive postures, gestures, and facial expressions.

JANE GOODALL

(b. April 3, 1934, London, Eng.)

British ethologist Baroness Jane van Lawick-Goodall is known for her exceptionally detailed and long-term research on the chimpanzees of Gombe Stream National Park in Tanzania.

Goodall, who was interested in animal behaviour from an early age, left school at age 18. She worked as a secretary and as a film production assistant until she gained passage to Africa. Once there, Goodall began assisting paleontologist and anthropologist Louis Leakey. Her association with Leakey led eventually to her establishment in June 1960 of a camp in the Gombe Stream Game Reserve (now a national park) so that she could observe the behaviour of chimpanzees in the region. In 1964 she married a Dutch photographer who had been sent in 1962 to Tanzania to film her work (later they divorced). The University of Cambridge in 1965 awarded Goodall a Ph.D. in ethology; she was one of very few candidates to receive a Ph.D. without having first possessed an A.B. degree. Except for short periods of absence, Goodall and her family remained in Gombe until 1975, often directing the fieldwork of other doctoral candidates. In 1977 she cofounded the Jane Goodall Institute for Wildlife Research, Education, and Conservation in California; the centre later moved its headquarters to Washington, D.C.

Over the years Goodall was able to correct a number of misunderstandings about chimpanzees. She found, for example, that the animals are omnivorous, not vegetarian; that they are capable of making and using tools; and, in short, that they have a set of hitherto unrecognized complex and highly developed social behaviours. Goodall wrote a number of books and articles about various aspects of her work, notably *In the Shadow of Man* (1971). She summarized her years of observation in *The Chimpanzees of Gombe: Patterns of Behavior* (1986). Goodall continued to write and lecture about environmental and conservation issues into the early 21st century. The recipient of numerous honours, she was created Dame of the British Empire in 2003.

INTELLIGENCE

Chimpanzees are highly intelligent and are able to solve many kinds of problems posed to them by human trainers and experimenters. A number of researchers have taught chimpanzees to use sign language or languages based on the display of tokens or pictorial symbols. The implications of these language studies have been contested, however. Critics charge that apes have not acquired true language in the sense of understanding "words" as abstract symbols that can be combined in meaningful new ways. Other investigators maintain that more recent language training has resulted in the chimpanzees' acquiring a true recognition of "words" as abstractions that can be applied in novel contexts.

Communication between chimps in the wild takes the form of facial expressions, gestures, and a large array of vocalizations, including screams, hoots, grunts, and roars. Males display excitement by standing erect, stamping or swaying, and letting out a chorus of screams. Chimps use louder calls and gestures for long-distance communication (such as drumming on tree buttresses) and quieter calls and facial expressions for short-distance communication. Similarities to human laughter and smiling might be seen in their "play panting" and grinning, respectively.

Various tools are used in several contexts. Chimpanzees "fish" for termites and ants with probes made of grass stalks, vines, branches, peeled bark, and midribs of leaves. They crack hard nuts open by using stones, roots, and wood as hammers or anvils, and they use leafy sponges to drink water. Branches and leaves are detached and displayed during courtship. In threat displays, chimps throw rocks and drag and throw branches. Sticks are used to inspect dead pythons or other unfamiliar objects that might be dangerous. Leaves are used hygenically in wiping the mouth or other soiled body parts. Chimpanzees also use different tools in succession as a "tool set." For example, chimpanzees of the Congo basin first dig into termite mounds with a stout stick and then fish for individual termites with a long, slender wand. Tools are also used in combination as "tool composites." Chimpanzees in the Guinea region push leafy sponges into hollows of trees containing water and then withdraw the wet sponges by using sticks. Chimps thus differ locally in their repertoire of tool use, with younger animals acquiring tool-using behaviours from their elders. Such cultural differences are also seen in food items consumed and in gestural communication. Chimpanzees indeed possess culture when it is defined as the transmission of information from generation to generation via social learning shared by most members of a single age or sex class in a given group.

Chimpanzees' intelligence, responsiveness, and exuberance have made them ideal nonhuman subjects for psychological, medical, and biological experiments. Young chimpanzees can become very attached to their human trainers, and their expressions of feeling resemble those of humans more closely than any other animal.

TAXONOMY

Genetic analysis suggests that humans and chimps diverged four million to eight million years ago and that at least 98 percent of the human and chimpanzee genomes are identical. Chimpanzees are classified taxonomically as a single species, *Pan troglodytes*. (The so-called pygmy chimpanzee, or bonobo, is a distinct and separate species, *P. paniscus*.) Three subspecies of *P. troglodytes* have traditionally been recognized: the tschego, or Central

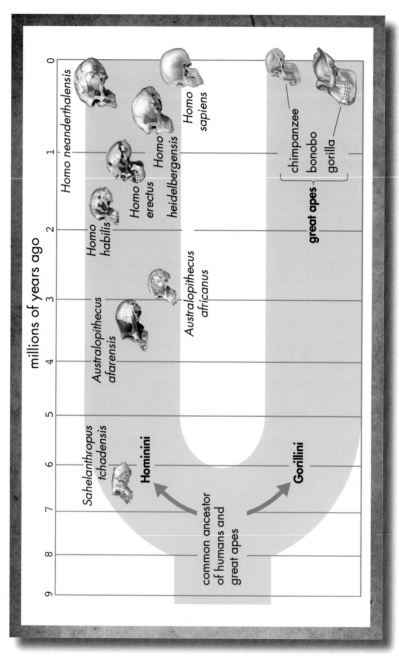

The divergence of humans and great apes from a common ancestor.
Encyclopædia Britannica, Inc.

African chimpanzee (*P. troglodytes troglodytes*), also known as the common chimpanzee in continental Europe; the West African, or masked, chimpanzee (*P. troglodytes verus*), known as the common chimpanzee in Great Britain; and the East African, or long-haired, chimpanzee (*P. troglodytes schweinfurthii*). A fourth subspecies, the Nigerian chimpanzee (*P. troglodytes vellerosus*), has also been proposed.

GIBBONS

The gibbons (family Hylobatidae) encompass a dozen or so species of small apes found in the tropical forests of Southeast Asia. Gibbons, like the great apes (gorillas, orangutans, chimpanzees, and bonobos), have a humanlike build and no tail, but gibbons seem to lack higher cognitive abilities and self-awareness. They also differ from great apes in having longer arms, dense hair, and a throat sac used for amplifying sound. Gibbon voices are loud, are musical in tone, and carry over long distances. The most characteristic vocalization is the "great call," usually a duet in which the female leads and the male joins in with less-complex notes, used as a territorial marker by both sexes.

Chinese white-cheeked gibbons (Hylobates leucogenys), *male and female.*
Encyclopædia Britannica, Inc.

Gibbons are arboreal and move from branch to branch with speed and great agility by swinging from their arms (brachiating). On the ground, gibbons walk erect with the arms held aloft or behind. They are active during the day and live in small monogamous groups that defend territories in the treetops. They feed mainly on fruit, with varying proportions of leaves and with some insects and bird eggs as well as young birds. Single offspring are born after about seven months' gestation and take seven years to mature.

Most gibbon species are about 40–65 cm (16–26 inches) in head and body length. The smaller species (both sexes) weigh about 5.5 kg (12 pounds); others, such the concolor gibbon, weigh about 7.5 kg (17 pounds). The various species of gibbons can be divided into four groups; molecular data indicate that the four groups are as different from one another as chimpanzees are from humans and thus should probably be classified as four genera.

The lars, a group of six or seven species, are the smallest and have the densest body hair. The dark-handed gibbon (*H. agilis*), which lives on Sumatra south of Lake Toba and on the Malay Peninsula between the Perak and Mudah rivers, may be either tan or black and has white facial markings. The white-handed gibbon (*H. lar*), of northern Sumatra and most of the Malay Peninsula northward through Thailand into Yunnan, China, is similar but has white extremities. The pileated gibbon (*H. pileatus*), of southeastern Thailand and western Cambodia, has white hands and feet; the male is black and the female buff with a black cap and chest patch. The difference in colour comes about with age; the juveniles are buff and both sexes darken with age, but the male does so much more rapidly. Kloss's gibbon (*H. klossii*), from the Mentawai Islands west of Sumatra, is completely black throughout its life. The sexes look alike in the silvery gibbon (*H. moloch*) of Java and in the white-bearded (*H. albibarbis*) and Müller's (*H. muelleri*) gibbons, both from different parts of Borneo.

In the concolor group both sexes are black as juveniles, but the females lighten to buff with maturity, so that the two sexes look quite different as adults. The males have an upstanding tuft of hair on top of the head and a small inflatable throat sac. All species live east of the Mekong River. The black crested gibbon (*H. concolor*) is found from southern China into northernmost Vietnam and Laos; the northern concolor (*H. leucogenys*) and southern concolor (*H. siki*) gibbons are found farther south, and the red-cheeked gibbon (*H. gabriellae*) lives in southern Vietnam and eastern Cambodia.

The remaining two groups each contain a single species. The hoolock gibbon (*H. hoolock*) is found from Burma west of the Salween River into Assam, India, and Bangladesh; adult males are black and females are brown, with colour changes similar to those seen in the concolor group. Both sexes have throat sacs and much harsher voices than those of the lar and concolor groups. The large and entirely black siamang is found alongside white- and dark-handed gibbons on the Malay Peninsula and Sumatra. Both sexes have a large throat sac, and their vocal repertoire includes a very harsh shrieking and booming call. The male has a prominent tassel of hair on the front of the lower abdomen.

Gibbons are still widely distributed in the rainforests and monsoon forests of Southeast Asia, but they are more and more under threat as their forest habitat is destroyed. They are sometimes hunted for food, but more often they are killed for their supposed medicinal properties; their long arm bones are especially prized.

SIAMANGS

Siamang (Hylobates syndactylus). Anthony Mercieca/Shostal Associates

The siamang (*Hylobates syndactylus*) is an arboreal ape of the gibbon family (Hylobatidae) found in the forests of Sumatra and Malaya. It resembles other gibbons but is more robust. The siamang is also distinguished by the webbing between its second and third toes and by a dilatable hairless air sac in its throat. The air sac is used in producing a resonant, booming call. The siamang is about 50–55 cm (20–22 inches) in head and body length, but can grow up to 90 cm (35 inches). The female siamang weighs 10.5 kg (23 pounds) and the male 12 kg (26 pounds); the siamang is the only gibbon with a significant size difference between the sexes. Its shaggy fur is completely black. Like the gibbon, the siamang is diurnal and arboreal and moves by brachiation, progressing from one point to another by swinging from its arms. It feeds mainly on fruit and has been observed to live alone or in small groups. The gestation period is about 230 days; births are typically single. Kloss' gibbon (*H. klossi*) is sometimes called a dwarf siamang; both it and the siamang were formerly classified in a separate genus, *Symphalangus*.

GORILLAS

The gorilla (*Gorilla gorilla*) is the largest of the apes and the closest living relative to humans, with the exception of the chimpanzee. Gorillas live only in tropical forests of equatorial Africa. Most authorities recognize a single species, *Gorilla gorilla*, with three races: the western lowland gorilla (*G. gorilla gorilla*) of the lowland rainforests from

Cameroon to the Congo River, the eastern lowland gorilla (*G. gorilla graueri*) of the lowland rainforests of the eastern Democratic Republic of the Congo (Kinshasa), and the mountain gorilla (*G. gorilla beringei*), found in the montane rainforests and bamboo forests of the highland terrain north and east of Lake Kivu, near the borders of Uganda, Rwanda, and Congo (Kinshasa).

Western lowland gorilla (Gorilla gorilla gorilla), *male.* Encyclopædia Britannica, Inc.

The gorilla is robust and powerful, with an extremely thick, strong chest and a protruding abdomen. Both skin and hair are black. The face has large nostrils, small ears, and prominent brow ridges. Adults have long, muscular arms that are 15–20 percent longer than the stocky legs. Males are about twice as heavy as females and may attain a height of about 1.7 metres (5.5 feet) and weight (in the wild) of 135–220 kg (300–485 pounds). Captive gorillas of both sexes may grow quite fat and hence become much heavier. A wild adult female typically is about 1.5 metres (about 5 feet) tall and weighs about 70–90 kg (154–198 pounds). Gorillas lack hair on the face, hands, and feet, and the chest of old males is bare. The hair of the mountain gorilla is longer than that of the other two subspecies. Adult males have a prominent crest on top of the skull and a "saddle" of gray or silver hairs on the lower part of the back—hence the term *silverback*, which is commonly used to refer to mature males. The saddle is much more conspicuous in eastern gorillas, which are jet black, than in western gorillas, which are more of a deep gray-brown.

Gorillas live in stable family groups numbering from 6 to 30. The groups are led by one or two (occasionally more) silverbacked males that are related to each other, usually a father and one or more of his sons. Occasionally brothers lead a group. The other members are females, infants, juveniles, and young adult males (blackbacks). Adult females join from outside the group, and the young are offspring of silverbacks.

The gorilla is active during the day (diurnal) and primarily terrestrial, usually walking about on all four limbs with part of its weight supported on the knuckles of its hands. This mode of locomotion, called knuckle walking, is shared with chimpanzees. Occasionally gorillas stand erect, mainly when displaying. Females and young climb more than males, mainly because much vegetation cannot support the weight of males.

Their diet is vegetarian; that of eastern gorillas includes leaves, stalks, and shoots, but western gorillas eat much more fruit. Gorillas generally dislike water, but in some areas, such as the Sangha-Ndoki region on the borders of Cameroon, the Republic of the Congo (Brazzaville), and the Central African Republic, they wade waist-deep into swampy clearings to feed on aquatic plants. Gorillas spend much of their time foraging and resting, with the group traveling a few hundred metres between several daily feeding bouts. Each group wanders through a home range of about 2–40 square km (0.77–16 square miles), though several different groups may share the same part of the forest. At dusk each gorilla builds its own crude sleeping nest by bending branches and foliage. A new nest is built every night either on the ground or in the trees.

The gorilla is much larger than its closest relative, the chimpanzee, and has a less-boisterous disposition. Although it is a relatively quiet animal, the repertoire of gorilla calls includes grunts, hoots, a terrifying alarm bark, and the roar, which is given by aggressive males. Much has been written about the ferocity of the gorilla, but studies indicate that it is unaggressive, even shy, unless unduly disturbed. Intruders may be faced by the leading silver-back of the group, which may make aggressive displays in attempting to protect his dependents. Such displays commonly involve chest beating, vocalization, or short rushes toward the intruder followed in most instances by a discreet withdrawal. Chest beating is performed by both males and females, but it is much louder in males owing to air sacs in the throat and chest that make the sound more resonant. Chest beating is often part of a ritual that may also include running sideways, tearing at vegetation, and slapping the ground. In addition to intimidating outsiders (gorilla or human), these displays also act as communication between groups and are often used to maintain the dominance hierarchy within the group.

Cognitively, gorillas lack the curiosity and adaptability of chimpanzees, but gorillas are calmer and more persistent. Captive gorillas have shown a capacity for problem solving and have demonstrated a degree of insight as well as memory and anticipation of experience. They appear to be as adept as chimpanzees at learning sign language from humans.

Wild female gorillas give birth about once every four years, and there is no fixed breeding season. The gestation period is about eight and a half months, and births are usually single, though twins occur on rare occasions. A newborn gorilla weighs only about 2 kg (4 pounds) and is utterly helpless for the first three months of life, during which it is carried in its mother's arms. The young gorilla sleeps in the mother's nest at night and rides on her back during the day. Female gorillas begin to reach reproductive maturity at about 10 years of age and then transfer to another group or to a lone silverback. Males reach sexual maturity at about age 9, but they do not reproduce until they become more physically mature silverbacks at about 12–15 years of age. Most male gorillas leave the group in which they were born and try to gather females to form their own family group. This may involve some aggression, since a young male may invade an established group and try to "kidnap" females, sometimes killing infants in the process. Occasionally a male will stay in his birth group and become its second silverback, breeding with some of the females and ultimately taking over its leadership when his father ages or dies. The life expectancy of wild gorillas is about 35 years, though captive gorillas have lived into their 40s.

The gorilla has become increasingly rare throughout its range, having suffered from human destruction of its forest habitat and from big-game hunting and overcollection by zoos and research institutions. A newer threat is hunting associated with the bushmeat trade, especially to feed logging crews. The International Union for Conservation of Nature (IUCN) has listed the eastern lowland gorilla as an endangered species and the mountain gorilla as critically endangered, its population estimated at only 700. Reasons for the near extinction of this race include continued loss of habitat as a result of human activities: farming, grazing, logging, and, recently, habitat destruction by refugees. At the same time, ecotourism involving visits by travelers to see gorillas in their natural habitat has contributed to the conservation of the mountain gorilla.

Population estimates of the western lowland gorilla, once classified by the IUCN as critically endangered, doubled in 2008 with the discovery of a previously unknown population. This population, numbering more than 100,000, inhabits the swamps of the Lac Télé Community Reserve in the Republic of the Congo.

Within the genus *Gorilla* it has been argued that eastern and western gorillas should be regarded as separate species: molecular genetic evidence indicates that eastern and western gorillas became separate more than a million years ago. It has also been proposed that the small population of gorillas in the Cross River mountains on the Nigeria-Cameroon border could be a separate subspecies of the western lowland gorilla. The mountain gorillas of the Bwindi Impenetrable Forest in Uganda might be an additional subspecies of the eastern gorilla.

DIAN FOSSEY

(b. Jan. 16, 1932, San Francisco, Calif., U.S.—d. Dec. 26, 1985, Rwanda)

Dian Fossey was an American zoologist who became the world's leading authority on the mountain gorilla. Fossey trained to become an occupational therapist at San Jose State College and graduated in 1954. She worked in that field for several years at a children's hospital in Louisville, Kentucky. In 1963 she took a trip to eastern Africa, where she met the anthropologist Louis Leakey and had her first glimpse of mountain gorillas. She returned to the United States after her trip, but in 1966 Leakey persuaded her to go back to Africa to study the mountain gorilla in its natural habitat on a long-term basis. To this end, she established the Karisoke Research Centre in 1967 and began a hermitlike existence in Rwanda's Virunga Mountains, which was one of the last bastions of the endangered mountain gorilla. Through patient effort, Fossey was able to observe the animals and accustom them to her presence, and the data that she gathered greatly enlarged contemporary knowledge of the gorilla's habits, communication, and social structure.

Fossey left Africa in 1970 to complete work for a doctorate at the University of Cambridge in England. In 1974 she received her degree in zoology with the completion of her dissertation, "The Behavior of the Mountain Gorilla." She returned to Rwanda with student volunteers who made broader kinds of research possible. Motivated by the killing of Digit, one of her favoured gorillas, Fossey generated international media coverage in 1978 in her battle against poachers.

In 1980 Fossey returned to the United States to accept a visiting associate professorship at Cornell University, Ithaca, New York. While teaching, Fossey also completed *Gorillas in the Mist* (1983; film 1988). Back in Rwanda, Fossey resumed her campaign against poachers, taking increasingly drastic measures to protect the Virunga gorillas. On Dec. 26, 1985, her slain body was discovered near her campsite. Though no assailant was ever identified, it is widely suspected that she was killed by the poachers against whom she had struggled for so long.

ORANGUTANS

The orangutan (*Pongo pygmaeus*) is the only Asian great ape. Orangutans are found in lowland rainforests on the Southeast Asian islands of Sumatra and Borneo. They possess cognitive abilities comparable to those of the gorilla

Male orangutan (Pongo pygmaeus) *with cheek pads.* Russ Kinne/Photo Researchers

and the chimpanzee, which are the only primates more closely related to humans.

The orangutan is not as powerfully built as the gorilla but is larger than the chimpanzee. The adult male is typically twice the size of the female and may attain a height of 1.3 metres (4.3 feet) and a weight of 130 kg (285 pounds) in the wild; females weigh 37 kg (82 pounds) or less. Older males develop wide cheek pads, a unique feature among primates. The typically dark tan or brownish skin is covered with relatively coarse and usually sparse red hair. Adult males and some older adult females may have partially or entirely bare backs, but the hair on a male can be so long as to look like a cape when he moves his arms.

Orangutans are the largest arboreal animals, spending more than 90 percent of their waking hours in the trees. During the day most of their time is divided equally between resting and feeding. Orangutans are predominantly ripe-fruit eaters, although they consume more than 400 different types of food, including invertebrates and, on rare and opportunistic occasions, meat. Almost every night orangutans construct a sleeping platform in the trees by bending and breaking branches, leaves, and twigs. Unlike the African apes, orangutans frequently use vegetation to protect themselves from the rain.

In addition to feeding and resting, orangutans also spend short periods of time traveling through the forest canopy, where they typically scramble by using all four hands and feet. Orangutans occasionally swing through the trees using only their arms (brachiation). Although their legs are short, their arms are proportionately the longest of those of the great apes. The hooklike hands have long fingers and palms with short thumbs. The feet resemble the hands in having opposable big toes that are similar to the thumbs. Another arboreal adaptation is flexible hip joints that allow orangutans similar movement in their legs and arms. On the ground orangutans are slow; a person can easily keep pace with them. They are not knuckle walkers like the African apes but instead walk on closed fists or extended palms.

There are two phases of sexual maturation among males—adult and subadult. Adult males are larger and exhibit striking secondary sexual characteristics, particularly the flat and prominent cheek pads that develop along the sides of the face. The pads enhance the size of the head and are linked with increased levels of testosterone. Adult males also have a throat pouch that serves as a resonating chamber for the "long call," a sequence of roars that can sometimes be heard for 2 km (1.2 miles). Males typically vocalize for a minute or more; calls up to five minutes in length have been recorded, giving the call its name. Females virtually never give the full sequence of the long call, as it serves to space males and attract sexually receptive females. Otherwise, orangutans are generally silent. Subadult males lack the wide cheek pads and large throat pouch, and they generally do not long call. Although smaller than adult males, subadults are still as large as or larger than adult females. Subadults may remain in this state for 10 to 20 years. This arrested development has been linked with stress associated with the presence of adult males.

Orangutans live in a semisolitary social organization that is unique among monkeys and apes. Population densities usually average only two to three individuals per square kilometre (about five to seven per square mile), with adult males having larger home ranges than females. Adult males are the most solitary, avoiding each other and associating only with consorting females or former consorts. Subadult males associate primarily with females. Adult females live with their dependent young, but adolescent females are almost gregarious. Sexually receptive females may attract several males, both adult and subadult. Males, adults in particular, behave aggressively toward other males at this time, with combat taking place in the presence of receptive females. Most mating takes place in the context of consortships that last 3 to 10 days and are correlated with ovulation. Subadult males often forcibly copulate with females at times other than during ovulation.

Female orangutans have the longest breeding interval of any mammal, giving birth on average once every eight years. Wild females generally first give birth when they are 15 or 16 years of age, but females as young as 7 have given birth in captivity. Gestation is about 8 months. Newborns weigh less than 1.5 kg (3 pounds) and have prominent white patches around their eyes and mouths as well as scattered over their bodies. Slow growth and development are consistent with the orangutan's long life span—60 years has been documented in captivity.

Orangutans are generally placid and deliberate, and in captivity they have shown considerable ingenuity and persistence, particularly in manipulating mechanical objects. They have demonstrated cognitive abilities such as causal and logical reasoning, self-recognition in mirrors, deception, symbolic communication, foresight, and tool production and use. In the wild, orangutans use tools, but at only one location in Sumatra do they consistently make and use them for foraging. In this context they defoliate sticks of appropriate size to extract insects or honey from tree holes and to pry seeds from hard-shelled fruit.

As recently as 1980, 100,000 orangutans existed in the wild. By the end of the 20th century, it was feared that there were 25,000 or fewer. Huge fires in the late 1990s, as well as conversion of tropical forest for agriculture, logging, and mining, have wiped out large areas of habitat. These factors, along with the poaching of orangutans for their infants, which are sold as pets, and the killing of orangutans as agricultural pests, prompted a massive survey of the orangutan population and its habitat in 2004. The results revealed that some 50,000 to 60,000 individuals remain in Borneo and Sumatra. Despite these encouraging figures, authorities maintain that the threats listed above could place wild orangutans in danger of extinction in the future.

Orangutans are classified with the African great apes, gibbons, and humans in the family Hominidae of the order Primates. Most authorities divide orangutans into two subspecies, the Bornean (*P. pygmaeus pygmaeus*) and the Sumatran (*P. pygmaeus abelii*), but others consider them as separate species. During the Pleistocene Epoch (about 2,600,000 to 11,700 years ago), the orangutan range was much more extensive, and orangutan remains have been found as far north as southern China.

CHAPTER 7
EARLY HOMININS

Hominins are members of the zoological "tribe" Hominini (family Hominidae, order Primates). Although there are many extinct members of this group, only one species exists today—*Homo sapiens*, or human beings. The term is used most often to refer to extinct members of the human lineage, some of which are now quite well known from fossil remains: *Homo neanderthalensis* (the Neanderthals), *Homo erectus*, *Homo habilis*, and various species of *Australopithecus*. In addition, many authorities place the genera *Ardipithecus*, *Orrorin*, and *Kenyanthropus* in Hominini. The primate group most closely related to Hominini today is Gorillini (the African apes), comprising the gorilla, the chimpanzee, and the bonobo. Gorillini and Hominini are part of the great ape family, Hominidae. Some characteristics that have distinguished hominins from other primates, living and extinct, are their erect posture, bipedal locomotion, larger brains, and behavioral characteristics such as specialized tool use and, in some cases, communication through language.

THE AUSTRALOPITHS

Identifying the earliest member of the human tribe (Hominini) is difficult because the predecessors of modern humans are increasingly apelike as the fossil record is followed back through time. They resemble what would be expected in the common ancestor of humans and apes in that they possess a mix of human and ape traits. For example, one of the earliest species, *S. tchadensis*, is humanlike in having small canine teeth and a face that does not

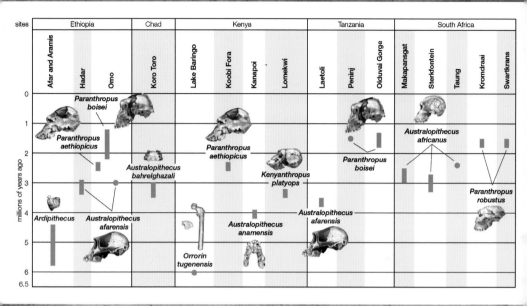

Approximate time ranges of sites yielding australopith fossils. Encyclopædia Britannica, Inc.

project very far. However, in most other respects, including brain size, it is apelike. Whether it walked upright is not known because only a single skull, jaw fragments, and teeth have been found. Bipedalism may have been established in the six-million-year-old *Orrorin tugenensis*, an australopith found in the Tugen Hills near Lake Baringo in central Kenya. In 2001 these fossils were described as the earliest known hominin. *O. tugenensis* is primitive in most if not all of its body except for femurs (thighbones) that appear to share traits of bipedalism with modern humans. Like later hominins, it has teeth with thick molar enamel, but, unlike humans, it has distinctively apelike canine and premolar teeth. The case for its hominin status rests on the humanlike features of the femur. According to its discoverers, features of the thighbone implying bipedalism include its overall proportions, the internal structure of the knee, and a groove on the bone for a muscle used in upright walking (the obturator externus).

The general term *australopith* (or *australopithecine*) is used informally to refer not only to members of the genus *Australopithecus* but also to other humanlike primates that lived in Africa between 6 and 1.2 million years ago. Other australopiths include *Sahelanthropus tchadensis* (7–6 million years ago), *Orrorin tugenensis* (6 million years ago), *Ardipithecus kadabba* and *Ardipithecus ramidus* (5.8–4.4 million years ago), *Kenyanthropus platyops* (3.5–3.2 million years ago), and three species of *Paranthropus* (2.3–1.2 million years ago). Remains older than 6 million years are widely regarded as those of fossil apes. Undisputed evidence of the genus *Homo*—the genus that includes modern human beings—does not appear until about 1.8 million years ago, in the form of *Homo ergaster*, also called *H. erectus* ("upright man"). The remains of *H. habilis* ("handy man") and *H. rudolfensis* are between 2.5 and 1.5 million years old, but these are difficult to differentiate from those of *Australopithecus*, and the identity of some of these remains is debated.

Another candidate for the earliest australopith is Ardipithecus (5.8–4.4 mya), found in 1992 at Aramis in the Afar region of Ethiopia. It too is primitive compared with later hominins, though it does share a few evolutionary novelties associated with hominins. Its cranial base is short like that of hominins, and the upper canines are shaped somewhat like those of later species. A well-preserved toe bone shows the characteristically bipedal feature of a base designed for hyperextension while walking, and bony protrusions that serve as muscle-attachment sites on the pelvis are similar to those found in more advanced hominins. Interestingly, Ardipithecus fossils have been found in association with animals usually found in closed woodland habitats rather than open grasslands.

Aramis is located about 100 km (60 miles) south of Hadar, where other australopith remains have been unearthed. About 10 km (6 miles) west of Aramis are sites that have yielded remains of *Ardipithecus kadabba* that date to between 5.2 and 5.8 million years ago. A toe bone recovered from this age range is unlike that of apes and has a diagnostically humanlike shape that indicates upright walking (bipedalism). This is part of the accumulating evidence confirming the hypothesis originally proposed by Charles Darwin and other 19th-century evolutionists that bipedalism preceded most other transformations in the human lineage.

AUSTRALOPITHECUS

Australopithecus (Latin: "southern ape") is a genus of extinct creatures closely related to, if not actually ancestors of, modern human beings. The genus is known from a series of fossils found at numerous sites in eastern, central, and southern Africa. The various species

of *Australopithecus* lived during the Pliocene (5.3 million to 2.6 million years ago) and Pleistocene (2.6 million to 11,700 years ago) epochs. As characterized by the fossil evidence, they bore a combination of human- and apelike traits. Like humans, they were bipedal (that is, they walked on two legs), but, like apes, they had small brains. Their canine teeth were small like those of humans, but their cheek teeth were large. The genus name meaning "southern ape" refers to the first fossils found, which were discovered in South Africa. Perhaps the most famous specimen of *Australopithecus* is "Lucy," a remarkably preserved fossilized skeleton from Ethiopia that has been dated to 3.2 million years ago.

Artist's rendering of Australopithecus afarensis, *which lived from 3.8 to 2.9 million years ago.* Encyclopædia Britannica, Inc.

Australopithecus Anamensis

The earliest member of the genus *Australopithecus* is *A. anamensis*, discovered in 1994 by a team led by Meave Leakey at Kanapoi and Allia Bay in northern Kenya. The fossils date to 4.2–3.9 million years ago, and, like *Ardipithecus*, *A. anamensis* is associated with woodland animals and a few grassland species as well. It is quite primitive with a strongly protruding lower face, but at the same time it has certain dental features not seen in *Ardipithecus ramidus*; most conspicuous is a thickening of tooth enamel that becomes characteristic of all later hominins. In addition, the ankle and knee are specialized for upright walking. Other skeletal features are very much like those of later hominins.

In 1998 Leakey's team also discovered *Kenyanthropus platyops* (3.5–3.2 million years ago) at Lomekwi on the western shore of Lake Turkana in northern Kenya. It too is associated with woodland fauna. It possesses some primitive skull features but shares with early *Homo* a flat and tall face. Though it overlaps in time with *A. afarensis*

ARDI

"Ardi" is the nickname for a partially complete, female hominin skeleton found by Ethiopian paleontologist Yohannes Haile-Selassie at Aramis, Ethiopia, in 1994. Ardi has been dated to 4.4 million years old, and she is one of more than 100 specimens belonging to *Ardipithecus ramidus*. Her form strongly suggests bipedal locomotion. She has a centrally located foramen magnum (that is, the opening in the skull through which the spinal cord enters) and a pelvis with features characteristic of later bipedal hominids. Each of her feet has an increased tarsal region (bones that form the sole of the foot) to facilitate upright walking. Ardi also possesses a small cranial cavity comparable to that of chimpanzees (*Pan troglodytes*), opposable great toes, small canine teeth, and a reduced upper jaw. Although she walked upright on the ground, her foot structure suggests at least a partially arboreal existence. She weighed about 50 kg (110 pounds) and stood about 1.2 metres (3.9 feet) tall.

(described below), it appears to be quite distinctive in its morphology and in some respects more primitive. In other respects it resembles much later hominins, particularly *H. rudolfensis*, in having a relatively flat face and small molars. These traits are related to chewing and thus may be related to diet. It is therefore possible that the resemblances between *H. rudolfensis* and *K. platyops* are the result of independent adaptations to similar situations. It is equally possible that the resemblances may imply an evolutionary link between the two.

Australopithecus Afarensis AND *A. Garhi*

The best-known member of *Australopithecus* is *A. afarensis*, discovered in deposits in East Africa and ranging in age from 3.8 to 2.9 million years old. Part of the earliest sample derives from the northern Tanzanian site of Laetoli, where specimens range from 3.8 to 3.5 million years ago and include footprints preserved in volcanic ash dating to 3.6–3.5 million years ago. These footprints are remarkably similar to those of modern humans in key details, including a forward-pointing big toe, relatively short lateral toes, and arched feet. The main fossil sample of this species comes from Hadar, a site in the Afar region of Ethiopia. Specimens here include a 40-percent-complete skeleton of an adult female ("Lucy") and the remains of at least nine adults and four juveniles buried together at the same time (the "First Family"). The animal fossils found in association with *A. afarensis* imply a habitat of woodland with patches of grassland.

The morphology of *A. afarensis* is a mosaic of primitive features and evolutionary developments shared by later hominins. Its skull is primitive in having a crest and a strongly projecting (prognathic) lower face. The brain was about one-third the size of a modern human's. The dentition is also mostly primitive, with canines that shear against the lower premolars and a gap (diastema) between the upper incisors and canines. There are, however, some dental features in common with later hominins. The rest of the body also combines ape and human traits, but the lower limbs are clearly meant for walking. The most conspicuous bipedal traits include greatly shortened and broadened pelvic blades with a forward-tilted sacrum, convergent knees, horizontally oriented ankles, and a convergent big toe. Primitive features include curved toes and hands, long toes (although much shorter than those of apes), a conical rib cage, and relatively short thighs. Sexual dimorphism was strong in *A. afarensis*, males weighing 45 kg (99 pounds) compared with 29 kg (64 pounds) for females. Males stood about 151 cm (4 feet 11 inches), whereas females were about 105 cm (3 feet 5 inches) tall.

In 1995 a lower jaw resembling that of *A. afarensis* came to light from Koro Toro, a site in the Baḥr el-Ghazāl region of northern Chad. It is 3.5–3.0 million years old and was assigned to a new species, *A. bahrelghazali*. In many respects it resembles East African *A. afarensis*, but it differs in significant details of the jaw articulation and teeth. *A. bahrelghazali* is the first Pliocene Epoch hominin known from central Africa and stretches the geographic range of *Australopithecus* 2,500 km (1,500 miles) westward.

A. garhi (2.5 million years ago), discovered near Hadar at Bouri in the Afar region of Ethiopia, resembles the more primitive *A. afarensis* more than it does *A. africanus* (described below). *A. garhi* has a projecting lower face, enormous cheek teeth, a shallow palate, a large gap (diastema) between the incisor and canine teeth, and forward-pitched incisors. Relative to the length of the upper arm, its thigh is elongated in a way approaching *Homo*, but its forearm is relatively long, as in apes. *A. garhi* is found in association with animal bones bearing cut marks that may indicate one of the earliest occurrences of tool use.

LUCY

"Lucy" is the nickname for a remarkably complete (40 percent intact) hominin skeleton found by Donald Johanson at Hadar on Nov. 24, 1974. The specimen was dated to 3.2 million years ago and is usually classified as *Australopithecus afarensis*. The specimen's existence suggests—by having long arms, short legs, an apelike chest and jaw, and a small brain but a relatively humanlike pelvis—that bipedal locomotion preceded the development of a larger (more humanlike) brain in hominin evolution. Lucy stood about 109 cm (3 feet 7 inches) tall and weighed about 27 kg (60 pounds).

Australopithecus Africanus

In 1925 anthropologist Raymond Dart coined the genus name *Australopithecus* to identify a child's skull recovered from mining operations at Taung in South Africa. He called it *Australopithecus africanus*, meaning "southern ape of Africa." From then until 1960 almost all that was known about australopiths came from limestone caves in South Africa. The richest source is at Sterkfontein, where Robert Broom and his team collected hundreds of specimens beginning in 1936. At first Broom simply bought fossils, but in 1946 he began excavating, aided by a crew of skillful workers. Excavation continues to this day. Sterkfontein is one of the richest sources of information about human evolution in the time period between about 3.0 and 2.5 million years ago. The *A. africanus* remains of Sterkfontein include skulls, jaws, and numerous skeletal fragments. In 1947 a partial skeleton was unearthed that revealed the humanlike specializations for bipedalism now known to be characteristic of all australopiths. Almost all of the *A. africanus* remains from Sterkfontein come from a deposit where there is a conspicuous absence of stone tools. An older deposit contains a beautifully preserved skeleton and skull of what might be an early variant of *A. africanus*.

Another source of *A. africanus* is at Makapansgat, South Africa, where Dart and his team collected about 40 specimens during expeditions from 1947 to 1962.

A. africanus is assigned only an approximate geologic age because the only dating method applicable is biostratigraphy. This indirect method compares accompanying animal fossils with those found in other African sites that have been dated more precisely using radiometric methods. The oldest dates are approximately 3.3 million years ago for hominin specimens (perhaps *A. africanus*) discovered in the late 1990s at Sterkfontein. Most of the samples of this species are between about 3.0 and perhaps 2.4 million years old.

A. africanus resembles *A. afarensis* in many respects but also shares unique features with early *Homo* that are not present in the more primitive *A. afarensis*. These include reduced facial projection (although there is considerable variation within *A. africanus*). It also possesses unique specializations not seen in *A. afarensis* or in early *Homo* that are related to powerful chewing, such as expansion of the cheek teeth, increased jaw size, and changes to the skull to accommodate the forces generated. Compared with those of *A. afarensis*, the lower limbs of *A. africanus* appear to be smaller and the upper limbs larger. Males weighed approximately 41 kg (90 pounds) and stood 138 cm (4 feet 6 inches) tall. Females weighed about 30 kg (66 pounds) and stood 115 cm (3 feet 9 inches) tall. Brain size averages 448 cc (27 cubic inches), closer to modern chimpanzees (395 cc) than to humans (1,350 cc).

Paranthropus Aethiopicus

Paranthropus aethiopicus (2.7–2.3 million years ago) is the earliest of the so-called "robust" australopiths, a group that also includes *P. robustus* and *P. boisei* (described below). *Robust* refers to exaggerated features of the skull, but it does not imply robusticity in any other aspects of the body. The expansion of cheek teeth and supporting structures for grinding hard, tough food continues in later australopiths.

Further specializations for strong chewing occur in *P. aethiopicus* fossils from the Omo remains, discovered in the Omo River valley in southern Ethiopia, and in remains found on the western shore of Lake Turkana in northern Kenya. Most of the remains are in the form of isolated teeth and fragmentary jaws, but one remarkably complete skull from 2.5 million years ago (the "Black Skull") was recovered from West Turkana. In features related to chewing, *P. aethiopicus* resembles the East African *P. boisei* (2.2–1.3 million years ago) in having enormous molars and premolars, a thick palate and jaws, and projecting cheekbones. In other respects, however, *P. aethiopicus* shares the primitive morphology of *A. afarensis* in having a projecting lower face, a large rear portion for attachment of the jaw muscle (temporalis), and flat cranial bones, among other features. Its resemblance to *P. boisei* may be attributable to their similar diets rather than to a closely shared descent.

Paranthropus Robustus AND *P. Boisei*

Paranthropus robustus and *P. boisei* are also referred to as "robust" australopiths. Some paleoanthropologists classify these two species as *Australopithecus*, but they appear to be closely related and distinctly different from other australopiths. In addition to a well-developed skull crest for the attachment of chewing muscles, other specializations for strong chewing include huge cheek teeth, massive jaws, and powerfully built cheekbones that project forward. These features make their skulls look very unlike those of modern humans.

Robert Broom recovered the first specimen of a robust australopith in 1938 from the South African cave site of

Kromdraai. He gave it the name *Paranthropus robustus* and noted its hominin features as well as its exaggerated chewing apparatus. Between 1948 and 1952 similar fossils were unearthed from Swartkrans, South Africa, which proved to be another of the richest sources of early hominins. A third source of *P. robustus* is the limestone cave of Drimolen, South Africa, where a team began collecting in 1992. All three sites are located within a few kilometres of one another in a valley about 30 km (18 miles) west of Johannesburg. As with the remains of *A. africanus*, the only method of dating the *P. robustus* remains is via biostratigraphy, which indicates that *P. robustus* dates from about 1.8–1.5 million years ago. Specimens attributed to *Homo* also occur in the same deposits, but these are much rarer.

Broom's choice of the name *Paranthropus* (meaning "to the side of humans") reflects his view that this genus was not directly ancestral to later hominins, and it has long been viewed as a distant side branch on the human evolutionary tree. Its specializations for strong chewing certainly make it appear bizarre. The choice of the name *robustus* referred to its heavily built jaws, teeth, and supporting structures. Its body was relatively petite, however, males weighing about 40 kg (88 pounds) and females about 32 kg (70 pounds). Its brain size is 523 cc, which is both absolutely and relatively larger than that of the earlier South African australopith, *A. africanus*, with its average brain of 448 cc.

The spectacular 1959 discovery of a nearly complete skull by Mary Leakey at Olduvai Gorge, Tanzania, first revealed the presence of a robust australopith in East Africa. It shares with its South African cousin the combination of chewing specializations and *Homo*-like evolutionary novelties not present in earlier australopiths. For this reason it is included in the same genus as the South African *Paranthropus*, but it is different enough to warrant its own species name, *P. boisei*. It dates to 2.2–1.3

million years ago, and in that interval it is the most abundant hominin species known, with specimens numbering in the hundreds. It has the greatest development of features related to chewing (mastication), possessing truly massive cheek teeth and jaws. It lived at the same time as species of early *Homo*, but there is some evidence that *Homo* and *P. boisei* preferred different habitats. Despite the enormity of its chewing apparatus, it had a relatively small body, with males weighing about 49 kg (108 pounds) and females 34 kg (75 pounds). *P. robustus* and *P. boisei* fossils are found with mammals that are usually associated with dry grassland habitats.

RELATIONSHIP TO HOMO

Paleontologists maintain that the emergence of genus *Homo* coincides with an increase in hominin brain size and a decrease in the size of cheek teeth. Other anatomical indicators include the lengthening of the femur and the development of a pelvis that closely resembles that of modern humans. The development of these anatomical features can be tracked through time using evidence in the fossil record. Although some humanlike limb and pelvic features occur in members of genus *Australopithecus*, the combination of these features with larger brains and reduced cheek teeth does not appear until the emergence of *H. habilis* about 2 million years ago.

QUALITY OF THE FOSSIL RECORD

Despite the fact that hominins were a rare and insignificant part of the mammalian fauna before about 40,000 years ago, Africans (anthropologists and nonanthropologists alike) and their international colleagues have had phenomenal success in exposing a rich fossil record of australopiths. However, abundant as the fossils are, there are still limitations. For example, the evidence is restricted geographically. The first two-thirds of the fossil record comes almost entirely from sites in the East African Rift Valley and from limestone caves in South Africa. The exceptions are *Sahelanthropus tchadensis* and the jaw fragment from Baḥr el-Ghazāl in Chad, which call attention to the strong likelihood that other hominins lived throughout tropical and subtropical Africa but left fossils that have not yet been found.

Even with comparatively rich samples of species such as *Australopithecus afarensis* and *A. africanus*, most of the specimens are very fragmentary, and even partial skeletons are rare. The *A. afarensis* skeleton "Lucy" stands almost alone in its completeness for the first several million years, joined by a skeleton from Sterkfontein and the *Ardipithecus ramidus* skeleton "Ardi." The rarity of skeletons makes the reconstruction of body size and shape dependent on many assumptions, which can be subject to interpretation. Another limitation to understanding arises from homoplasy, the appearance of similarities in separate evolutionary lineages. Homoplasy was common in hominin evolution. Various evolutionary novelties appear in the record over time, but many must have evolved independently—for example, extreme expansion of the cheek teeth and all the chewing structures of "robust" australopith species and, to a lesser extent, of *A. afarensis*, *A. africanus*, and *A. garhi*. Extreme development of such traits links the robust australopiths—*P. aethiopicus*, *P. boisei*, and *P. robustus*—into a separate lineage.

A related difficulty is the limited understanding of character transformations. Are all traits truly independent evolutionary novelties, or are some of them part of complexes that change together? Jaw size and tooth size, for example, are not independent, and flexion of the base of the skull and being flat-faced are generally correlated. Taxonomic grouping based on shared evolutionary novelties (cladistic analysis) brings these correlations into focus. Research on developmental biology will provide important clues about the evolutionary independence of characteristics.

Australopith and Homo *fossil sites in eastern and southern Africa.* Encyclopædia Britannica, Inc.

The limitations outlined above are important, but they must be balanced by appreciation of successes. These successes can be organized in many ways. For example, the accumulation of evolutionary novelties can be followed over time. This approach appears obvious, but it has its subtlety, acknowledging that any known sample of fossils represents a species that was successful at the time but was not necessarily the direct ancestor of later species. Speciation probably occurred in small, isolated, peripheral populations that the fossil record has not sampled. What we collect is what was successful at the time. Therefore, we might expect to find many unique characteristics (autapomorphies) of fossil species that exclude them from direct ancestry but that also provide keys to reconstructing the common ancestor of later species.

From this point of view, the fossil record is superb. One can follow the hominin lineage step by step as the accumulation of humanlike characteristics. Oddities may be autapomorphies of a particular species, but they do not necessarily exclude the possibility that it and subsequent species shared a common ancestor. It is important to realize that this accumulation has no predetermined direction. We look back on history and see patterns, but these patterns were not established in advance, as evolution has no predetermined direction.

CHANGES IN ANATOMY

The hominin fossil record does not include a truly intermediate form between an apelike and a humanlike body, although *Ardipithecus ramidus* presents a strong case in the minds of some paleontologists. *Australopithecus* retains many primitive apelike traits, but, unlike any ape, it is fundamentally reorganized and highly specialized for walking upright. This state of development required a profound alteration in the genetic template to produce short pelvic blades, a forward-pointing big toe (adducted hallux), and other bipedal traits. The precise sequence of these transformations may in fact never be known from the fossil record, because different parts of the bipedal body may have changed at different rates. For example, the pelvic blades may have shortened before the big toe straightened. Such is the case with the extinct and distinctly nonhuman ape, *Oreopithecus*, which appears to have had reduced pelvic blades but retained a divergent big toe.

Regardless of when or how traits arose, bipedalism is the diagnostic criterion for the evolutionary departure of the human tribe from apes. Bipedal behaviour, however, would have arisen before any fossil evidence of adaptations to it. Thus, the very first hominins most likely had rather apelike bodies without the adaptations for bipedalism that later became the hallmark of the human lineage. These African and possibly European species dating to the late Miocene Epoch (11.6 million to 5.3 million years ago) came, in Charles Darwin's words, "to live somewhat less on trees and more on the ground," owing to "a change in its manner of procuring subsistence, or to a change in the conditions of its native country."

Although Darwin and his contemporaries predicted much of what the human fossil record would eventually reveal, no one anticipated the discovery of hominins with massive jaws. African apes and modern humans have small cheek teeth relative to body size. Australopiths, on the other hand, had huge molars and premolars with concomitantly gigantic jaws, buttressed cheekbones and face bones, and large areas on the skull for the attachment of chewing muscles.

There appear to be two major structural shifts in the evolution of the human body. The first was the transition to bipedalism that is documented in *A. anamensis*, *A. afarensis*,

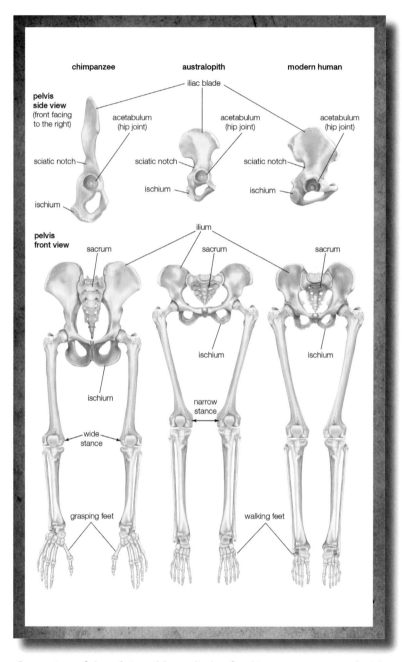

Comparison of the pelvis and lower limbs of a chimpanzee, an australopith, and a modern human. Encyclopædia Britannica, Inc.

A. africanus, and *A. garhi*, which span a time frame from 4.2 to 2.5 million years ago. The limbs and torsos among these species are difficult to assess because of the incompleteness of the fossil record. All share features with *Homo*, but only *A. afarensis* and *A. africanus* are complete enough to make detailed comparisons. These two species share a similar mixture of apelike, humanlike, and unique features in their wrists, hips, and knees. They apparently differ in limb joint sizes, however, with *A. africanus* appearing to be more apelike even though it lived later in time and had a more *Homo*-like skull and teeth. Both species appear to share a combination of specialized bipedal traits but are not exactly like modern humans in that they possess upper limb features associated with climbing.

The second major change in evolution appears at about 1.9 million years ago with the appearance of hips that are uniquely *Homo*. Long femurs and relatively enlarged hip joints mark a significant change in locomotion that is related, perhaps, to long-distance, efficient striding more like that seen in modern *H. sapiens*. The discovery of *A. garhi* reveals the complexity of tracing evolution of limb proportions in that it had a humanlike femur-to-upper-arm ratio yet a long, apelike forearm.

There are opposing interpretations of the primitive body traits retained in the early species of *Australopithecus*. One view emphasizes the bipedal specializations, whereas the other calls attention to the many primitive skull characteristics. Even so, both camps agree that all species of *Australopithecus* were bipedal and thus did not climb like apes. Australopiths did, however, retain features associated with tree-dwelling for at least a million years. Their different hip architecture implies some difference from modern humans in gait and climbing ability. The divergence between *Australopithecus* and later-appearing *Homo* became clearer with the discoveries of lower-body fossils associated with *Homo erectus*, particularly the "Strapping Youth," also called "Turkana Boy," found at Nariokotome, Kenya, in 1984. The striking difference between the pelvis and femur of *Australopithecus* and those of *Homo* probably registers a major shift in adaptation between the two groups. From this perspective, *Australopithecus* appears to have had the hands free for carrying but was adapted only to traveling short distances. It likely had a healthy appreciation of trees for safety, feeding, and sleeping. The longer femur and more humanlike pelvis that appear by 1.9 million years ago in *Homo* mark the beginning of an important change.

Not only were there numerous species of human predecessors long ago, but many of these overlapped in time and space. Habitats favourable for hominin occupation undoubtedly appeared and disappeared throughout much of Africa over and over again with the drastic fluctuations in tropical climates that occurred during the Pliocene and Pleistocene epochs. More species presumably await discovery, because there were probably many evolutionary experiments in these varied and changing habitats. Although the current sample of fossil hominins leads some to the impression that there were only a few hominin lineages, it is far more likely that the human family tree will turn out to be quite "bushy." Species names may need to multiply to accommodate the diversity, although a balance needs to be maintained between excessive splitting groups apart and lumping them together.

Evidence regarding the relationship of *Australopithecus* to the origin of the genus *Homo* may appear to conflict, but, from the perspective of accumulated shared traits, the fossil record is less perplexing. Put simply, brains expand and cheek teeth shrink. In *H. habilis* (2.3–1.6 million years ago) the body appears to remain like that of

Australopithecus—small with relatively large upper limbs and small lower limbs. If the lower limb fossils found with the skulls and teeth of a 1.9-million-year-old specimen of *H. rudolfensis* also belong to this species, then the more humanlike body proportions and hip architecture first appear in this species just after 2 million years ago. Both *H. habilis* and *H. rudolfensis* are transitional, with some primitive and some derived characteristics of later *Homo* species. Other skeletal remains are critical here because body size appears to be very different. *H. habilis* was very small (35 kg [77 pounds]), and *H. rudolfensis* was large (55 kg [121 pounds]). Scaling cheek-tooth size to body weight shows that they both had reversed the trend of ever-increasing cheek-tooth size. Relative brain size expanded, especially in *H. habilis*. Brain size expanded further with the appearance of *H. erectus* by at least 1.8 million years ago, but body size also increased, so that relative brain size apparently was not so dramatically expanded. The early African form of *H. erectus* is often referred to as *H. ergaster* to contrast it with the well-known Asian *H. erectus*. Body size and especially hind limb length reach modern proportions in this species. Other traits *Australopithecus* has in common with later *Homo* include a further reduction in facial projection as well as other features, including reduction in the size of the cheek teeth. Brains then continue to expand and cheek teeth become progressively smaller through the evolution of the genus *Homo*.

CHAPTER 8
EARLY HUMANS

The members of *Homo* are distinguished from other hominins by a unique set of anatomical and behavioral features. All of the species in this group have a relatively large cranial capacity, a limb structure adapted to a habitual erect posture and a bipedal gait, well-developed and fully opposable thumbs, hands capable of power and precision grips, and the ability to make standardized precision tools, using one tool to make another. Together with modern man, *Homo sapiens*, the genus includes the extinct species *H. habilis*, *H. erectus*, and *H. heidelbergensis* as well as the extinct Neanderthals (*H. neanderthalensis*) and the early form of *H. sapiens* called Cro-Magnon. Two species of early humans, *H. habilis* and *H. erectus* (whose origins date back to over 1.7 million years ago), are considered below.

HOMO HABILIS

Homo habilis (Latin: "able man" or "handy man") is an extinct species of human and the most ancient representative of the genus *Homo*. *H. habilis* inhabited parts of sub-Saharan Africa from perhaps 2 to 1.5 million years ago. In 1959 and 1960 the first fossils were discovered at Olduvai Gorge in northern Tanzania. This discovery was a turning point in the science of paleoanthropology because the oldest previously known human fossils were Asian specimens of *Homo erectus*. Many features of *H. habilis* appear to be intermediate in terms of evolutionary development between the relatively primitive *Australopithecus* and the more-advanced *Homo* species.

The first *H. habilis* remains found at Olduvai consist of several teeth and a lower jaw associated with fragments of a cranium and some hand bones. As more specimens were unearthed at locations such as Koobi Fora in northern Kenya, researchers began to realize that these hominins were anatomically different from *Australopithecus*, a genus of more-apelike creatures whose remains had been found at many African sites. Formal announcement of the discoveries was made in 1964 by anthropologists Louis S.B. Leakey, Phillip Tobias, and John Napier. As justification for designating their new creature *Homo* rather than *Australopithecus*, they described the increased cranial capacity and comparatively smaller molar and premolar teeth of the fossils, a humanlike foot, and hand bones that suggested an ability to manipulate objects with precision—hence the species name *Homo habilis*, or "handy man." Furthermore, simple stone tools were found along with the fossils. All these characteristics foreshadow the anatomy and behaviour of *H. erectus* and later humans, making *H. habilis* extremely important, even though there are few remnants of it.

Artist's rendering of Homo habilis, *which lived from 2 to 1.5 million years ago.* Encyclopædia Britannica, Inc.

The Fossil Evidence

Apart from the original discovery of the jaw, cranial, and hand bones from a juvenile individual called Olduvai Hominid 7 (OH 7), additional fossils from Olduvai have been ascribed to *H. habilis*. Pieces of another thin-walled cranium along with upper and lower jaws and teeth came to light in 1963. Just a month later a third skull was found, but these bones had been trampled by cattle after being washed into a gully. Some of the teeth survived, but the cranium was broken into many small fragments; only the top of the braincase, or vault, has been pieced back together. These two skulls are called OH 13 and OH 16.

Since 1964 more material has been discovered, not only at Olduvai but at other African localities as well. One intriguing specimen is OH 24. This cranium is more complete than others from Olduvai. Because some of the bones are crushed and distorted, however, the face and braincase are warped. OH 24 may differ from *Australopithecus* in brain size and dental characteristics, but it resembles the australopiths of southern Africa in other features, such as the shape of the face. Complete agreement concerning its significance has not been reached, partly because the fossil is damaged.

Important discoveries made in the Koobi Fora region include a controversial skull called KNM-ER 1470 (Kenya National Museum–East Rudolf), which resembles both *Australopithecus* and *Homo*. As in the case of OH 16, this specimen had been broken into many fragments, which could be collected only after extensive sieving of the deposits. Some of the pieces were then fitted into the reconstruction of a face and much of a large vault. Brain volume can be measured rather accurately and is about 750 cc (46 cubic inches). This evidence prompted some paleoanthropologists to describe ER 1470 as one of the

KOOBI FORA

Koobi Fora is a region of paleoanthropological sites in northern Kenya near Lake Turkana (Lake Rudolf). The Koobi Fora geologic formation consists of lake and river sediments from the eastern shore of Lake Turkana. Well-preserved hominin fossils dating from between 2.1 and 1.3 million years ago include at least one species of robust australopith (*Paranthropus boisei*) and three species of *Homo* (*H. habilis*, *H. rudolfensis*, and African *H. erectus*, which is also called *H. ergaster*). Stone tools dating to 2 million years ago resemble certain Oldowan industry artifacts from Olduvai Gorge in Tanzania. Koobi Fora's archaeological record dates to as recently as 1.4 million years ago, but there are very few Acheulean hand axes.

In other fossil-bearing sites west of Lake Turkana, several other species of hominins have been found, including *Kenyanthropus platyops* (3.2 million years ago), which has facial traits similar to those of the controversial 1.9-million-year-old *H. habilis* skull KNM-ER 1470—a skull that in some ways resembles *Australopithecus*. In sediments from 2.5 million years ago comes the "Black Skull" belonging to the robust australopith *P. aethiopicus*. In later beds occur representatives of *P. boisei* (2.3–1.6 million years ago), *H. habilis* (c. 2 million years ago), and *H. ergaster/erectus* (1.6 million years ago), including a nearly complete skeleton of an 11–13-year-old male called "Turkana Boy." A 1.44-million-year-old jawbone ascribed to *H. habilis* and a 1.55-million-year-old skull belonging to *H. erectus* have been found east of Lake Turkana. These fossils suggest that *H. habilis* and *H. erectus* coexisted at this location for a time. Oldowan tools have been discovered near Lake Turkana as well, in sediments estimated to be 2.34 million years old; Acheulean tools appear by 1.65 million years ago.

most ancient undoubted representatives of the genus *Homo* because some other features of the braincase are also *Homo*-like. At the same time, it is apparent that the facial skeleton is relatively large and flattened in its lower parts. In this respect, the Koobi Fora specimen resembles *Australopithecus* anatomically.

Among other key finds from the Koobi Fora region are KNM-ER 1813 and KNM-ER 1805. The former, which is most of a cranium, is smaller than ER 1470 and resembles OH 13 in many details, including tooth size and morphology. The latter skull exhibits some peculiar features. Although the braincase of ER 1805 is close to 600 cc in volume and is thus expanded moderately beyond the size expected in *Australopithecus*, a bony crest runs along the top of the skull. This sagittal crest is coupled with another prominent crest oriented across the rear of the skull. These ridges indicate that the chewing muscles and neck muscles were powerfully developed. A similar if more exaggerated pattern of cresting appears in the so-called robust australopiths but not in *Homo*. Other features of ER 1805, however, are *Homo*-like. As a result, there has been disagreement among anatomists regarding the hominin species to which this individual should be assigned. Despite its anomalies, ER 1805 is often discussed along with other specimens grouped as *H. habilis*.

Several mandibles resembling that of OH 7 have been recovered from the Koobi Fora area, and teeth that may belong to *H. habilis* have been found farther to the north, in the Omo River valley of Ethiopia. Some additional material, including a badly broken cranium, are known from the cave at Swartkrans in South Africa. At Swartkrans the fossils are mixed with many other bones of robust australopiths. An early species of *Homo* may also be present at Sterkfontein, not far from Swartkrans. Here again the remains are fragmentary and not particularly informative.

A more valuable discovery was reported from Olduvai Gorge in 1986. A jaw with teeth and skull fragments as well as pieces of a right arm and both legs were found. The bones seem to represent one individual, called OH 62. Although the skull is shattered, enough of the face is preserved to suggest similarities to early *Homo*. The find is especially important because of the limbs, which show that OH 62 was a very small hominin. The arm is long relative to the leg, resulting in body proportions that differ dramatically from those of more modern hominins.

BODY STRUCTURE

Olduvai and Koobi Fora fossils have allowed researchers to make some determinations about the anatomy of early humans. It is clear that the braincase of *H. habilis* is larger than that of *Australopithecus*. The original finds from

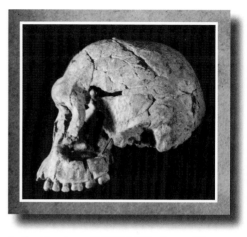

Left side view of KNM-ER 1813, a Homo habilis *cranium found in 1973 at Koobi Fora, Kenya, and dated to some 1.9 million years ago.* G. Philip Rightmire

Olduvai Gorge include two sizable bones from the skull of OH 7. An incomplete brain cast was molded by putting the bones together to form a partial cranium. This cast has been used to estimate a total brain volume of about 680 cc. A brain cast from ER 1470, which has a more complete cranium, can be measured directly; its volume is about 775 cc. One or two additional fragmentary skulls appear to be about the same size as that of ER 1470. Others—such as ER 1813, which has a cranial capacity of only about 510—are much smaller. Thus, brain sizes ranging from slightly more than 500 to nearly 800 cc seem to characterize *H. habilis*.

The skulls by and large have thin walls and are rounded, rather than low and flattened; they do not have the heavy crests and projecting browridges characteristic of later *H. erectus*. The underside of the cranium is shortened from the back of the palate to the rear of the skull, as in all later *Homo* species. This is an important contrast to the so-called gracile australopiths, in which the cranial base is relatively narrow and elongated.

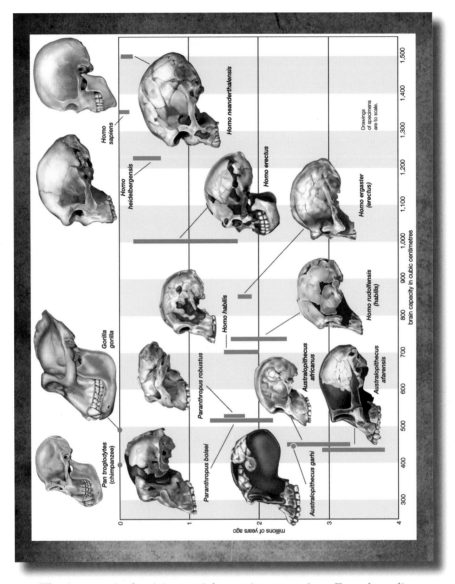

The increase in hominin cranial capacity over time. Encyclopædia Britannica, Inc.

The facial bones of several specimens are at least partly preserved, and facial proportions vary considerably. One of the Olduvai hominins, OH 24, seems anatomically similar to *Australopithecus* in having

AVERAGE CAPACITY OF THE BRAINCASE IN FOSSIL HOMININS		
HOMININ	NUMBER OF FOSSIL EXAMPLES	AVERAGE CAPACITY OF THE BRAINCASE (CC)
Australopithecus	6	440
Paranthropus	4	519
Homo habilis	4	640
Javanese *Homo erectus* (Trinil and Sangiran)	6	930
Chinese *Homo erectus* (Peking man)	7	1,029
Homo sapiens	7	1,350

prominent cheekbones and a flat nasal region. This gives the central region of the face a depressed, or "dished," appearance, and the upper part of the nasal profile is obscured by the cheek when the specimen is viewed from the side. Such hollowing of the face is characteristic of some South African australopiths but is not seen in later *Homo*. The facial skeleton of ER 1470 is large relative to the braincase, and it shows flattening below the nose—*Australopithecus*-like features. The walls of the nasal opening, however, are slightly everted, and there is at least an indication that the nose stands out in more relief than would be expected in australopiths. The face of ER 1813 is even more modern.

The front teeth of *H. habilis* are not much different in size from those of *Australopithecus*, but the premolar and molar crowns—particularly in the lower jaw—are narrower. The jaw itself may be quite heavily constructed like that of gracile australopiths. This is the case for OH 7 and also for at least one specimen from Koobi Fora. Other jaws are smaller but still robust in the sense of being thick relative to height. For example, the mandible of OH 13 is similar in many respects to that of *H. erectus*, and this individual might have been called *H. erectus* if its jaw had not been found along with small, thin vault bones.

Only a few other skeletal parts have been discovered. Some limb bones from Olduvai and Koobi Fora have been grouped tentatively with *H. habilis* on the basis of general anatomic similarity to later humans. These fossils, however, are not associated with any teeth or skulls, and it is probably not appropriate to use them as the basis for describing early *Homo*. One individual for which body parts are more fully represented is OH 62. Arm and leg bones of OH 62 are fragmentary, but the arm is relatively long. The skeleton may be similar in its proportions to small australopiths. OH 62 probably walked on two legs as efficiently as other early hominins, but this diminutive individual was unlike later humans in many respects.

Another important specimen is the immature hand of OH 7. These bones, found with skull bones, are still apelike in some aspects, but it is almost certain that the individual from which they came had dextrous hands. Stone artifacts and early *Homo* fossils have been found at Olduvai and other sites. These tools are called the Oldowan industry, and, though they are crude, they indicate that *H. habilis* could shape stone.

Behavioral Inferences

The stone tools and unused waste materials (mainly crude chopping tools and sharp flakes) left by *H. habilis* provide important clues about the behaviour of these early humans. Olduvai Gorge has been a rich source of Oldowan tools, and the tools are often found with animal fossils. Originally, the occurrence of artifacts with bones was interpreted to mean that *H. habilis* hunted animals and brought the carcasses to where it lived for butchering, but it is now known that the situation was more complicated. Assemblages such as those found at Olduvai can be created through various means, not all of which are related to hominin activities. Olduvai *H. habilis* certainly used animal products, however. With the aid of a scanning electron microscope, it has been shown that cut marks on some of the bones must have been made by stone tools, but this does not prove that animals were hunted. Analysis of Olduvai animal fossils also shows that some marks were made by either rodent or carnivore teeth, the indication being that at least some of the animals were killed by nonhominin predators. In all likelihood, the hominins at Olduvai could obtain larger carcasses only after the animals had been killed and partially eaten by other predators. *H. habilis* may have hunted small prey, such as antelope, but definitely was a scavenger.

It is debatable whether or not the Olduvai sites were home bases. Nothing recovered indicates that people resided where the animal bones accumulated. Such areas were presumably dangerous since they undoubtedly attracted numerous predators. These sites may have been caches of stone tools and raw materials that were established in areas convenient for rapid processing of animal parts. Therefore, where the hominins lived or whether their social structure was prototypical of later hunter-gatherers remains unknown, although *H. habilis* must have engaged in cultural activities.

Whether or not early *Homo* had acquired language is another fundamental question, and the indirect evidence on this issue has been variously interpreted. It is the belief of some anatomists that endocranial casts of *H. habilis* fossils indicate that the regions associated with speech in modern humans are enlarged. Others disagree with this assessment, particularly since the number of braincases preserved well enough to make detailed casts is small. Anthropologists have also based their interpretations on the archaeological record. According to some, the crude Oldowan artifacts indicate the ability to use language. Critics of this view assert that the Oldowan industry represents only opportunistic stonework. They argue that, because the later Acheulean tools of *H. erectus* are more carefully formed and are often highly symmetrical, this later hominin was the first to use symbols and language. One of the problems with this theory is that no clear link between technological and linguistic behaviour has been established—even the more sophisticated tools could have been made by nonspeaking hominins. Thus, it is not certain when *Homo* developed the linguistic skills that characterize modern humans.

EVOLUTIONARY IMPLICATIONS

The general interpretation of the fossil evidence is that *H. habilis* is not only substantially different from *Australopithecus* but that it represents the beginning of the trends characterizing human evolutionary history, particularly expansion of the brain. Some specimens clearly have a larger cranial capacity than that of *Australopithecus*, and the capacity increases progressively afterward with *H. erectus*, archaic *H. sapiens*, and modern humans. *H. habilis* is also thought to exhibit the origins of other trends such as smaller teeth and changes in facial structure, especially the nasal region.

The theory that *H. habilis* is intermediate between relatively primitive *Australopithecus* and more advanced *Homo* appears to be generally accurate, but several aspects of this view can be challenged. Although there are not many *H. habilis* fossils, it is becoming clear that there are anatomic differences among the East African assemblages. Some of the newer discoveries have confirmed the expectation that early *Homo* craniums should be relatively large, with the rear of the skull being rounded and its base shortened. Other fossils have proved less easy to assign to *H. habilis*, and there has been controversy over their interpretation. Some braincases are considerably smaller, and it is frequently suggested that this variation is one of the differences between males and females (sexual dimorphism), the larger skulls being ascribed to males. But there are differences in shape as well as size, and several of the smaller skulls depart from the morphology of large-brained *H. habilis* in ways that are not obviously related to sex. There are also facial similarities between some specimens and *Australopithecus*. Thus, there is the possibility that two different species rather than one sexually dimorphic group are actually represented by the fossils.

DATING THE FOSSILS

Several approaches have been used to date *H. habilis* fossils from Olduvai, and a reasonably accurate timescale for Olduvai has been developed. The oldest remains, including OH 24, are from about 1.85 million years ago. Others such as OH 7 and OH 62 are not quite so ancient. The youngest Olduvai skull that is representative of early *Homo* is OH 13. No radiometric date for it is available, but other dating methods estimate it to be about 1.5 million years old.

In the Koobi Fora region a number of important fossils have been located near a level of volcanic ash that also contains stone tools. This ash bed was dated to about 2.6 million years ago. When ER 1470 was discovered several metres below this layer in 1972, it was thought that the newfound cranium must document *Homo* from a time well before the Olduvai deposits had accumulated. This assumption was soon questioned on the basis of other evidence, however, and before 1980 it was clear that the age had been overestimated. A series of radiometric determinations done subsequently has yielded a date of 1.88

million years ago. The ER 1470 skull and other *H. habilis* specimens recovered below this ash layer, therefore, must be close to two million years old. Evidence from East Africa thus suggests that *H. habilis* lived for a half-million years or so before giving way to later *Homo* species.

Classifying the various specimens separately means that each must be fitted into a scheme of hominin descent, or phylogeny. One interpretation assigns specimens with smaller craniums to a gracile species of *Australopithecus*. According to this scenario, only the larger skulls represent early *Homo* evolution. Others, questioning the notion that all species of *Homo* proceed along a simple linear progression, believe that early human populations were more diverse than has been recognized; although these researchers recognize two separate species, they prefer to lump both in the genus *Homo*. In this view, two species may have lived contemporaneously 2.0–1.5 million years ago. Only one could be the direct ancestor of *H. erectus*, and so perhaps it was the large-brained form that evolved further, while the smaller hominin became extinct.

DATING HOMININ FOSSILS WITH MOLECULAR CLOCKS

Before about 1980 it was widely thought that distinctively hominin fossils could be identified from 14 to 12 million years ago. However, during the 1970s geneticists introduced the use of molecular clocks to calculate how long species had been separated from a common ancestor. The molecular clock concept is based on an assumed regularity in the accumulation of tiny changes in the genetic codes of humans and other organisms. Use of this concept, together with a reanalysis of the fossil record, moved the estimated time of the evolutionary split between apes and human ancestors forward to as recently as about 5 million

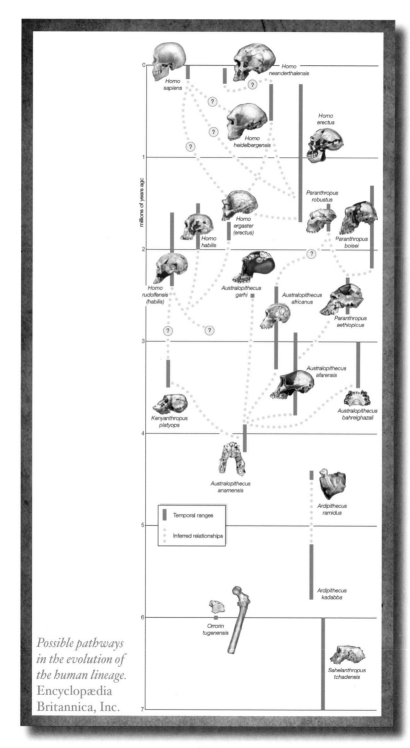

Possible pathways in the evolution of the human lineage. Encyclopædia Britannica, Inc.

years ago. Since then the molecular data and a steady trickle of new hominin fossil finds have pushed the earliest putative hominin ancestry back in time somewhat, to perhaps 8–7 million years ago.

HOMO ERECTUS

Homo erectus (Latin: "upright man") is an extinct species of the genus *Homo* and perhaps an ancestor of modern humans (*H. sapiens*). *H. erectus* most likely originated in Africa, though Eurasia cannot be ruled out. Regardless of where it first evolved, the species seems to have dispersed quickly, starting about 1.7 million years ago near the middle of the Pleistocene Epoch, moving through the African tropics, Europe, South Asia, and Southeast Asia. This history has been recorded directly if imprecisely by many sites that have yielded fossil remains of *H. erectus*. At other localities, broken animal bones and stone tools have indicated the presence of the species, though there are no traces of the people themselves. *H. erectus* was a human of medium stature that walked upright. The braincase was low, the forehead was receded, and the nose, jaws, and palate were wide. The brain was smaller and the teeth larger than in modern humans. *H. erectus* seems to have flourished until some 200,000 years ago or perhaps later before giving way to other humans including *Homo sapiens*.

FOSSIL EVIDENCE

The first fossils attributed to *Homo erectus* were discovered by a Dutch army surgeon, Eugène Dubois, who began his search for ancient human bones on the island of Java (now part of Indonesia) in 1890. Dubois found his first specimen in the same year, and in 1891 a well-preserved skullcap

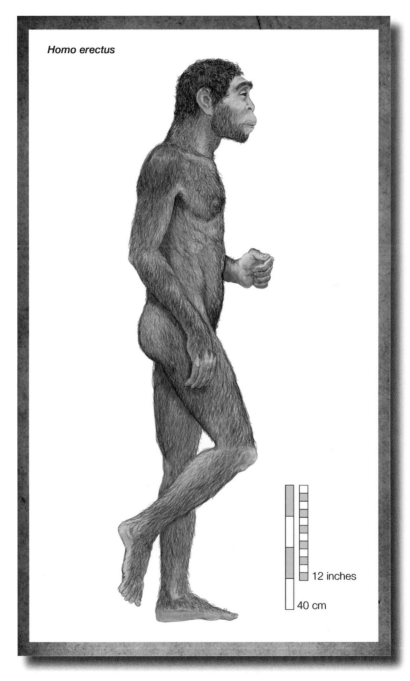

Artist's rendering of Homo erectus, *which lived from approximately 1,700,000 to 200,000 years ago.* Encyclopædia Britannica, Inc.

was unearthed at Trinil on the Solo River. Considering its prominent browridges, retreating forehead, and angled rear skull, Dubois concluded that the Trinil cranium showed anatomic features intermediate between those of humans (as they were then understood) and those of apes. Several years later, near where the skull was discovered, he found a remarkably complete and modern-looking femur (thighbone). Since this bone was so similar to a modern human femur, Dubois decided that the individual to which it belonged must have walked erect. He adopted the name *Pithecanthropus* (coined earlier by the German zoologist Ernst Haeckel) and called his discoveries *Pithecanthropus erectus* ("upright ape-man"), but the colloquial term became "Java man." Only a few other limb fragments turned up in the Trinil excavations, and it would be some three decades before more substantial evidence appeared. Most paleontologists now regard all of this material as *H. erectus*, and the name *Pithecanthropus* has been dropped.

OTHER ASIAN FOSSILS

Subsequent discoveries continued to establish a case for this new and separate species of fossil hominin. At first these discoveries were centred largely in Asia. For example, similar fossils were found during the early 20th century at several different locations in Java: Kedung Brubus, Mojokerto (Modjokerto), Sangiran, Ngandong (Solo), Sambungmacan (Sambungmachan), and Ngawi. Another series of finds was made in China beginning in the 1920s, especially in the caves and fissures of Zhoukoudian (Chou-k'ou-tien), near Beijing. Remains found at Zhoukoudian by Davidson Black became popularly known as Peking man; virtually all of these remains were subsequently lost by 1941 during the Sino-Japanese War (1937–45), though casts of them still exist. Newer discoveries have since been made in the Zhoukoudian caves and at four other Chinese sites: Gongwangling

(Kung-wang-ling) and Chenjiawo (Ch'en-chia-wo) in the Lantian (Lan-t'ien) district of Shaanxi province, Hulu Cave near Nanjing, and Hexian (Ho-hsien) in Anhui province. By the end of World War II the pattern of early discovery had given rise to the idea that *H. erectus* was a peculiarly Asian expression of early humans. Subsequent discoveries in Africa changed this view, and by the end of the 20th century it was confirmed that Europe also harboured *H. erectus*.

AFRICAN FOSSILS

In North Africa in 1954–55, excavations at Tighenif (Ternifine), east of Mascara, Algeria, yielded remains dating to approximately 700,000 years ago whose nearest affinities seemed to be with the Chinese form of *H. erectus*. Other Moroccan hominin fragments from this region—parts of a skull found in 1933 near Rabat and jaws

ZHOUKOUDIAN

Zhoukoudian is an archaeological site near the village of Zhoukoudian, Beijing municipality, China, which lies 42 km (26 miles) southwest of the central city. The site, including some four residential areas, has yielded the largest known collection of fossils of the extinct hominin *Homo erectus*—altogether some 40 incomplete skeletons, which are commonly known as the Peking man fossils. Remains of anatomically modern humans (*H. sapiens*) have also been excavated there. The discoveries at Zhoukoudian have proved vital to advancing the study of human evolution.

The hominin remains were found within a series of scree- and loess-filled clefts (inaccurately referred to as "caves") in a limestone cliff. In 1921 the Swedish geologist and fossil hunter J. Gunnar Andersson became intrigued by tales of "dragon bones" that local people found in the clefts and used for medicinal purposes. Andersson explored the clefts and discovered some quartz pieces that could have been used as early cutting tools. This discovery lent credence to his theory that the bones were actually human fossils. In 1927 the Canadian anthropologist Davidson Black retrieved a hominin molar from the site. On the basis of that finding, he identified a previously unknown hominin group, which he named *Sinanthropus pekinensis* (i.e., Peking man). Large-scale excavations began in 1929.

In the years that followed, archaeologists uncovered complete skulls, mandibles, teeth, leg bones, and other fossils from males and females of various ages. The specimens were eventually classified as *H. erectus*. Many of the fossil-bearing layers have been dated, and the results suggest that the site was first occupied more than 770,000 years ago and then used intermittently by *H. erectus* until perhaps 230,000 years ago. If these dates are correct, Zhoukoudian documents the relatively late survival of this species.

Further discoveries at the site demonstrated that Peking man was fairly technologically sophisticated. Stone scrapers and choppers as well as several hand axes indicated that Peking man devised various tools for different tasks. Excavators also claimed to have uncovered ash deposits consisting of charred animal bones and stones indicating that Peking man had learned to use fire for lighting, cooking, and heating. This discovery resulted in a drastic revision of the date for the earliest human mastery of fire. A reanalysis of the site in 1998, however, revealed no evidence for hearths, ash, or charcoal and indicated that some of the "ash" layers were in fact water-laid sediments washed into the sites from the surrounding hillsides. The bones and stones were charred not by human activity but by lightning-induced fire.

During World War II the more notable fossils were lost during an attempt to smuggle them out of China for safekeeping; they have never been recovered. Following the war, excavations resumed, and many more fragments of *H. erectus* were unearthed; however, some areas remain unexcavated. In 1987 Zhoukoudian was placed on the list of UNESCO World Heritage sites. In 1995 concern over the deterioration of the clefts, parts of which were in danger of collapsing, led to the establishment of a joint UNESCO-China project aimed at preserving the site and encouraging investigations there.

and teeth from Sīdī ʿAbd al-Raḥmān (Sidi Abderrahman) in Morocco—show features reminiscent of *H. erectus*, though they are rather more advanced in structure than those of Tighenif and Asia. Another fossil likened to *H. erectus* is a 400,000-year-old cranium found in 1971 at Salé, Morocco.

Although nearly all of the face and part of the forehead have broken away, it is an important specimen.

Some of the more convincing evidence for the existence of *H. erectus* in Africa came with the discovery in 1960 of a partial braincase at Olduvai Gorge in Tanzania. This fossil, catalogued as OH 9, was excavated by Louis S.B. Leakey and is probably about 1.2 million years old. Olduvai Gorge has since yielded additional cranial remains, jaws, and limb bones of *H. erectus*. Much of this material is fragmentary, but gaps in our knowledge of East African *H. erectus* have been filled to some extent through finds made by Louis Leakey's son, Richard Leakey. Since 1970 a number of important fossils have been unearthed at localities on the eastern shore of Lake Turkana (Lake Rudolf) in northwestern Kenya, now commonly referred to as the Koobi Fora sites. The fossils recovered there may be about 1.7 million years old, based on radiometric dating of the associated volcanic material. Included in these assemblages are the remains of *Australopithecus* and probably some representatives of early *Homo*. Of several specimens that are clearly *Homo*, one cranium (KNM-ER 3733) is quite complete and well-preserved. Dated to 1.75 million years ago, it is likely to be one of the most ancient *H. erectus* fossils discovered in Africa. It and other specimens from Koobi Fora are considered by some paleontologists to be a separate species they call *H. ergaster*. Other significant finds in this area include a partially intact skeleton (KNM-ER 1808), although it comes from a diseased individual. A more complete skeleton named "Turkana Boy" (KNM-WT 15000) was found nearby at Nariokotome, a site on the northwestern shore of Lake Turkana. The remains of this juvenile male have provided much information about growth, development, and body proportions of an early member of the species.

Although it has been recognized for some time that Africa as well as Asia was peopled by at least one form of *H. erectus*, the situation in Europe is less clear. One of the oldest European hominin fossils is an isolated mandible (lower jawbone) with teeth, found in 1907 in a sandpit just north of Mauer, Germany, near Heidelberg. Dating to about 500,000 years ago, it has been given a variety of names over the years, but its exact relationship to other fossils remains uncertain, partly because no associated cranium was found. Some investigators have come to regard the Mauer mandible as representing *H. erectus*. Although its age is perhaps comparable to that of the older Zhoukoudian hominins in China, this European specimen shows more modern structural features than do the Asian and African jaws of *H. erectus*. The exact significance of these features in the Mauer jaw is still being debated, and some consider it a separate species (*H. heidelbergensis*) that is slightly more advanced in its anatomy than the African and Asian populations. Another fossil that may tentatively be grouped with the Mauer mandible is a lower leg bone (tibia) found in 1993 during excavations at Boxgrove, West Sussex, England.

More convincing evidence for the presence of *H. erectus* in Europe has come from Ceprano in central Italy, where a skull lacking its face was found in 1994. Clay deposits surrounding it contain no volcanic material that is directly datable, but the fossil is probably somewhat older than the Mauer mandible. The Ceprano individual displays the heavy continuous brow, low braincase, angled rear skull, and thick cranial bones that are characteristic of *H. erectus*.

Other important fossils have been recovered in the southern Caucasus region of Georgia. Excavations at the medieval village of Dmanisi revealed a jaw with a full set of teeth in 1991. Found along with animal bones and crude stone tools, this specimen has been likened to *H. erectus*, and it is much more ancient than the remains from Mauer or Ceprano. In 1999 two more craniums were reported from the same site. These well-preserved individuals confirm the presence of *H. erectus* at the gates to Europe and seem to resemble the fossils from the Koobi Fora sites in Kenya. Dated to 1.7 million years ago, the Dmanisi hominins are among the oldest known outside of Africa, and they bear directly on the question of how *H. erectus* evolved and dispersed across the Old World.

DATING THE FOSSILS

To reconstruct the position of *H. erectus* in hominin evolution, it is essential to define the place of this species in time, and modern paleoanthropologists have at their disposal a variety of techniques that permit them to do so with great precision. Potassium-argon dating, for instance, can provide the age of a specimen by clocking the rate at which radioactive isotopes of these elements have decayed. When radiometric methods cannot be applied, investigators may still ascribe a relative age to a fossil by relating it to the other contents of the deposit in which it was found.

Such lines of evidence have led to the tentative conclusion that *H. erectus* flourished over a long interval of Pleistocene time. The fossils recovered at Koobi Fora are from about 1.7 million years ago, and OH 9 from Olduvai is probably 1.2 million years old. The specimens from Sangiran and Mojokerto in Java may approach the age of the Koobi Fora skeletons, and one from the Lantian localities in China is roughly contemporary with OH 9. The youngest hominins generally accepted as *H. erectus* are from Tighenif in Algeria (800,000–600,000 years ago), Zhoukoudian in China (770,000–230,000 years ago), and Sambungmacan and Ngandong (Solo) in Java (perhaps less than 250,000 years ago).

For the most part, fossils older than 1.7 million years are the remains of *H. habilis* and *H. rudolfensis*. These species are also known from Olduvai Gorge and Koobi Fora in Africa, the oldest specimens being about 2.0 to 1.8 million years in age. On the other hand, there is a group of later specimens that show some features of *H. erectus* but are commonly regarded either as "archaic" representatives of *Homo sapiens* or as belonging to *H. heidelbergensis*; these include specimens from Europe (Mauer, Arago, Bilzingsleben, and Petralona), northwestern Africa (Rabat and perhaps Salé and Sīdī 'Abd al-Raḥmān), eastern and southern Africa (Kabwe, Elandsfontein, Ndutu, Omo, and Bodo), and Asia (the Dali find of 1978).

BODY STRUCTURE

Much of the fossil material discovered in Java and China consists of cranial bones, jawbones, and teeth. The few broken limb bones found at Zhoukoudian have provided little information. It is possible that the complete femur excavated by Dubois at Trinil is more recent in age than the other fossils found there and not attributable to *H. erectus*. It comes as no surprise, therefore, that the greatest descriptive emphasis has been on the shape of the skull rather than other parts of the skeleton. The continuing discoveries in Africa (particularly at the Olduvai and Lake Turkana sites) have yielded a more complete picture of *H. erectus* anatomy.

The cranium of *H. erectus*, with its low profile and average endocranial (brain) capacity of less than 1,000 cubic cm (61 cubic inches), is distinctly different from that of other humans. The average endocranial capacity of modern *Homo sapiens*, for example, is 1,350 cubic cm (82 cubic inches), although the range for recent humans is appreciable, perhaps 1,000 to 2,000 cubic cm (61 to 122 cubic inches). The upper part of the maximum estimated range for *H. erectus* endocranial capacity (1,200 cubic cm [73 cubic inches]) thus overlaps with the lower values expected for *Homo sapiens*.

Some difference in estimated brain size is apparent between the Javanese and the Zhoukoudian populations of *H. erectus*. That is, the average capacity of the Zhoukoudian fossils exceeds that of the Javanese by about 160 cubic cm (10 cubic inches). There is, however, an earlier, anomalous cranium from Gongwangling, China, that is approximately contemporary with some Java fossils. It shares with the Javanese group a smaller cranial capacity (780 cubic cm [48 cubic inches]). Theoretically, the difference in brain size between the two groups of Asian fossils may be the consequence of further evolution in later populations of *H. erectus*. Alternatively, it may simply be interpreted as representing the variation expected between sexes or between two separate populations or subspecies of *H. erectus*. Several African values are also available, and in the case of the Koobi Fora and Olduvai individuals these range from about 850 to 1,067 cubic cm (52 to 65 cubic inches).

While the cranial capacity of *H. erectus* falls short of that of *Homo sapiens*, it far exceeds the capacities of the australopiths. The difference between *Australopithecus* and *H. erectus* is slightly greater than that between *H. erectus* and *Homo sapiens*. Into the former gap fit the cranial capacities of *H. habilis* and *H. rudolfensis*. Clearly, the last word has not been written on their relationships.

Besides their brain capacity, the skulls of *H. erectus* show a number of other distinctive features. The face, which is preserved in only a few specimens, is massively constructed, and its lower parts project forward. The bone forming the wall of the nose is thinner and more everted than in earlier *Homo* or *Australopithecus*, and the nasal bridge is relatively high and prominent. This development suggests that *H. erectus* was well-equipped to conserve moisture that would otherwise be lost during exhalation. Such a physiological advantage would have allowed early African *H. erectus* to travel for longer periods in an arid environment. The braincase is low, with thick bones and sides that taper upward. Over the eye sockets is a strongly jutting browridge (supraorbital torus). There is a flattened forehead, and the part of the cranium immediately behind the browridge is appreciably constricted from side to side. A low ridge or crest of bone extends from the frontal bone along the midline of some skulls, and there tend to be strongly developed crests in the ear region. The broad-based skull has another ridge running across it. The area where the neck muscles attach is much larger than in *H. habilis* or *Homo sapiens*. Other distinguishing features in *H. erectus* can be found on the underside of the skull, especially at the jaw joint. The lower jaw itself is deep and robust and lacks chin development. The teeth are on the whole larger than those of *Homo sapiens*.

The femur is the most commonly recovered noncranial fossil. Apart from the puzzling Trinil specimen, a number of femurs have been found at Zhoukoudian, and more have been recovered from sites in Africa. These bones resemble those of modern humans, and *H. erectus* must have walked upright efficiently. Its skeleton is robust, suggesting that the lifestyle of *H. erectus* was physically demanding. The limb bones also supply information about the size of *H. erectus*. Size influences behaviour and various aspects of anatomy, including bodily proportions. One measure of size is stature, or height. The femurs found at Zhoukoudian and Koobi Fora are too broken to yield a good estimate of the height of these individuals, but accurate measurements of the boy's skeleton found at Nariokotome have been made. Although he was not fully grown, it is thought that the boy would have reached 180 cm (6 feet) in height.

The total pattern of the bodily structure of *H. erectus*, as preserved in the fossils, is different from that of

Artist's depiction of what Homo erectus *may have looked like.* Painting by Zdenek Burian; reproduced with permission

Homo sapiens, hence its classification as a separate species. Parts of its skeleton are more robust, but it is otherwise comparable to that of modern humans. The brain is relatively small, though not so small as that of *Australopithecus* and *H. habilis*. Unlike *Homo sapiens* and *H. habilis*, later species of *Australopithecus* and *H. erectus* have thick skull bones and extraordinarily developed browridges. Some paleoanthropologists maintain that *H. erectus* has features not present in its presumed ancestors or in *Homo sapiens* and that Asian *H. erectus*, with a thick cranium and large adornments on the skull, could not have been on any direct evolutionary line to *Homo sapiens*, noting that early *Australopithecus* and *H. habilis* are more ancient but had skulls more like ours, with thin bones and only modest enhancements on the cranium. These scientists point instead to early African *H. erectus*, sometimes referred to as a distinct species named *H. ergaster*, as the more probable ancestral form. This species is considered to have evolved, perhaps through an intermediate step (*H. heidelbergensis*), in the direction of modern humans.

Such a reading of the fossil record may be incorrect. In fact, there is very little evidence about the variability of features such as cranial thickness and external embellishments of the skull among even one population of *H. erectus*, let alone among different populations dispersed through two or three large continents. Practically nothing is known about the climatic or ecological conditions under which cranial thickening occurred. Also unknown is the relationship between skull growth and the brain enlargement that is such a striking feature of hominin evolution. These and many other questions must be answered before *H. erectus* can be either confirmed or written off as an ancestor of *Homo sapiens*. In the meantime, all that can be said with any certainty is that *H. erectus*, in a broad geographic sense over the course of more than one million years, evolved from pre-*Homo erectus* (probably *H. habilis* or *H. rudolfensis*) to post-*Homo erectus*—that is, to *H. heidelbergensis* or perhaps directly to archaic *Homo sapiens*.

BEHAVIORAL INFERENCES

At Zhoukoudian the remains of *H. erectus* were found in cave and fissure deposits. Although this does not prove that these hominins were habitual cave dwellers, the additional evidence of associated remains—such as stone, charred animal bones, collections of seeds, and what could be ancient hearths and charcoal—all points to *H. erectus* as having spent periods of time in the grottoes of Zhoukoudian. On the other hand, the remains of Lantian, Trinil, Sangiran, and Mojokerto, as well as Tighenif, Olduvai, and Koobi Fora, were all found in open sites, sometimes in stream gravels and clays, sometimes in river sandstones, and sometimes in lake beds. These suggest that *H. erectus* also lived in open encampments along the banks of streams or on the shores of lakes and also that proximity to water was crucial to survival. These presumed campsites were revealed by excavation, and they contain abundant stone implements and stone chips that surely resulted from human manufacture. Fractured and partly burned bones of animals found at the sites indicate that *H. erectus* may have either hunted or scavenged meat.

There is little doubt that mastery of fire was an important factor in colonizing cooler regions. Indeed, this discovery may have sped the migrations of ancient humans into the chilly, often glaciated expanses of prehistoric Europe. Sooner or later humans started cooking their food, thus reducing the work demanded of their teeth. This in turn may have played an important part in minimizing the evolutionary advantage of big teeth, since cooked food needs far less cutting, tearing, and grinding than does raw food. This relaxation of the selective pressure favouring the survival of people with large, strong teeth may have led directly to a reduction in the size of the teeth—an important consideration given that this is one of the features distinguishing *Homo sapiens* from *H. erectus*.

Zhoukoudian has been cited as providing signs that humans had mastery of fire 400,000 years ago. Investigators reported ash and charcoal accumulations that resemble hearths, and it is possible that *H. erectus* used fire in the caves for warmth and for preparing food. However, more recent research shows that at least some of the "ash" is instead sediment probably deposited by water. Nevertheless, burned bones are present, and these relics may still speak to the ability of the Zhoukoudian inhabitants to roast meat.

Other signs of the culture of *H. erectus* are implements found in the same deposits as their bones. Chopping tools and flakes made from split pebbles characterize both the Zhoukoudian and Dmanisi deposits; both are members of a so-called Chopper chopping-tool family of industries. At Tighenif in northwestern Africa, *H. erectus* was found in association with totally different kinds of stone implements; these comprise double-edged hand axes and scrapers that have been characterized as representing what archaeologists call an early Acheulean industry. This is part of the great Acheulean hand-ax industrial complex, remnants of which are found widely spread over large parts of Europe and Africa. An Acheulean industry is known also from Olduvai Gorge, as is a local, more ancient form of stone chopper manufacture known as the Oldowan industry, but the exact cultural associations of these stone tools with African *H. erectus* (as exemplified by OH 9) are uncertain.

Hence, *H. erectus* has been found associated in some parts of the world with a Chopper chopping-tool tradition and in other places with an Acheulean double-edged hand-ax industrial complex. Numerous animal bones occur also with the remains of *H. erectus*, and sometimes these bones seem to have been deliberately broken or charred. From this evidence it is sometimes inferred that *H. erectus* was a hunter. The brain, body size, and manufactured equipment of *H. erectus* were so superior to those of *Australopithecus* and *H. habilis* that it is highly probable that food-collecting techniques, including hunting, were also better. Many scientists hold that *Australopithecus* and *H. habilis* were more scavengers than hunters, perhaps at best opportunists who seized their chance when a weak, young, sick, or aged animal crossed their paths. Indeed, many of the animal bones found in australopith deposits are of juvenile and old individuals. Although larger animal bones have been recovered from *H. habilis* deposits, these have exhibited tooth marks of nonhuman predators as well as cut marks. *H. erectus*, on the other hand, seems to have been a confirmed hunter whose prey included animals of all age groups.

It can credibly be supposed that, as with present-day hunters such as the African San (Bushmen) and the Australian Aboriginals, meat from the hunt formed only a part of the diet of *H. erectus*. Other juicy morsels may have been furnished by snakes, birds and their eggs, locusts, scorpions, centipedes, tortoises, mice and other rodents, hedgehogs, fish, and crustaceans. Even children could have caught many of these—as they still do in Africa's Kalahari Desert today, before being allowed to accompany the older men on the hunt. Vegetable food—such as fleshy leaves, fruits, nuts, roots, and tubers—also must have been important in the diet of *H. erectus*. Accumulations of hackberry seeds, for example, were found in the Zhoukoudian cave deposits. There seems to be little doubt that *H. erectus* was omnivorous, for such a diet is the most opportunistic of all, and modern humans are the most opportunistic of all living primates. *H. erectus* was probably one of the earliest of the great opportunists, and it is likely that this attribute endowed the species with adaptability and evolutionary flexibility.

Another question that may be asked about *H. erectus* culture is whether there is any evidence of ritual. There is no sign that they buried their dead: no complete burials have been found, nor have graves, grave goods, or red ochre (a mineral used as a paint by later forms of hominins), either on or around any bones. Cannibalism was once inferred from the Ngandong (Solo) and Zhoukoudian finds, but little credible evidence remains to support such a hypothesis.

RELATIONSHIP TO *Homo Sapiens*

Although *H. erectus* is widely regarded as a direct ancestor of later species, including *Homo sapiens*, a few researchers have opposed this view. Louis Leakey argued energetically that *H. erectus* populations, particularly in Africa, overlap in time with more advanced *Homo sapiens* and therefore cannot be ancestral to the latter. Some support for Leakey's point of view has come from analysis of anatomic characteristics exhibited by the fossils. By emphasizing a distinction between "primitive" and "derived" traits in the reconstruction of relationships between species, several paleontologists have attempted to show that *H. erectus* does not make a suitable morphological ancestor for *Homo sapiens*. Because the braincase is long, low, and thick-walled and presents a strong browridge, they claim that *H. erectus* shows derived (or specialized) characteristics not shared with more modern humans. At the same time, it is noted, *Homo sapiens* does share some features, including a rounded, lightly built cranium, with earlier hominins such as *H. habilis*. For these reasons, some paleontologists (including Leakey) consider the more slender, or "gracile," *H. habilis* and *H. rudolfensis* to be more closely related to *Homo sapiens* than is *H. erectus*. These findings are not widely accepted, however. Instead, studies of size in human evolution indicate that representatives of *Homo* can be grouped into a reasonable ancestor-to-descendant sequence showing increases in body size. Despite having a heavier, more flattened braincase, *H. erectus*, most particularly the African representatives of the species sometimes called *H. ergaster*, is not out of place in this sequence.

If this much is agreed, there is still uncertainty as to how and where *H. erectus* eventually gave rise to *Homo sapiens*. This is a major question in the study of human evolution and one that resists resolution even when hominin fossils from throughout the Old World are surveyed in detail. Several general hypotheses have been advanced, but there is still no firm consensus regarding models of gradual change as opposed to scenarios of rapid evolution in which change in one region is followed by migration of the new populations into other areas.

THEORIES OF GRADUAL CHANGE

A traditional view held by some paleontologists is that a species may be transformed gradually into a succeeding species. Such successive species in the evolutionary sequence are called chronospecies. The boundaries between chronospecies are almost impossible to determine by means of any objective anatomic or functional criteria; thus, all that is left is the guesswork of drawing a boundary at a moment in time. Such a chronological boundary may have to be drawn arbitrarily between the last survivors of *H. erectus* and the earliest members of a succeeding species (e.g., *Homo sapiens*). The problem of defining the limits of chronospecies is not peculiar to *H. erectus*; it is one of the most vexing questions in paleontology.

Such gradual change with continuity between successive forms has been postulated particularly for North Africa, where *H. erectus* at Tighenif is seen as ancestral to later populations at Rabat, Temara, Jebel Irhoud, and elsewhere. Gradualism has also been postulated for Southeast Asia, where *H. erectus* at Sangiran may have progressed toward populations such as those at Ngandong (Solo) and at Kow Swamp in Australia. Some researchers have suggested that similar developments could have occurred in other parts of the world.

The supposed interrelation of cultural achievement and the shape and size of teeth, jaws, and brain is a theorized state of affairs with which some paleoanthropologists disagree. Throughout the human fossil record there are examples of dissociation between skull shape and size on the one hand and cultural achievement on the other. For example, a smaller-brained *H. erectus* may have been among the first humans to tame fire, but much bigger-brained people in other regions of the world living later in time have left no evidence that they knew how to handle it. Gradualism is at the core of the so-called "multiregional" hypothesis, in which it is theorized that *H. erectus* evolved into *Homo sapiens* not once but several times as each subspecies of *H. erectus*, living in its own territory, passed some postulated critical threshold. This theory depends on accepting a supposed *erectus-sapiens* threshold as correct. It is opposed by supporters of the "out of Africa" hypothesis, who find the threshold concept at variance with the modern genetic theory of evolutionary change.

THEORIES OF PUNCTUATED CHANGE

A gradual transition from *H. erectus* to *Homo sapiens* is one interpretation of the fossil record, but the evidence also can be read differently. Many researchers have come to accept what can be termed a punctuated view of human evolution. This view suggests that species such as *H. erectus* may have exhibited little or no morphological change over long periods of time (evolutionary stasis) and that the transition from one species to a descendant form may have occurred relatively rapidly and in a restricted geographic area rather than on a worldwide basis. Whether any *Homo* species, including our own, evolved gradually or rapidly has not been settled.

The continuation of such arguments underlines the need for more fossils to establish the range of physical variation of *H. erectus* and also for more discoveries in good archaeological contexts to permit more precise dating. Additions to these two bodies of data may settle remaining questions and bring the problems surrounding the evolution of *H. erectus* nearer to resolution.

CHAPTER 9
RECENT HUMANS

Between 1 million years ago and the present, three species of humans—possibly as many as four species—have evolved. *Homo heidelbergensis* was the most primitive of this group. Chronologically, it evolved some 600,000 years ago, and it is thought to be the shared ancestor of Neanderthals (*H. neanderthalensis*) and modern humans (*H. sapiens*). Neanderthals emerged next, appearing between 200,000 and 100,000 years ago and disappearing sometime between 35,000 and 28,000 years ago. Modern humans, the only hominin not yet extinct, followed, emerging sometime less than 150,000 years ago.

HOMO HEIDELBERGENSIS

Homo heidelbergensis is an extinct species of archaic human (genus *Homo*) known from fossils dating from 600,000 to 300,000 years ago in Africa, Europe, and possibly Asia. The name first appeared in print in 1908 to accommodate an ancient human jaw discovered in 1907 near the town of Mauer, 16 km (10 miles) southeast of Heidelberg, Germany. Among the fossils found with the Heidelberg jaw were those of several extinct mammals that lived about 500,000 years ago.

The Heidelberg jaw, also called the Mauer jaw, lacks a chin and is exceptionally thick and broad. The teeth are surprisingly small for such a massive mandible. The jaw is also long, and this feature may imply that the individual had a projecting lower face. Among other examples of *H. heidelbergensis*, the best are specimens from Bodo (Ethiopia), Kabwe (Zambia), Ndutu (Tanzania), Petralona

(Greece), Arago (France), and possibly Dali (China). The craniums have massive browridges, long and low braincases, and thick vault bones like *H. erectus*. Their braincases are larger than what is typical for *H. erectus*, but the skulls lack the unique specializations that characterize the Neanderthals. The expanded brain necessitates the modern features seen in the skull, such as the more-rounded rear of the skull (occipital), expanded sides (parietals), and broadened forehead.

Until the 1990s it was common to place these specimens either in *H. erectus* or into a broad category along with Neanderthals that was often called archaic *H. sapiens*. A problem with the latter designation was the growing recognition that Neanderthals were unique to and relatively isolated in Europe and western Asia. It therefore became common to categorize the Neanderthals as a separate and morphologically well-defined species, *H. neanderthalensis*. At the same time, lumping specimens such as those found at Bodo and Petralona with modern *H. sapiens* would have created an unreasonably heterogeneous species, since modern *H. sapiens* is remarkably homogeneous in morphology and behaviour and differs strongly from archaic *Homo* species. Designating the Bodo and Petralona specimens as *H. heidelbergensis* emphasizes the uniqueness of modern *H. sapiens*, Neanderthals, and *H. erectus*. Using this taxonomy, it appears to many researchers that *H. heidelbergensis* is the common ancestor of both Neanderthals and modern man, with the transition from *H. heidelbergensis* to *H. sapiens* having occurred in Africa between 300,000 and 200,000 years ago.

NEANDERTHALS

The Neanderthal is the most recent species of archaic humans. Neanderthals emerged between 200,000 and

ATAPUERCA

Atapuerca is a complex of several limestone caves near Burgos in northern Spain. It is known for the abundant human (genus *Homo*) remains discovered there beginning in 1976. The site called Sima del Elefante ("Pit of the Elephant") contains the earliest evidence of humans in western Europe—fragments of a jawbone and teeth date to 1.1–1.2 million years ago. The nearby site of Gran Dolina contains human remains dating to about 800,000 years ago and some of the earliest tools found in western Europe.

Paleoanthropologists who first described the fossils attributed them to a new species, *H. antecessor*, which they proposed as the ancestor of modern humans (*H. sapiens*) owing to certain distinctly modern facial features. Other researchers, however, hesitate to accept this assertion and group the fossils with similar remains classified as *H. heidelbergensis*. One of the most astonishing discoveries at Atapuerca is a cave called Sima de los Huesos ("Pit of the Bones"), where more than 1,600 human fossils, including several nearly complete skulls, have been found. The age of this material is at least 300,000 years and may be as old as 600,000 years. Brain sizes are within the range of both Neanderthals (*H. neanderthalensis*) and modern humans. The skeletons possess several traits unique to Neanderthals, including a projecting midface, long and narrow pubic bones, and thick finger bones. Unlike later Neanderthals, however, they do not fully express the characteristic Neanderthal form.

Atapuerca was designated a UNESCO World Heritage site in 2000.

100,000 years ago and were replaced by early modern humans between 35,000 and 28,000 years ago. They inhabited Eurasia from the Atlantic regions of Europe eastward to Central Asia and from as far north as present-day Belgium southward to the Mediterranean and southwest Asia. Similar human populations lived at the same time in eastern Asia and Africa. Because Neanderthals lived in a land of abundant limestone caves, which preserve bones well and where there has been a long history of prehistoric research, they are better known than any other archaic

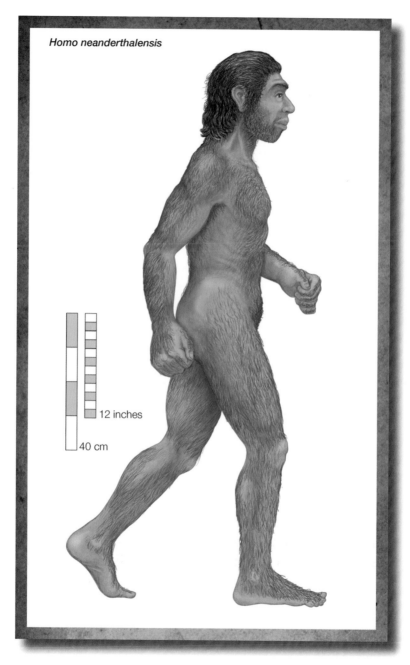

Homo neanderthalensis

12 inches

40 cm

Artist's rendering of Homo neanderthalensis, *who ranged from western Europe to Central Asia for some 100,000 years before dying out approximately 30,000 years ago.* Encyclopædia Britannica, Inc.

human group. Consequently, they have become the archetypal "cavemen." The name Neanderthal (or Neandertal) derives from the Neander Valley near Düsseldorf, Germany, where quarrymen unearthed portions of a human skeleton from a cave in 1856.

THE FOSSIL EVIDENCE

The remains from the Neander Valley consist of 16 pieces, which were scientifically described shortly after their discovery. Immediately there was disagreement as to whether the bones represented an archaic and extinct human form or an abnormal modern human. The former view was shown to be correct in 1886, when two Neanderthal skeletons associated with Middle Paleolithic stone tools and bones of extinct animals were discovered in a cave at Spy, Belgium.

From shortly after the Spy discovery to about 1910, a series of Neanderthal skeletons were discovered in western and central Europe. Using those skeletons as a basis, scholars reconstructed the Neanderthals as semihuman, lacking a full upright posture and being somewhat less intelligent than modern humans. According to that view, the Neanderthals were intermediate between modern humans and the apes, as no older human forms were then generally recognized. They were also considered to be too different from modern humans to be their ancestors. Only after World War II were the errors in this perception of Neanderthals recognized, and the Neanderthals have since come to be viewed as quite close evolutionarily to modern humans. This view has been reflected in the frequent inclusion of the Neanderthals within the species *Homo sapiens*, usually as a distinct subspecies, *H. sapiens neanderthalensis*; more recently they have often been classified as a different but closely related species, *H. neanderthalensis*. Neanderthal skeletons have been found in caves and shelters across Europe, in southwest Asia, and eastward to Uzbekistan in Central Asia, providing abundant skeletal remains and associated archaeological material for understanding these prehistoric humans. The Neanderthals are now known from several hundred individuals, represented by remains varying from isolated teeth to virtually complete skeletons.

NEANDERTHAL ORIGINS AND ANATOMY

The fossil evidence for the few hundred thousand years leading up to the time of the Neanderthals shows a gradual decrease in the size and frequency of anatomic characteristics of *H. erectus* and an increase in features more representative of Neanderthals. A gradual emergence of the Neanderthals from earlier regional populations of archaic humans can be inferred, probably across their entire geographic range. The changes between Neanderthal ancestors and the Neanderthals themselves highlight their characteristics. Brain size gradually increased to reach modern human volumes relative to body mass, although Neanderthal brains and braincases tended to be somewhat longer and lower than those of modern humans. Neanderthal faces remained large and especially long, similar to those of their ancestors, and they retained browridges and a projecting dentition and nose and had a receding chin. Their chewing teeth (premolars and molars)

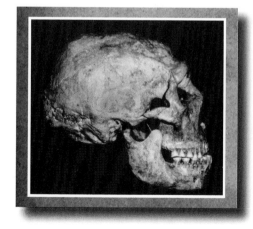

The Shanidar 1 Neanderthal skull found at Shanidar Cave, northern Iraq. © Erik Trinkaus

were small like those of early modern humans, and their chewing muscles and cheek regions had shrunk accordingly. Their incisor and canine teeth, however, remained large, like those of their ancestors, indicating their continued use as a vise or third hand.

LA CHAPELLE-AUX-SAINTS

La Chapelle-aux-Saints is a cave site near the village of La Chapelle-aux-Saints in central France where the bones of an adult Neanderthal male were found in 1908. Studies of the remains published in 1911–13 by French anthropologist Marcellin Boule became the classic early 20th-century description of Neanderthals as apelike and evolutionarily divergent from modern humans. Despite decades of subsequent research that has revised and rejected this semihuman depiction, Boule's description still lingers as the popular image of the Neanderthals.

The well-preserved skull and less-complete trunk and limb bones exhibit a suite of characteristics in common with other Neanderthals: stocky, cold-adapted body proportions; a skull with a large and projecting midface (especially the teeth and nose), a rounded browridge, and a large but long, low, and rounded braincase; and stout limb bones with strongly marked attachments for the arm and hand muscles.

The La Chapelle-aux-Saints skeleton shows evidence that Neanderthals led stressful lives with high risk of injury and that they experienced considerable bodily degeneration from daily activities. Such evidence includes the loss of most of the cheek teeth and associated degeneration of the jaw joint; inflammation of the ear canals, indicating a possible loss of hearing; serious osteoarthritis of one shoulder; massive osteoarthritic degeneration of the neck vertebrae; a damaged hip joint; and a healed rib fracture. Though this individual died in his 30s, he survived for years with these degenerative conditions and injuries. The skeleton therefore demonstrates not only that Neanderthals had the physical strength partly to compensate for limitations in their technology but also that they had a social network that enabled long-term survival of injured and infirm members of the group. The skeleton also provided the first evidence of mortuary ritual among the Neanderthals, as the body was intentionally buried in a pit in the middle of the small cave.

The bodies of the Neanderthals changed little from those of their ancestors. They retained broad shoulders, extremely muscular upper limbs, large chests, strong and fatigue-resistant legs, and broad, strong feet. There is nothing in their limb anatomies to indicate less dexterity than modern humans or any inability to walk efficiently. The details of their hand bones, however, do suggest greater emphasis on power rather than precision grips. All of these features appear to have been maintained from their ancestors.

The Neanderthals differed in facial appearance from other archaic humans of East Asia and Africa, primarily in their retention of large incisors and canines, large noses, and long faces to support those teeth. In all archaic populations, facial massiveness and the size of premolars and molars were diminishing.

THE FATE OF THE NEANDERTHALS

The evolutionary fate of the Neanderthals is closely related to the origins of modern humans. Over the years, the Neanderthals have been portrayed as everything from an evolutionary dead end to the direct ancestors of modern European and western Asian populations. Fossil evidence indicates that modern humans first evolved in sub-Saharan Africa sometime prior to 100,000 years ago. Subsequently they spread northward after 40,000 years ago, displacing or absorbing local archaic human populations. As a result, the southwest Asian, Central Asian, and central European Neanderthals were absorbed to varying degrees into those spreading modern human populations and contributed genetically to the subsequent early modern human populations of those regions. Even in western Europe—a cul-de-sac where the transition to modern humans took place relatively late—there is fossil evidence for interbreeding between late Neanderthal and early modern humans.

The anatomic changes between the Neanderthals and early modern humans involved largely a loss of the sturdiness characteristic of all archaic humans. Upper limbs became more gracile, although they were still very muscular by the standards of today's humans. The hand anatomy shifted to emphasize precision grips. Leg strength remained high, reflecting the mobility that characterized all Pleistocene hunting-and-gathering human populations. Front teeth became smaller and faces shortened, producing full chins and brows without ridges. Braincases became more elevated and rounded but not larger. Tool use and culture became more elaborate, but there are no anatomic features directly indicating that Neanderthals were smarter or less smart than other humans living at the time.

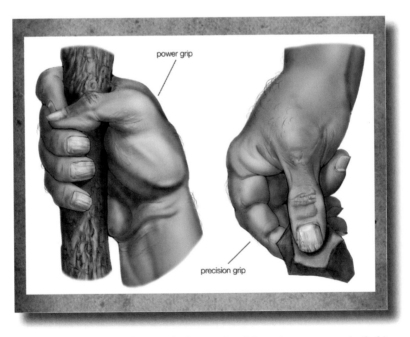

A fully opposable thumb gives the human hand its unique power grip (left) *and precision grip* (right). Encyclopædia Britannica, Inc.

NEANDERTHAL BEHAVIOUR

The behavioral patterns of the Neanderthals can be inferred from their anatomy in combination with their archaeological record. From their fossil remains and the debris they left behind at hundreds of sites they created— in cave entrances, rock shelters, and the open air—an accurate view of their way of life can be put together.

The Neanderthals appear to have lived in relatively small groups, moving frequently on the landscape but reusing the same locations often. This is indicated by the small sizes of their sites and by the considerable depth of debris at a number of sites. The materials left behind show only minor variations among sites, suggesting that there was little planned differential use of the landscape—one site seemed to serve as well as another for most purposes.

Most of their early tool kits are described as those of a Paleolithic technological complex called the Mousterian industry (or Middle Paleolithic industry). They include carefully made chipped stone tools or broad flakes and simple spears made of wood. Although much of their stone technology was simple and crude, they occasionally made high-quality stone tools by first preparing the block of raw material so as to strike off symmetrical and relatively uniform stone flakes. They rarely used bone as a raw material, despite its abundance at their sites as kitchen debris, and few of their tools were hafted. The predominance of handheld thick stone flakes in their tool kits is associated with the strength of their arms and hands; such tools would have required great strength to perform the same tasks that modern humans accomplish with mechanically more-efficient implements and with less strength. It also fits with their tendency to use their front teeth as a vise, augmenting their hands and tools.

This pattern changes after about 40,000 years ago, when Neanderthals in Europe began making a variety of more-advanced (Upper Paleolithic) tools from bone and stone that were frequently hafted. They also made personal ornaments. Although such sophistication is a late phenomenon for this group of archaic humans, it nonetheless shows clearly that they were fully capable of complex technological and social behaviours. This is all the more important as the earliest modern humans in southwest Asia left behind an archaeological record that is essentially indistinguishable from that of the Neanderthals.

Information about the Neanderthal diet consists mostly of the animal bones that they left behind, but there is rare evidence that they ate nuts, tubers, and other plant foods when available. The animal bones they abandoned indicate that they were able to hunt small and moderately large animals (goats, horses, and cattle) but were able to eat larger animals (e.g., rhinoceroses and mammoths) only by scavenging from natural deaths. The bone chemistry of European Neanderthals indicates that they were highly carnivorous and therefore must have been reasonably effective hunters. The animals exploited for food closely reflect what was available in the surrounding countryside. Consumption of fish, birds, or shellfish appears to have been rare. There is simply no evidence for any systematic harvesting of wild plant or animal resources—a characteristic of modern hunter-gatherers in similar environments.

Neanderthals were the first human group to survive in northern latitudes during the cold (glacial) phases of the Pleistocene. They had domesticated fire, as evidenced by concentrations of charcoal and reddened earth found at their sites. Their hearths were simple and shallow, however, and must have cooled off quickly, providing little warmth through the night. Not surprisingly, Neanderthals exhibited anatomic adaptations to cold conditions, especially in Europe. Such features included large torsos and relatively short limbs, both of which maximized heat production and minimized heat loss.

The Neanderthals exhibited some uniquely modern features despite their archaic anatomy and their less-efficient foraging systems (as compared with those of modern human hunter-gatherers). They were the first humans to bury their dead intentionally, usually in simple graves. This indicates social systems sufficiently elaborate to make some kind of formal disposal of the dead desirable. They also occasionally created simple forms of personal decoration such as pierced pendants. Creation of artistic objects became well-developed among late Neanderthals associated with early Upper Paleolithic technologies.

The difficult existence of the Neanderthals is reflected in their high frequency of traumatic injury. The remains of all older individuals show signs of serious wounds, sprains, or breaks. There are abundant signs of nutritional deprivation during growth, more than 75 percent of individuals showing evidence of growth defects in their teeth. Life expectancy was low; few Neanderthals lived past 40 years of age, and almost none lived past 50. Still, they were able to keep severely injured individuals alive, in some cases for decades. This again reflects a more advanced social organization.

The overall image of the Neanderthals, therefore, is one of archaic humans who shared a number of important characteristics with modern humans, including their large brains, manual dexterity and walking ability, and social sophistication. Like their archaic predecessors, however, their foraging systems were considerably less efficient than those of modern human hunter-gatherers, necessitating more-muscular limbs, greater endurance, and large front teeth. It was only with the emergence of modern humans that these archaic features disappeared, being superseded by more elaborate cultural behaviours and technologies.

HOMO FLORESIENSIS

Homo floresiensis is the taxonomic name given to an extinct hominin that is presumed to have lived on the Indonesian island of Flores as recently as 18,000 years ago, well within the time range of modern humans (*Homo sapiens*).

Skeletal remains of an adult female and other individuals were found at the Liang Bua cave on Flores in 2004 by a team of Australian and Indonesian anthropologists. An initial analysis of the remains indicated that *H. floresiensis* stood only some 100 cm (40 inches) tall and had long arms and a skull with a cranial capacity of a mere 380 cc, comparable to that of a modern chimpanzee; yet the delicate skeletal bones, nonprojecting face, and reduced dentition placed them squarely within the human family. On the basis of these findings, the hominin's discoverers classified it as a distinct species of genus *Homo* and theorized that it may have descended from *H. erectus*, a much older and larger hominin that may also be the ancestor of modern humans.

They further hypothesized that the diminutive size of *H. floresiensis* may have been caused by island dwarfing, or endemic dwarfing, a process whereby some creatures confined to isolated habitats such as islands are known to have become smaller over time. Such dwarfing has never been seen in the remains of other members of the human family, which show that stature and brain size have generally increased from the earliest hominins up to modern humans.

Public curiosity about the new species abounded, and, in homage to a short-statured race in J.R.R. Tolkien's novels, it was soon dubbed "hobbit-like." However, the initial analysis of the find and the dwarfing hypothesis were immediately challenged by the scholarly community. Some subsequent examinations of the remains contradicted the original conclusions, suggesting instead that they represent a population of modern humans that was quite gracile (slender) but of normal height. In contrast, other investigations, which compared the specimen's gait, foot size, and skull size to that of modern humans, suggested that the remains belong to a new species, perhaps one that descended from an ancestor more primitive than *H. erectus*.

HOMO SAPIENS

Homo sapiens (Latin: "wise man") is the species to which all modern human beings belong. *Homo sapiens* is one of several species grouped into the genus *Homo*, but it is the only one that is not extinct.

The name *Homo sapiens* was applied in 1758 by the father of modern biological classification, Carolus Linnaeus. It had long been known that human beings physically resemble the primates more closely than any other known living organisms, but at the time it was a daring act to classify human beings within the same framework used for the rest of nature. Linnaeus, concerned exclusively with similarities in bodily structure, faced only the problem of distinguishing *Homo sapiens* from apes (gorillas, chimpanzees, orangutans, and gibbons), which differ from humans in numerous bodily as well as cognitive features. (Charles Darwin's treatise on evolution, *On the Origin of Species*, would come 101 years later.)

Since Linnaeus's time, a large fossil record has been discovered. This record contains numerous extinct species that are much more closely related to humans than to today's apes and that were presumably more similar to us behaviorally as well. Following our ancestors into the distant past raises the question of what is meant by the word *human*. *Homo sapiens* is human by definition, whereas apes are not. But what of the extinct members of the human tribe (Hominini), who were clearly not us but were nonetheless very much like us? There is no definitive answer to this question. Although human evolution can be said to involve all those species more closely related to us than to the apes, the adjective *human* is usually applied only to ourselves and other members of our genus, *Homo* (e.g., *H. erectus*, *H. habilis*). Behaviorally, only *Homo sapiens* can be

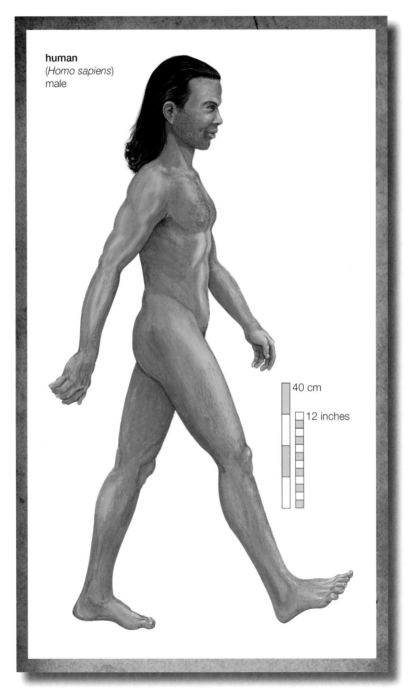

human
(*Homo sapiens*)
male

40 cm

12 inches

Human being (Homo sapiens), *male.* Encyclopædia Britannica, Inc.

said to be "fully human," but even the definition of *Homo sapiens* is a matter of active debate. Some paleoanthropologists extend the span of this species far back into time to include many anatomically distinctive fossils that others prefer to allocate to several different extinct species. In contrast, a majority of paleoanthropologists, wishing to bring the study of hominins into line with that of other mammals, prefer to assign to *Homo sapiens* only those fossil forms that fall within the anatomic spectrum of the species as it exists today. In this sense, *Homo sapiens* is very recent, probably originating less than 150,000 years ago.

BEHAVIORAL INFLUENCES

The story of hominin evolution is one of increasing behavioral complexity, but, because behaviour does not leave direct fossil evidence, clues must be sought in other sources. The most obvious candidates are in the archaeological record, which begins with the appearance of Paleolithic (Old Stone Age) tools about 2.5 million years ago. These early tools were simple indeed: stone flakes a few centimetres long that were chipped off of one small cobble by a blow from another. But, for all their simplicity, they marked a major advance in lifestyle: for the first time, the carcasses of dead animals could be dismembered quickly, and favoured parts could be taken for consumption to safer places, where blows from hammerstones allowed the extraction of nutritious marrow from bones. These tools also signify a cognitive advance in hominins; even with intensive training, no ape has yet mastered the notion of hitting one rock with another at precisely the angle needed to detach a sharp flake. Furthermore, the early toolmakers had the ability to anticipate their needs, since they often carried suitable rocks long distances before making them into tools.

The history of stone toolmaking ushers in a pattern seen throughout the paleoanthropological record until the emergence of behaviorally modern *Homo sapiens*: in general, technological innovations have been sporadic and rare. Moreover, behavioral novelties have tended not to coincide with the appearance of new species. For almost a million years following the introduction of stone tools, the methods used for making them remained largely unchanged. It is only at about 1.6 million years ago, in Africa (well after the appearance of *Homo ergaster*), that a larger type of tool is introduced: the hand ax. Shaped carefully on both sides to a standard and symmetrical form, it was usually teardrop- or egg-shaped. It is the characteristic tool of the Acheulean industry. Although the notion has been contested, it does seem fairly clear that these implements bear witness to another cognitive advance: the existence in the toolmaker's mind of a standard "mental template" to which the tools were made. Hand axes were manufactured in Africa by the thousands—sometimes at apparent workshops—until quite recent times. Stone tools of this kind have always been rare in eastern Asia. It is only at about 300,000 years ago that another major technological (and possibly cognitive) advance is found. This is the "prepared-core" tool, whereby a stone core was elaborately shaped until a single blow, perhaps with a hammer made of a "soft" material such as bone, would detach a virtually finished tool with a continuous cutting surface around its periphery. The great masters of this technique were the Neanderthals, whose possession of language has long been debated. Regardless, it has been demonstrated (in studies with people) that language is not required for the transmission of the skills needed to make tools of this kind.

The stone tool record is well-preserved, but it is only an indirect reflection of overall lifestyle and cognitive capacities. It is still unknown, for example, whether the earliest tool users hunted extensively or merely scavenged animal remains. It is likely that, if they hunted, it was for small prey. Nonetheless, metabolic studies of bone suggest that some *Australopithecus* may have eaten substantially more meat than chimpanzees do today.

Most authorities had guessed that efficient ambush-hunting was an invention of *Homo sapiens*, but 400,000-year-old wooden throwing spears found in 1995 at Schöningen, Germany, may suggest otherwise. Unlike thrusting spears, which must be used at close range and with considerable risk, these 2-metre (6.6-foot) javelin-like weapons have their weight concentrated at the front and therefore could have been hurled from a safe distance. The age of the location at which these spears were found puts them within the period of *H. heidelbergensis*.

Also at 400,000 years ago, there is the first convincing evidence of two other innovations: the domestication of fire in hearths and the construction of artificial shelters. At Terra Amata in southern France, traces of large huts have been found. The huts were formed by embedding saplings into the ground in an oval and then bringing their tops together at the centre. Stones placed in a ring around the hut braced the saplings. Some of these huts were found to contain hearths scooped in the ground and lined with burned stones and blackened bones. These sites represent some of the earliest definitive proof of fires deliberately maintained and used for cooking, although 700,000-year-old hearths are reported from a site in Israel. (Reports of most earlier fire domestication have been contested on various grounds.)

Prior to the advent of *Homo sapiens*, archaeological sites are generally random scatterings of detritus of various types — mostly butchery sites and sites where groups lived at later times. In the dwelling places of behaviorally modern early *Homo sapiens*, on the other hand, there is a definite pattern in the use of space: toolmaking was done in one place, cooking in another, sleeping elsewhere. The earliest intimations of such partitioning are found at the South African site of Klasies River Mouth, dating to more than 100,000 years ago. This pattern is also typical of sites left behind by the earliest European *Homo sapiens*, who colonized that continent many tens of thousands of years later. Also found at African sites are the first suggestions of symbolism and the complex behaviours that characterize *Homo sapiens* worldwide today—behaviours that were effectively absent from the repertoires of their predecessors. At Blombos Cave, near Africa's southern tip, was found an ochre plaque more than 70,000 years old that is engraved with an unmistakably geometric motif. This and other early African sites have produced engraved ostrich eggshells and snail shells pierced for stringing and bodily adornment; these date from 70,000 to 50,000 years ago. It is also in Africa that the earliest evidence appears for such modern behaviours as long-distance trade and the mining of flint for artifact production.

The most striking evidence for a distinct cognitive contrast between modern humans and all their predecessors, however, comes from Europe. *Homo sapiens* came late to this continent, entering about 40,000 years ago, and brought a new kind of stone tool based on striking long, thin "blades" from a carefully prepared long core. These Aurignacian tools were accompanied by a kit of implements that for the

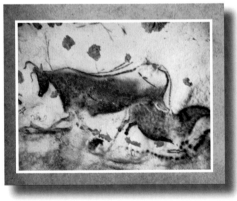

Cave painting of a bull and a horse; in Lascaux Grotto, near Montignac, France. Hans Hinz, Basel

first time were made out of materials such as bone and antler and that were treated with exquisite sensitivity to their particular properties. In short order these Europeans, the so-called Cro-Magnons, left a dazzling variety of symbolic works of prehistoric art. The earliest known sculptures— delicate small carvings in ivory and bone—are about 34,000 years old. From about the same time come the earliest musical instruments, bone flutes with complex sound capabilities. Also from this time come the first known notations. These markings were made on bone plaques, one of which has been interpreted as a lunar calendar. By 30,000 years ago the Cro-Magnons were already creating spectacular animal paintings deep in caves, most of which are accompanied by numerous geometric symbols.

Domestic items were regularly decorated and engraved by the Cro-Magnons. Burials, already practiced by the Neanderthals in a simple form, became complex, and graves were often crammed with goods that were likely thought to be useful to the deceased in an afterlife. Clay figurines were soon baked in primitive but remarkably effective kilns, and by about 27,000 years ago delicate eyed needles made of bone heralded the advent of couture. It is hard to ask for better proof that the Cro-Magnons were modern *Homo sapiens* cognitively equipped with all the intellectual faculties of today's people. Nobody would dispute, for example, that the Cro-Magnons had language; such a claim is highly arguable in earlier Stone Age *Homo sapiens* and Neanderthals.

The Cro-Magnons contrasted strikingly with the Neanderthals, the hominins they had found already living in Europe upon their arrival and whom they replaced entirely over the next 10,000 to 12,000 years. While symbolic behaviours are typical of all groups of living humans, not all such groups have left behind symbolic records as dramatic as those of the Cro-Magnons. Nonetheless, there is no doubt that the Cro-Magnons and the Neanderthals perceived and interacted with the world in entirely different ways. The Cro-Magnons were people with whom we could relate on our own terms; as such, *Homo sapiens* is not simply an incremental improvement on previous hominins. As the archaeological record eloquently indicates, our species is an entirely unprecedented phenomenon.

Exactly when and where this new phenomenon initially occurred is problematic, but again the earliest evidence for the new behavioral pattern comes from Africa, and, as is discussed in the section below, the earliest anatomic intimations for the origin of *Homo sapiens* also come from that continent. However, anatomic and cognitive "modernities" do not seem to have developed hand in hand; evidently there was a time lag between the establishment of modern anatomy (which appears to have come first) and modern behavioral patterns. While perhaps counterintuitive, this observation actually makes sense. Any innovation must take place within a species, since there is no place else it can do so. Natural selection is, moreover, not a creative force. It merely works on variations that come into existence spontaneously—it cannot call innovations into existence just because they might be advantageous. Any new structure or aptitude has to be in place before it can be exploited by its possessors, and it may take some time for those possessors to discover all the uses of such novelties. Such seems to have been the case for *Homo sapiens* in that the earliest well-documented members of our species appear to have behaved in broadly the same manner as Neanderthals for many tens of thousands of years. It is highly unlikely that another species anatomically indistinguishable from *Homo sapiens* but behaviorally similar to Neanderthals was supplanted worldwide in an extremely short span of time. Therefore, it seems appropriate to conclude that a latent capacity for symbolic reasoning was present when anatomically modern *Homo sapiens* emerged and that our forebears discovered their radically new behavioral abilities somewhat later in time.

A cultural "release mechanism" of some sort was necessarily involved in this discovery, and the favoured candidate for this role is language, the existence of which cannot be inferred with any degree of confidence from the records left behind by any other species but our own. Language is the ultimate symbolic activity, involving the creation and manipulation of mental symbols and permitting the posing of questions such as "What if?" Not all components of human thought are symbolic (the human brain has a very long accretionary, evolutionary history that still governs the way thoughts and feelings are processed), but it is certainly the addition of symbolic manipulations to intuitive processes that makes possible what is recognized as the human mind.

The origins of this mind are obscure indeed, especially as scientists are still ignorant of how a mass of electrochemical signals in the brain gives rise to what we experience as consciousness. But the invention of language would plausibly have released the earliest of the cultural and technological innovations that symbolic thought makes possible—in the process unleashing a cascade of discoveries that is still ongoing. One of the most striking features of the archaeological record that accompanies the arrival of behaviorally modern *Homo sapiens* is a distinct alteration in the tempo of innovation and change. Significant cultural and technological novelties had previously been rare, with long periods of apparent stability intervening between relatively sudden episodes of innovation. But once behaviorally modern *Homo sapiens* arrived on the scene, different local technological traditions—and, by extension, other forms of cultural diversity—began to proliferate regularly, setting a pace that is still gathering today.

BODILY STRUCTURE

As intimated above, the physical definition of *Homo sapiens* is bedeviled by a basic divergence of views among paleoanthropologists. One school of thought derives its philosophy from the "single-species hypothesis" popular in the 1960s. This hypothesis held that two kinds of culture-bearing hominins could not, on principle, exist at any one time and that, as a result, all hominin fossils had necessarily to be accommodated within a single evolving lineage. By the mid-1970s, however, a rapidly expanding fossil record had begun to reveal a variety of extinct hominins that simply could not be contained within this linear construct. The proponents of the single-species hypothesis thus began to shift to the notion that *Homo sapiens* is in fact an enormously variable species with roots extending far back in time to the era of *H. habilis*, some 2 million years ago. All subsequent hominins (including *H. erectus*, *H. neanderthalensis*, etc.) are in this view classifiable within *Homo sapiens*. The tremendous anatomic variety among the populations that would compose this single species are then credited to separate evolutionary and adaptive histories in different parts of the Old World. Meanwhile, the reproductive integrity of this huge and diversifying species would have been maintained over time by interbreeding between local populations in the peripheral areas where they would have come into contact. According to those who support such regional continuity, modern variants of humankind would have resulted from long quasi-separate evolutionary histories. In this so-called "multiregional" scenario, Australian Aboriginals are derived from Java man (i.e., Javanese *H. erectus*), modern Chinese from Peking man (Chinese *H. erectus*), today's Europeans from the Neanderthals (*H. neanderthalensis*) with some admixture from Cro-Magnons, and so on.

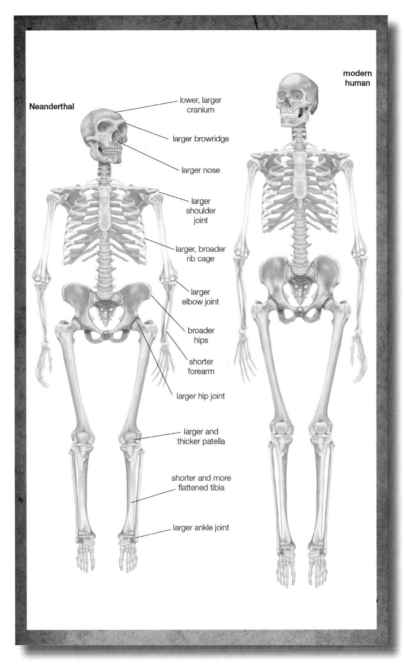

Skeleton of a Neanderthal (Homo neanderthalensis) *compared with a skeleton of a modern human* (Homo sapiens). Encyclopædia Britannica, Inc.

This formulation, which places the roots of today's geographically distinctive groups of *Homo sapiens* extremely deep in time, does not accord well with how the evolutionary process is known to work. Anatomic innovations can become fixed only within small, effectively isolated populations; large populations simply have too much genetic inertia for changes to occur throughout the species. This multiregional notion, moreover, implies an evolutionary pattern that is at variance with that of all other successful mammalian groups, not to mention the diversity that is already recognized among the very early hominins. Taxonomically, it also stretches the morphological notion of species beyond its limits.

The alternative model, called the "out of Africa"—or, more cautiously, the "single-origin"—theory of human emergence, sees the anatomic diversity of the hominin fossil record as representing a substantial diversity of species. In its bony structure, *Homo sapiens* is quite distinctive, boasting a relatively lightly built skeleton distinguished in many anatomic details from its closest relatives. In the cranium a high, rounded, and quite thin-boned braincase overhangs a greatly reduced face that is not expanded by large air sinuses. This face is topped by small or only modestly pronounced browridges that are uniquely divided into distinct central and lateral halves. In the lower jaw, the chin is not simply a swelling in the midline of the mandible (as can be found in certain other hominins) but a complex and distinctive structure that does not exist in other members of the human tribe. This list could continue with many other features.

If we define ourselves in terms of a suite of anatomic characteristics, few representatives of *Homo sapiens* appear in the fossil record until comparatively recent times. Indeed, the first intimations of our distinctively modern anatomy come from southern and eastern Africa only in the period between about 160 and 100 thousand years ago. Unfortunately, most of the fossils concerned (from such sites as Klasies River Mouth, Border Cave, and Omo) are fragmentary, or their dates are questionable. Still, the unmistakable signal they send is that *Homo sapiens*, in the sense of a creature that looked just like us in its essential bony attributes, did not exist in Africa before about 160,000 years ago.

This conclusion of the single-origin hypothesis matches the one reached by molecular geneticists who analyze the distributions of different types of mitochondrial DNA (mtDNA) in the cells of living human populations. This form of DNA consists of a tiny ring of hereditary material that actually lies outside the nucleus of the cell and is passed solely through the maternal line. It is not recombined between generations, as is nuclear DNA, and it seems to accumulate changes quite rapidly, which makes it ideal for analysis of recent evolutionary events. Comparisons of mtDNA samples derived from people all over the world point to the common descent of all modern humans from a small population that existed about 150,000 years ago. In addition, the African samples show more variability in their mtDNA than do those of other continents, suggesting that African populations have been diversifying longer. Finally, the mtDNA types of native Asians and Europeans are subsets of the African mtDNA types, again suggesting that other populations of modern humans ultimately derived from an African one. For all these reasons, it appears that we originated as an anatomically distinctive species quite recently and probably somewhere in the continent of Africa.

The distinctiveness of *Homo sapiens* has also been emphasized by a remarkable technological achievement in molecular genetics: the extraction of small stretches of undegraded mtDNA from Neanderthal samples. The few Neanderthal mtDNA sequences obtained so far lie entirely outside the envelope of variation offered by modern human samples from all over the world. Indeed, they are different enough to suggest that the lineages leading to *H. neanderthalensis* on the one hand and to *Homo sapiens* on the other split approximately 500,000 years ago. This observation supports a scenario whereby a European diversification of hominins culminating in the Neanderthals was descended from a population of *H. heidelbergensis* that had exited Africa. Similarly, East Asian hominins such as *H. erectus* were descended from an earlier wave of African émigrés (perhaps *H. ergaster* or a related species) that had spilled forth more than a million years earlier. Later, between about 100,000 and 50,000 years ago, a final exodus of *Homo sapiens* (or successive waves of such emigrations) ultimately led to the replacement of those indigenous (albeit ultimately African-derived) Asians and Europeans. There is ample evidence from Europe that the previously successful Neanderthals succumbed quite rapidly to the arrival of the Cro-Magnons, and new dates of about 40,000 years ago for late-surviving *H. erectus* in Java suggest that invading *Homo sapiens* may have accomplished a similar feat of replacement in Indonesia about the same time.

One of the best-preserved early fossils that bears all the anatomic hallmarks of *Homo sapiens* is a skull dated to about 92,000 years ago from the Israeli site of Jebel Qafzeh. This part of the Middle East, called the Levant, is often regarded as a biogeographic extension of Africa, so perhaps the discovery of this fossil in this particular location is not surprising. The specimen is a fractured but quite complete example of an individual whose skeleton is typically *Homo sapiens* but whose cultural context is Mousterian—the name also given to the stone tool industry of the Neanderthals. Indeed, all hominin fossils known from the Levant in the period between about 100,000 years ago and 50,000 to 40,000 years ago are associated with Mousterian tool kits, whether they belonged to *H. neanderthalensis* or *Homo sapiens*. Apparently, these two physically distinctive hominin species managed to conduct a long coexistence in the limited confines of the Levant for upward of 50 millennia—about five times as long as it took the Cro-Magnons to eliminate the Neanderthals from the vast area of Europe. Exactly how the two forms managed this is unknown, but one suggestion involves a kind of time-sharing, for the sparse record contains no definite evidence of temporal coexistence. If the Neanderthals evolved in comparatively frigid Europe, it is possible that they were "cold-adapted," as their rather stocky frames might suggest. Perhaps early *Homo sapiens*, having originated in Africa, was "heat-adapted." It is thus possible that the Neanderthals withdrew from the Levant in warmer times while the *Homo sapiens* population advanced northward. In colder times, on the other hand, the reverse might have occurred. Whatever the case, what seems most significant is that once blade-based tools, similar though not identical to those later used by the Cro-Magnons, were introduced in the Levant around 45,000 years ago, the Neanderthals rapidly disappeared. This is not absolutely conclusive evidence, but it does appear that when the Levantine *Homo sapiens* had devised a technology that in at least one way is associated with modern humans, there is no longer evidence of coexistence.

The fact that modern anatomy and modern behaviour were not established at the same time is not entirely surprising, but it does complicate attempts to define *Homo sapiens*. We tend to pride ourselves on our unique cognitive qualities rather than anatomic minutiae. Yet, biologically speaking, we are most sensibly defined by physical appearance. This is especially true if our cognitive potential was born with the genetic changes that determined our distinctive modern anatomy rather than later, when our unusual cognitive capacity finally began to be expressed. Our earliest anatomically modern ancestors may have behaved in their day very much like Neanderthals, but would one of them, transplanted as a child to a modern society, develop cognitively into a recognizably modern adult—as almost certainly no Neanderthal would have been able to do? Probably so, but the answer to this question can never be known with certainty.

MODERN POPULATIONS

Homo sapiens is now crammed into virtually every habitable region of Earth, yet our species still bears the hallmarks of its origin as a tiny population inhabiting one small corner of the world. The variation in DNA among all the widespread human populations of today is less than what is found in any population of living apes. This is very surprising, given that there are so few apes in such small geographic areas—conditions that one might expect to produce a more homogeneous gene pool. The inevitable conclusion is that ancestral *Homo sapiens* quite recently passed through a "bottleneck" in which the entire human population was reduced to a few hundred or perhaps a couple of thousand individuals, perhaps approximately 150,000 years ago. Such a population size would be sufficiently small for a set of unique traits to become established, making it plausible that one small group would be the population from which *Homo sapiens* emerged as a new, isolated reproductive entity.

The past few hundred thousand years have been a period during which climates have oscillated constantly between warmer and colder and also between wetter and drier. During these times, sea levels have repeatedly risen and fallen, creating islands and expanding landmasses. These are precisely the conditions in which small populations could become isolated and then expand to recolonize territories as conditions changed. In other words, conditions were most propitious for evolutionary innovation. *Homo sapiens* appears to be a typical product of such a process.

From a tiny population that most likely lived in Africa, our species spread, directed in its wanderings by the vagaries of climate, environment, and competition with species both human and nonhuman. This population spread first out of Africa, then throughout the Eurasian landmass and into Australasia, and finally into the New World and the Pacific Islands. The initial expansion was almost certainly the result of population increase as opposed to nomadic travels. This spread was assuredly not uniform but episodic and opportunistic, with frequent false starts, mini-isolations, and recoalescences. The physical variety of humankind today, while striking, is actually superficial, and it reflects this checkered history.

During the history of *Homo sapiens*, local populations have developed various physical as well as cultural and linguistic differences. Some of these physical variations must have been controlled by the environment, others by purely random factors. It is clear, for example, that variations in skin colour are responses to variations in the intensity of sunlight in different climates. The dark pigment melanin protects against the highly damaging effects of the sun's ultraviolet (UV) radiation, and the darkest skins occur in the tropics, where such radiation is highest. In contrast, skins at higher latitudes tend to be pale, which allows the less-intense UV radiation to penetrate the skin and promote the synthesis of essential factors such as vitamin D. Similarly, populations living in hot, dry areas tend to be taller and more slender than those living in very cold climates, because they need to lose heat rather than retain it as a rounder body does. On the other hand, nobody knows why some populations have thinner lips than others or why many Asians have an additional fold of skin above their upper eyelids. These and other variations are inconsequential to fitness and are likely to be the mere results of random chance.

Scientists have always had difficulty classifying people into groups on the basis of variation, and the reason is simple. Genetically, only two processes can take place within a species. One of these processes is the diversification of local populations—a routine and unremarkable event that requires some degree of isolation of local groups. The other is the reintegration of populations and the consequent blending of characteristics via interbreeding when contact is reestablished. Human populations show the results of both processes as driven by the climatic shifts of ice ages. Today, although it is generally possible to tell an Asian from a European from an African, many individuals defy such categorization, and boundaries are impossible to draw. This is why, from a biologist's point of view, trying to define "races" is impossible if not pointless. Race is instead a social construct addressed by cultural anthropology.

Still, tracing the history of our species' spread and diversification is undeniably fascinating, and several genetic approaches have been used to try to unravel it. In addition to mtDNA and its male counterpart, the Y chromosome, DNA from the Human Genome Project will also help clarify our relatively short but astonishingly complex history. The interpretation of mtDNA divergence shows the *Homo sapiens* branch of the family tree to be rooted in Africa some 150,000 years ago. It identifies four descendant mtDNA lineages (A, B, C, and D) among

Classification of Homo sapiens *within the order Primates.* Encyclopædia Britannica, Inc.

Native Americans. These four lineages are also present in continental Asians, as are lineages designated E, F, G, and M. Europeans show a different set of lineages, called H, I, J, and K as well as T through X. Africans present one principal lineage called L, with three major variants. One of these, L3, seems to have been the founder of both the Asian and the European groupings. Using the differences (genetic substitutions) observed among the lineages, the L3 emigrants are calculated to have reached Europe between about 51,000 and 39,000 years ago, a date that is in good agreement with the archaeological record. But there are some apparent anomalies in these data. For example, the rare European X lineage has been identified in some northern Native Americans. This cannot be explained by recent intermarriage, since this lineage appears to have originated in America in pre-Columbian times. As the genes of more populations are studied, a more detailed picture of past human population movements and integrations around the world will emerge.

CONCLUSION

Primates are the mammalian order to which humans belong. By virtue of their culture-bearing and tool-making abilities, it is possible to set humans apart from other primates and the rest of the natural world. Anatomically speaking, however, *Homo sapiens* shares many physical and behavioral traits with its primate relatives.

Humans view themselves as exceptional forms of life. Since they have explored and settled most of Earth's surface, traveled to the deepest parts of the ocean, and journeyed to the Moon, the case for human exceptionalism is strong. On Earth, the effects of human activities are widespread. The global reach of humanity's influence is exemplified by the trace amounts of pollution found throughout the atmosphere and the recent changes in Earth's climate caused in part by the release of greenhouse gases from industry and transportation. In addition, vast areas of natural lands, such as forests and wetlands, have been converted to agriculture and urban use. No other primate can remake Earth's surface on such a scale.

As greater numbers of their lemur, monkey, and ape relatives are threatened with extinction, humans should carefully consider the potential for the demise of their own species. Fossil evidence has shown that *Homo sapiens* was not the first human species. Others, such as *H. habilis*, *H. erectus*, and the Neanderthals, have come and gone, their exit resulting from an inability to adapt to changing environmental conditions. Consequently, if *Homo sapiens* continues to disrupt and degrade the very ecosystems it depends on for food, water, and other resources, it risks meeting the same fate as its ancestors.

GLOSSARY

allele One of several forms of a gene that can be found at a particular location on a chromosome. Each allele produces a specific characteristic, such as eye color or blood type. Usually one form of the allele will be expressed more than another in an individual.

allometric The way that size affects the proportions of different organs and body structure in a living being.

basal Basic or foundational.

Catarrhini Old World apes, humans, and monkeys.

catholicity Wide ranging.

cladistic Referring to a scientific method of classifying living organisms by shared ancestry.

couture The art of making fashionable clothes, or the clothes themselves.

endocrinology A branch of medical science concerning the endocrine system, in particular hormones and their role in regulating body functions.

epiphyte A plant that grows on another plant or a different object gets its nutrients from the air and rain instead of the ground.

estrus A time in the sexual cycle of certain female mammals when they are physically ready to mate.

hallux A big toe.

Haplorrhini The suborder of primates that includes tarsiers, monkeys, and apes (including humans).

hominin A member of a taxonomic tribe that includes *Homo sapiens* (human beings) and extinct species of early humans.

homogeneous Something that is either exactly the same or like something else.

homology A similarity between different organisms caused by a shared ancestor.

immutability The state of being unchangeable.

innervation Containing or being supplied with nerves.

mitochondrial DNA Also mtDNA. A type of DNA located in mitochondria. The genes contained in mtDNA allow cells to create energy.

morphologically Referring to the physical structure of plants and animals.

parturition Giving birth.

peripatetic Related to moving, especially by walking.

phylogeny The history of the evolution of a certain kind of organism.

Platyrrhine New World monkeys.

quadrupedalism Locomotion involving four limbs.

sobriquet Nickname.

Strepsirrhini A suborder of primates that includes lemurs, lorises, aye-ayes and pottos.

taxonomy The formal way scientists classify plants and animals.

tortuous Twisted.

turbinates Thin plates on the walls of the nasal chambers that are covered by membranes and are made either of bone or cartilage.

turgidity The state of being swollen or distended.

vascularity Relating to channels such as veins that transmit body fluid throughout a living plant or animal.

xerophilous A living thing that thrives in a dry environment.

zygote A recently fertilized egg before it divides into smaller cells.

BIBLIOGRAPHY

PRIMATES

J.R. Napier and P.H. Napier, *The Natural History of the Primates* (1985, reissued 1994), provides a general overview of the order, with many photographs. Ronald M. Nowak, *Walker's Primates of the World* (1999), is concisely written and contains information on all aspects of primates at the genus level. Noel Rowe, *The Pictorial Guide to the Living Primates* (1996), describes the primates species by species and includes summary information and a colour photo of almost all of them. *Monkey in the Mirror* (1995), coproduced by WNET and the British Broadcasting Corporation as part of the television series *Nature*, compares humans with other primates. Barbara B. Smuts et al. (eds.), *Primate Societies* (1987), functions as a source book on primate social behaviour and ecology.

Colin Groves, *Primate Taxonomy* (2001), comprehensively reconstructs primate classification from the species level upward. Phyllis Dolhinow and Agustín Fuentes (eds.), *The Nonhuman Primates* (1999), is a collection of essays devoted largely to behavioral topics but covering all aspects of primatology, including conservation. John G. Fleagle, *Primate Adaptation and Evolution*, 2nd ed. (1999), provides separate chapters for current and paleontological information on major primate groups: prosimians, Old World monkeys, New World monkeys, and apes (including humans). Friderun Ankel-Simons, *Primate Anatomy: An Introduction*, 2nd ed. (2000), also includes coverage of taxonomy and molecular biology.

Prudence Hero Napier and Paulina D. Jenkins, *Catalogue of Primates in the British Museum (Natural History)*, 5 vols. (1976–90), the first three by Napier, the last two by Jenkins, are full treatments of the primates, with each volume covering a different taxonomic group.

LEMURS

Russel A. Mittermeier, *Lemurs of Madagascar* (1994), is a field guide including maps and 36 colour plates; and *Spirits of the Forest* (1987), produced by WNET as part of the *Nature* television series, portrays several species and behaviours.

BABOONS

Hans Kummer, *In Quest of the Sacred Baboon: A Scientist's Journey*, trans. from German (1995), is a narrative account of this primatologist's study of the hamadryas baboon. *Baboon Tales* (1998), directed by Gillian Darling Kovanic, explains and portrays on video the life of a baboon troop during a newborn's first year.

APES

William C. McGrew, Linda F. Marchant, and Toshisada Nishida, *Great Ape Societies* (1996), consists of a series of accounts covering all aspects of the lives of the great apes as observed in the wild. *Great Apes* (1997), produced and directed by Nigel Ashcroft, is a video documentary examining morphology, evolution, and natural history. Holger Preuschoft et al. (eds.), *The Lesser Apes: Evolutionary and Behavioural Biology* (1984), is an account by numerous experts on all aspects of the anatomy, taxonomy, and behaviour of gibbons. Robert M. Yerkes and Ada W.

Yerkes, *The Great Apes: A Study of Anthropoid Life* (1929, reprinted 1970), remains a classic and accessible work. Paola Cavalieri and Peter Singer (eds.), *The Great Ape Project: Equality Beyond Humanity* (1993, reissued 1996), draws ethical conclusions about the treatment of our closest living relatives based on recent scientific findings.

BONOBOS AND CHIMPANZEES

Takayoshi Kano, *The Last Ape: Pygmy Chimpanzee Behavior and Ecology* (1992; originally published in Japanese, 1986), is the most extensive description of bonobos in their natural habitat. Frans de Waal, *Bonobo: The Forgotten Ape* (1997), compares the behaviour of captive and wild bonobos with that of other chimpanzees and humans. Sue Savage-Rumbaugh and Roger Lewin, *Kanzi: The Ape at the Brink of the Human Mind* (1994), describes the remarkable intellect of a bonobo living in a primate research laboratory in Atlanta, Georgia.

Richard W. Wrangham et al. (eds.), *Chimpanzee Cultures* (1994, reissued 1996), compares differences in behaviour observed among various groups of chimps and bonobos both in captivity and in the wild. Jane Goodall, *In the Shadow of Man*, rev. ed. (1988, reissued 2000), is a scientific yet personal account of the author's pioneering research on wild chimpanzees in Tanzania and is considered a classic, as is *The Chimpanzees of Gombe: Patterns of Behavior* (1986), which synthesizes 25 years of observations made in the chimpanzees' natural habitat. Toshisada Nishida (ed.), *The Chimpanzees of the Mahale Mountains: Sexual and Life History Strategies* (1990), summarizes the field studies conducted by Japanese scientists in Tanzania since the 1960s. Christophe Boesch and Hedwige Boesch-Achermann, *The Chimpanzees of the Taï Forest: Behavioural Ecology and Evolution* (2000), analyzes

15 years of observation of West African chimpanzees in the context of human evolution. Roger Fouts and Stephen Tukel Mills, *Next of Kin: What Chimpanzees Have Taught Me About Who We Are* (1997), traces Fouts's experiences during his 30 years of language research with chimpanzees. *The New Chimpanzees*, produced by the National Geographic Society (1995), portrays on video the differences in behaviour between chimpanzees of different sites and between chimps and bonobos.

GORILLAS

A.F. Dixson, *The Natural History of the Gorilla* (1981), is the most complete treatment available in English. William C. McGrew, Linda F. Marchant, and Toshisada Nishida (eds.), *Great Ape Societies* (1996), devotes some chapters to gorillas; other chapters compare gorillas' social behaviour with that of chimpanzees, bonobos, and orangutans. Terry L. Maple and Michael P. Hoff, *Gorilla Behavior* (1982), describes ethological studies of both captive and wild gorillas along with providing information on their biology, conservation, and care. *Gorillas: Tender Giants*, presented by Discovery Channel Pictures and Silverback Productions Ltd. (1996), captures on video the daily activities of western lowland gorillas in the wild; whereas the video *Gorillas*, hosted by George Page for WNET (1989, reissued 1997), documents the life of mountain gorillas.

ORANGUTANS

Jeffrey H. Schwartz (ed.), *Orang-Utan Biology* (1988), is a detailed description of orangutan anatomy, physiology, and evolution. Birute Galdikas, *Reflections of Eden: My Years with the Orangutans of Borneo* (1995), is a narrative account of the primatologist's study of orangutans in Borneo. H.D. Rijksen and E. Meijaard, *Our Vanishing Relative: The Status of Wild Orang-utans at the Close of the Twentieth Century* (1999), comprehensively discusses data on the distribution and population of orangutans, threats to their survival, and plans for their conservation. *Orangutans: Just Hangin' On*, produced by Argo Films for WNET and National Geographic Television as part of the PBS television series *Nature*, documents on video the research being done on both captive and wild orangutans, including studies of intelligence.

AUSTRALOPITHECUS

Donald C. Johanson and Maitland A. Edey, *Lucy: The Beginnings of Humankind* (1981, reissued 1990), recounts the field expeditions of Lucy's discoverer (Johanson) and provides background on other human ancestors in addition to *Australopithecus afarensis*. Meave G. Leakey and Friedemann Schrenk, *History of the Anthropoid: The Search for the Beginning* (1997), produced by Films for the Humanities, is a video documentary in which Meave Leakey discusses human evolutionary theory at Tanzanian paleontological sites. William H. Kimbel, Yoel Rak, and Donald C. Johanson, *The Skull of Australopithecus afarensis* (2004), is a complete scientific text.

HOMO ERECTUS

Noel T. Boaz and Russell L. Ciochon, *Dragon Bone Hill: An Ice-Age Saga of Homo erectus* (2004), investigates the science and saga of the remains found at Zhoukoudian, China. Alan Walker and Pat Shipman, *The Wisdom of the Bones: In Search of Human Origins* (1996), is a similar treatment of the Nariokotome skeleton of Kenya. G. Philip Rightmire, *The Evolution of Homo erectus: Comparative*

Anatomical Studies of an Extinct Human Species (1990, reissued 1993), is a more advanced examination of *Homo erectus* fossil evidence.

NEANDERTHALS

Erik Trinkaus and Pat Shipman, *The Neanderthals: Of Skeletons, Scientists, and Scandal* (1993), recounts the history of Neanderthal research since the first discovery in 1856. Ian Tattersall, *The Last Neanderthal: The Rise, Success, and Mysterious Extinction of Our Closest Human Relatives*, rev. ed. (1999), examines the points of argument surrounding Neanderthals while defining them as a separate species rather than as a subspecies of *Homo sapiens*. Juan Luis Arsuaga, *The Neanderthal's Necklace: In Search of the First Thinkers*, trans. by Andy Klatt (2002), emphasizes recent findings from Sierra de Atapuerca, Spain. *Neanderthals on Trial* (2001), directed by Mark J. Davis for the PBS television series *NOVA*, is a video documentary that presents evidence for both sides of the evolutionary debate: Neanderthals as our ancestors and Neanderthals as a separate group of humans.

Clive Finlayson, *Neanderthals and Modern Humans: An Ecological and Evolutionary Perspective* (2004), emphasizes the role of climate and ecological change in the extinction of Neanderthals. Paul Mellars, *The Neanderthal Legacy: An Archaeological Perspective from Western Europe* (1996), is a detailed presentation of Neanderthal archaeology and the behaviours that can be inferred from it.

HOMO SAPIENS

Ian Tattersall, *Becoming Human: Evolution and Human Uniqueness* (1998, reissued 2000), examines common yet specific questions often posed about the nature of

Homo sapiens. H.J. Deacon and Janette Deacon, *Human Beginnings in South Africa: Uncovering the Secrets of the Stone Age* (1999), examines early human history from an archaeological standpoint. Jeffrey H. Schwartz, *Sudden Origins: Fossils, Genes, and the Emergence of Species* (1999), considers human evolutionary theories within the larger framework established by paleontology, genetics, and zoology. Jonathan Marks, *What It Means to Be 98% Chimpanzee: Apes, People, and Their Genes* (2002), is a lively description of molecular genetics and its relevance to understanding humankind's place in nature. Luigi Luca Cavalli-Sforza, *Genes, Peoples, and Languages*, trans. from the French by Mark Seielstad (2001), integrates findings from several disciplines with the author's landmark study of genetic differences among peoples of the world. Ian Tattersall and Jeffrey H. Schwartz, *Extinct Humans* (2000), emphasizes morphology in a richly illustrated account of the human fossil record.

M.J. Aitken, Chris Stringer, and Paul Mellars (eds.), *The Origin of Modern Humans and the Impact of Chronometric Dating* (1992), reviews through a series of research papers the advances in dating fossils and sites that are relevant to the evolution of *Homo sapiens.* Luigi Luca Cavalli-Sforza, Paolo Menozzi, and Alberto Piazza, *The History and Geography of Human Genes* (1994, reissued 1996), painstakingly maps and analyzes genetic data drawn from populations throughout the world. Jeffrey H. Schwartz and Ian Tattersall, *The Human Fossil Record: Craniodental Morphology of Genus Homo*, vol. 1 and 2 (2002 and 2003), definitively compiles the fossil evidence as it applies to human skulls. Christopher Stringer and Robin McKie, *African Exodus: The Origins of Modern Humanity* (1996, reissued 1998), interprets the evidence supporting the out-of-Africa model of *H. sapiens* evolution. Milford H. Wolpoff, *Paleoanthropology*, 2nd ed. (1999), is a college textbook that outlines the multiregional hypothesis of *H. sapiens*. Ian Tattersall, "Paleoanthropology: The Last Half-century," *Evolutionary Anthropology*, 9(1):2–16 (2000), reviews developments of the science to the close of the 20th century.

The Mind's Big Bang (2001), produced by WGBH Video and Clear Blue Sky Productions, vol. 6 of the series *Evolution*, delves into possible explanations for the emergence of the human mind between 50,000 and 100,000 years ago. *Journey of Man* (2003), produced by PBS Home Video and Tigress Productions, presents results of the genetic analysis of human populations and offers commentary from anthropologists, archaeologists, and historians. *The Human Animal: A Natural History of the Human Species* (2003), produced by Films for the Humanities, British Broadcasting Corporation, and Discovery Channel, is a six-part documentary series that examines the evolution of physical as well as behavioral traits such as language, culture, and creativity.

INDEX